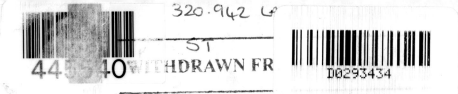

FIFTY KEY  IN
TWENTIETH-CENTURY
BRITISH POLITICS

This accessible guidebook provides a complete overview of the lives and influence of fifty major figures in modern British political history. Reflecting the changes within British society and politics over the past century, the entries chart the development of key contemporary issues such as women's rights, immigration and the emergence of New Labour. Figures covered include:

- Tony Blair
- Barbara Castle
- Winston Churchill
- John Maynard Keynes

- David Lloyd George
- Emmeline Pankhurst
- Enoch Powell
- Margaret Thatcher

With cross-referenced entries and helpful suggestions for further reading, this book is an essential guide for all those with an interest in understanding the most prominent issues of modern British politics.

Keith Laybourn is Professor of History at the University of Huddersfield.

ROUTLEDGE KEY GUIDES

Routledge Key Guides are accessible, informative and lucid handbooks, which define and discuss the central concepts, thinkers and debates along a broad range of academic disciplines. All are written by noted experts in their respective subjects. Clear, concise exposition of complex and stimulating issues and ideas make *Routledge Key Guides* the ultimate reference resource for students, teachers, researchers and the interested lay person.

FIFTY KEY FIGURES IN TWENTIETH-CENTURY BRITISH POLITICS

Keith Laybourn

London and New York

First published 2002
by Routledge
11 New Fetter Lane, London EC4P 4EE

Simultaneously published in the USA and Canada
by Routledge
29 West 35th Street, New York, NY 10001

Routledge is an imprint of the Taylor & Francis Group

© 2002 Keith Laybourn

Typeset in Bembo by Taylor & Francis Books Ltd
Printed and bound in Great Britain by TJ International Ltd, Padstow, Cornwall

British Library Cataloguing in Publication Data
A catalogue record for this book is available from the British Library

Library of Congress Cataloging in Publication Data
A catalog record for this book has been requested

ISBN   0–415–22676–7 (hbk)
ISBN   0–415–22677–5 (pbk)

ALPHABETICAL LIST
OF CONTENTS

PREFACE

This book contains relatively brief essays (from 800 to 3,000 words) on fifty of the political figures of the twentieth century whom I consider have made a significant political impact, for good or ill. Undoubtedly, other historians would have produced a different list – and would possibly have included the likes of Tony Benn and Shirley Williams – which may, from their point of view, have been as justified as final list that I have produced. Indeed, my original listing of more than 70 politicians included both Benn and Williams. Yet the listing of any historian would certainly have differed on the more marginal figures. What is certain is that all lists would have included at least half of those examined: for example, Clement Attlee, Winston Churchill and David Lloyd George.

All the biographical sketches outline the career and political importance of the particular figure being examined. They also indicate the most relevant related biographies to read and list, in a bibliography, the most useful books on the subject. There are no footnotes but the sources of precise quotes are bracketed in the main text and often listed in the bibliography.

Keith Laybourn

FIFTY KEY FIGURES IN TWENTIETH-CENTURY BRITISH POLITICS

HERBERT HENRY ASQUITH 1852–1928

The career and reputation of Herbert Henry Asquith are creditably associated with the reforms of the pre-First World War period, which saw the emergence of the Liberal welfare state. Less auspiciously, they are also associated with the failure to tackle the women's suffrage issue and Irish Question of the same period. However, whilst Asquith's period as Prime Minister inaugurated political and constitutional change, much of the political credit he gained disappeared with his career and reputation during the First World War. He was the last Prime Minister of a purely Liberal government, and in his conflict with Lloyd George over the premiership, in December 1916, split the Liberal Party and brought forward its almost inevitable decline.

Asquith came from a northern industrial family and was born on 12 September 1852, the second of two sons and five children of Joseph Dixon Asquith, owner of a woollen mill at Morley, near Leeds. On Joseph's sudden death in 1860 his widow, Emily, took her four surviving children to Huddersfield, where her father, William Willans, was a prominent citizen and a man with National Liberal and Congregationalist connections. When Willans died, in 1863, Emily moved to Sussex, and the boys were entrusted to the care and support of her eldest brother, John, in London. When John returned to Yorkshire, the boys were boarded with a London family. They attended the City of London School, where Herbert Henry was an outstanding pupil and exhibited the 'intellectual effortlessness' that was to characterize his academic career. In 1869 he won a scholarship to Balliol College, Oxford, where he excelled in Union debates, becoming President of the Oxford Union, was attracted by the advanced Liberal ideas of T. H. Green, rowed and played golf. He gained 'easy Firsts' and prizes in his degree examinations in Classics/ Greats; and eventually became a Fellow of his college.

Asquith retained his Fellowship until 1881, but in 1875 moved to London to practise as a lawyer. In 1877, aged 25, he married Helen Melland, daughter of a Manchester physician, with whom he had four children between 1878 and 1887. Asquith was attracted to the Liberal Party and was elected to Parliament in 1886 as Liberal MP for East Fife (Edinburgh), which he represented for the next thirty-two years. His powerful speeches, and his association with the Eight Club of young Radical Imperialists, brought him to prominence in Parliament. With the death of his wife in 1891, driven to distraction, after the 1892 general election he became more deeply involved in politics, becoming Home Secretary in Gladstone's fourth ministry. He remained Home Secretary throughout that government and in the succeeding Rosebery government of 1894–5.

Asquith earned a reputation as a cautious reformer, although this was marred by his use of troops to control the Featherstone disturbances of 1893, during the national coal strike of that year. About this time he moved from the Radical Liberalism of his nonconformist background to a more Liberal Imperialist position, and his lifestyle also changed when in 1894, he married Margot Tennant, a socialite who introduced him to London's high society and the country-house life. To finance his new way of life he resumed his legal practice.

The 1895 general election returned a Conservative government and, with the resignation of Rosebery, Asquith now supported Henry Campbell-Bannerman as Liberal Leader, in his efforts to maintain unity within the Liberal Party. Asquith often maintained a moderate stand on the issues which most divided the Liberal Party – Irish Home Rule and the Empire. His inclination was to be a 'Liberal Imperialist' rather than 'pro-Boer' at the turn of the century when the Dutch-descended Boer farmers sought to exclude British 'Uitlanders', or newcomers. War broke out in October 1899, and in the general election of 1900 the Liberals were divided over the conflict. The Conservatives (or 'Unionists') were victorious. In June 1901 Campbell-Bannerman worsened the Liberal turmoil by denouncing British treatment of the Boers, and the internment of many in concentration camps, as 'methods of barbarism'. Asquith now found himself acting as a moderating influence in the Party against the extremist pro-Boers.

The Liberal Party's political fortunes revived from 1902 onwards, more because of the reaction against Conservative/Unionist policies than any favour towards their own. They united against Balfour's Education Act, which 'put Church schools on the rates' as well as replacing school boards with local education authorities. In 1903 they again united, this time against Joseph Chamberlain's 'protective tariff' campaign to favour Empire trade, Asquith's attack upon Chamberlain carrying more weight because of his moderate Imperialist credentials. The Unionist government collapsed in December 1905, and Campbell-Bannerman headed a Liberal Cabinet in which Asquith was Chancellor of the Exchequer. After the January 1906 general election the Liberals and their Irish Nationalist and Labour allies held a Commons majority of 400, in what was a Liberal landslide victory.

Asquith was Chancellor for two-and-a quarter years and presented three Budgets, the third a month after becoming Prime Minister.

Their underlying policy was the promotion of 'Peace, Retrenchment and Reform'. In 1906 he inherited a surplus from the previous Budget and used it to remove the coal export tax imposed at the time of the Boer War and reduce the tea duty from 6d to 5d. In 1907 he reduced income tax from one shilling (5p) in the pound to 9d (3.8p) on incomes up to £2,000 (probably about £120,000 to £150,000 in modern-day terms). He also introduced graduated tax on estate duty on inheritance. Between 1906 and 1908 he gained a reputation for prudence as a result of paying off about £47 million of debt. However, his greatest achievement as Chancellor, for which he has not been given due credit, was state provision of old-age pensions. On Campbell-Bannerman's resignation and death, in April 1908, Asquith's succession as Prime Minister was unchallenged.

As Premier, Asquith was ring-master to a Cabinet/Government which included such talented politicians as David Lloyd George and Winston Churchill. Although not an innovator, in the Cabinet his authority was unchallenged and he dominated in the Commons. His government introduced new principles of state responsibility for social justice and the redistribution of income and wealth which were the basis of a welfare state. 'New Liberalism', its driving force, accepted the need to establish a harmony of interests within society and eschewed the class conflict explicit in strikes. The arbiter of social conflict in society, New Liberalism offered the Liberal reforms, although the working classes were often alienated from the movement by its lack of support of their right to strike. Nevertheless, the great legislative issues for Liberals were education, old age, national insurance, temperance, land reform, Welsh Church Disestablishment and Irish Home Rule, and when, in 1908–9, the Cabinet divided over naval and military expenditure in the face of German rearmament, a looming clash with the House of Lords was a welcome diversion from mounting internal tensions.

The conflict arose out of the fact that Lloyd George, the Chancellor of the Exchequer, needed to raise money in order to pay for social reform. Moving the burden of taxation from indirect to direct taxation, and the levying of new taxes on land, led to a simmering conflict with the House of Lords. The Lords then rejected the Finance Bill arising from Lloyd George's 'People's Budget'. A resulting general election, in January 1910, left Asquith's government heavily dependent upon Irish and Labour votes to command a Commons majority. The Lords did not pass the 1909 Budget until April 1910, and Asquith was under pressure, particularly from David Lloyd George, to reduce their powers. As fortune would have it,

Edward VII died, and Asquith had to persuade a reluctant George V – after a further indecisive general election in December 1910 and rowdy scenes in Parliament – to agree to create enough new peers, if necessary, to overcome the Lords' opposition to a Bill to reduce their constitutional powers. This became the Parliament Act of 1911.

By that time Asquith was facing a new crisis on the industrial front. From 1910 to 1913 there was a continuous sequence of strikes, by miners, dockers and railwaymen, which generated fierce class hatred and damaged the economy: 40,980,000 working days were lost in 1912 alone in what, mistakenly, was referred to as 'industrial syndicalism', which sought revolution by the workers through a general strike of all industrial workers. Because it depended on the support of Irish Nationalist MPs, the government also had to reactivate its Home Rule policy, which provoked strong Conservative and Unionist reaction. This brought closer the prospect of civil war in Ireland. In March 1913 there was a 'mutiny' of Ulster Protestant army officers, which Asquith countered by imposing obedience, against the wishes of the King and protests by the Unionists. In his handling of these domestic crises, Asquith has been both lauded for his statesmanship and denounced for his inertia in what proved to be a difficult time for his Liberal governments whose progressive policies were also being increasingly challenged by the emergent Labour Party. In the end, the third Home Rule Bill was abandoned on the outbreak of war in 1914.

Even more critical were the problems abroad that brought war in 1914. These began with German aggression in Morocco in 1905–6, renewed in 1911, which intensified the Anglo-German 'naval race'. As well as divisions over the domestic issues, there were Cabinet splits on the financing of rearmament and involvement in the Balkans crises that culminated in the assassination of the Archduke Franz Ferdinand and the Austrian ultimatum to Serbia, and pitted Britain against Germany and Austria-Hungary, in alliance with Tsarist Russia as well as France. However, only German violation of Belgian neutrality allowed Asquith to lead a partly-pacifist Liberal Party into a war that was more enthusiastically supported by the Opposition. Nor were his calm and deliberative moderation and his disposition to 'wait and see' to fit him for life as a wartime leader.

Widespread discontent at the Asquith government's inaction and incompetence developed as the war dragged on in its early months. In Asquith's re-formed Cabinet of August 1914, Lord Kitchener, the country's most famous soldier, became War Minister, but proved to be 'a terrible muddler', and found himself in conflict with David Lloyd George. Asquith lost prestige by repeating Kitchener's false assurance that there was no shortage of shells. He erred in establishing a War Council that was too large and unwieldy. The adoption of a strategy of attacking Turkey when stalemate set in on the Western front produced the disastrous amphibious operation to capture the Dardanelles straits and the Gallipoli peninsula. This and the scandal of the munitions shortage precipitated a crisis by May 1915 and the formation of a Coalition Cabinet, containing Unionists and one Labour member (Arthur Henderson), as a gesture of national unity. For a Cabinet riddled with intrigue, the chief war issue became that of conscription. Kitchener's greatest achievement had been to create a volunteer army of two and a half million by March 1916. Liberals were opposed ideologically to compulsory service, and felt betrayed when Asquith's inner War Council of three Liberals and two Unionists pushed a Conscription Bill through Parliament, although he himself only accepted the measure when faced with the threat of resignation from Lloyd George. From May, Asquith was under siege. The Gallipoli fiasco had ended in January 1916; the 'Easter Rebellion' of Irish republicans in Dublin was not anticipated and ended in brutal repression; and the Somme offensive in France, begun in July, ended in disaster. The death of Asquith's eldest son worsened his own personal gloom. Finally, in November a brief clash of battleships off Jutland only made the Germans turn to their more-effective submarines. Indeed, Lloyd George complained that Asquith was 'absolutely hopeless'. He continued: 'He came to Cabinet with no policy which he had decided to recommend, listened to what others said, summed it up ably and then as often as not postponed the decision. It was a futile method of carrying on a war'. On 5 December Asquith was forced to resign when he was outmanoeuvred in Cabinet intrigues by the Liberal Lloyd George and the Unionist leader Andrew Bonar Law, although it has been suggested that he had a nervous breakdown or was simply testing the level of his support. Lloyd George became Prime Minister, the only Liberal in a War Cabinet of five. Exhibiting the qualities of wartime leadership Asquith had lacked, Lloyd George became virtual dictator and 'The Man Who Won The War', but suffered Asquith's wrath for his betrayal.

From then onwards, Asquith's reputation suffered by comparison. His one attempt to challenge in Parliament the government's conduct of the war, through the Maurice Debate which questioned the government's figures on army strength at the Western Front, left him discredited and Lloyd George triumphant, deepening further the division between the Asquith and Lloyd George Liberals. When the First World War ended in November 1918 Lloyd George called an election, in which Liberal candidates were divided between 'Asquithian' and 'Coalition' (supporting Lloyd George in coalition with the Unionists). In a landslide defeat, Asquith lost his own seat at East Fife, and there were only 29 non-Coalition Liberals, not even all of those 'Asquithian', so that Lloyd George, leading 129 'Coalition Liberals', could have claimed the Party leadership had he so wished.

Asquith returned to the Commons in a by-election at Paisley in February 1920, but he made little impact, and attempts at reconciliation with Lloyd George to reunite Liberal resources foundered on Asquith's distractions and ineptitude, and on mutual suspicion. However, in October 1922 the Conservative/Unionists rejected Lloyd George's leadership, replacing him with Andrew Bonar Law, and in the ensuing general election the two Liberal factions fought separately, and with little success. Further limited attempts at reunion were made in a general election in 1923, through the efforts of C. P. Scott, owner of the *Manchester Guardian*. Asquith and Lloyd George campaigned together to defend free trade, the one issue on which they agreed even though it was rumoured at the time that Lloyd George was willing to contemplate protectionism. Labour was now the main party of the Left, and MacDonald's government of January 1924 was sustained by Liberal votes. Yet when MacDonald called an election in October, following the loss of Liberal support, the Liberals won only 40 seats, and Asquith lost his own seat for the last time. At this point it was clear that the Liberal Party had lost to the Labour Party any credible claim to being the progressive party of British politics.

This humiliation effectively ended Asquith's political career. With no hope of returning to the Commons, he accepted the Earldom of Oxford and Asquith. His forays into politics became increasingly rare, although he did give his support to the Stanley Baldwin Conservative government at the time of the General Strike in 1926. Asquith suffered strokes in 1926 and 1927, which impaired his powers. He retired from active politics, and the leadership of the Liberal Party, in October 1926 and died on 15 February 1928, leaving a reputation achieved in peacetime by outstanding intellectual powers, but tarnished by the failures on the battlefields in the First World War and by a succession of political defeats thereafter. An effective politician in the Edwardian era, he failed to continue with that success through the dramatically changing world of the Georgian era of George V.

See also: Churchill, Lloyd George

Further reading

Asquith, H. H., 1928, *Memories and Reflections, 1852–1927*, 2 vols, Toronto: McClelland & Stewart.
Jenkins, R., 1964, *Asquith*, London: Collins.
Koss, S., 1976, *Asquith*, London: Allen Lane.
McCallum, R. B., 1936, *Asquith*, London: Duckworth.
Spender, J. A., and Asquith, C., 1932, *The Life of Hubert Henry Asquith, Lord Oxford and Asquith*, London: Hutchinson.

NANCY (WITCHER LANGHORNE) ASTOR 1879–1964

Nancy Astor was the first woman to take up a seat in the House of Commons when she was returned for Plymouth in a parliamentary by-election in 1919, remaining Conservative MP for that constituency until her retirement in 1945. Indeed, she is best remembered for being the first woman to breach that male preserve the House of Commons, and thus emerged as a figurehead in the political development of the feminist movement.

Nancy Langhorne, born in 1879, was an American divorcee with a young child when she came to Britain at the beginning of the twentieth century. She married Waldorf Astor, a rising Conservative politician who was raised to the House of Lords on the death of his father in 1919. In the Commons Lady Astor became a strong advocate of feminist issues and worked hard to promote the 1923 legislation that equalized the grounds for divorce between men and women. She was equally determined in getting the voting age for women reduced from 30 in 1918 to 21, the same age as for men, in 1928. She was also a constant defender of the rights of married women to work and advocated, with little prospect of success, equal pay for women. Indeed, she was at the forefront of issues that affected the conditions and opportunities for women, and especially concerned with developing nursery school provision.

Although Nancy Astor was a Conservative politician she held a wide range of views beyond those normally associated with the Conservative Party. She was conventionally aristocratic and Conservative during the General Strike of 1926, which saw the Trades Union Congress call out on strike about one and three-quarter million workers between 3 and 12 May 1926. During that period she was regularly photographed with the female volunteers, some of them aristocrats, working to feed the volunteer male workers in Hyde Park. Yet she was much more unconventional as a Conservative on the issue of alcoholic drink. Her first husband had been an alcoholic and she became a determined champion of temperance throughout her life. Indeed, Oswald Mosley recalls how on the issue of alcoholic drink she stated to him that she would rather 'commit adultery than drink a glass of beer', to which Mosley replied 'Who wouldn't?' Other accounts suggest that this exchange took place when she was addressing a meeting with naval ratings in Plymouth and that the response came from one of those ratings concerned at the possible loss of the rum ration. Her political agenda was also driven partly by her religious views, for she was also an ardent Christian Scientist.

In the 1930s Nancy Astor was a close friend of Neville Chamberlain and gathered around her a social circle, famously dubbed by the press as the Cliveden Set, which was closely identified with Neville Chamberlain's policy of appeasement towards the fascist powers in Europe. On the outbreak of the Second World War, in September 1939, she came to accept that appeasement had not been the right course of action to pursue and was soon to be found giving her unbending support to Winston Churchill's wartime Coalition Government. Throughout the war she did much to build up public morale, particularly in her own constituency of Plymouth, which was bombed heavily.

Nancy Astor retired from politics in 1945. Though she was too eclectic a politician to make a broadly based political impact, her commitment to feminist and female issues was important and deserves to be her political epitaph. Above all, she opened up the possibilities for the political citizenship of women. She died in 1964, a respected, though largely forgotten, pioneer of women's rights.

See also: Chamberlain (Neville), Churchill

Further reading

Grigg, J., 1980, *Nancy Astor: A Lady Unashamed*, Feltham: Hamlyn.
Harrison, B., 1987, 'Nancy Astor: Publicist and Communicator', in *Prudent Revolutionaries*, Oxford: Clarendon.
Sykes, C., 1972, *Nancy: The Life of Lady Astor*, London: Collins.

(RICHARD) CLEMENT ATTLEE 1883–1967

On his death in 1967 *The Times* concluded that Attlee was 'one of the least colourful but most effective of the British Prime Ministers of this century'. Indeed, as Prime Minister he presided over the granting of independence to India, the formation of the North Atlantic Treaty Organization (NATO), the development of Britain's modern welfare state, and the formation of the National Health Service (NHS). His impact upon the Labour Party, which he led from 1935 to 1955, was similarly dramatic to the extent that, in the 1980s, prominent figures in the then-declining Labour Party looked back to the Attlee era, establishing some sort of mythology around a reticent and unassuming leader. Yet the gibes against him still stick, most obviously the Winston Churchill one that 'An empty taxi drew up outside 10 Downing Street, and out walked Mr. Attlee'.

Attlee was born in Putney on 3 January 1883, the seventh child of Henry Attlee and Ellen Watson. He was raised in an upper-middle-class family and educated at Haileybury School, a public school founded by the East India Company, between 1896 and 1901, where he enjoyed cricket and literature. He then went to University College, Oxford, emerging with a second-class degree in History. At this point he studied law, the profession of his father, and became a barrister in 1906. However, in October 1905 he went to Haileybury House (associated with his public school), a boys' club in the East End of London and by 1907 he had become manager of the club. At this point he joined the socialist Stepney Independent Labour Party and decided upon a political career. This meant both the abandonment of his legal career and his political commitment to the Conservative Party. From this point onwards, Attlee promoted the Poor Law Minority Campaign of Sidney and Beatrice Webb, campaigned for the trade unions during the Dock Strike of 1911, and lectured on trade unionism for Ruskin College, Oxford, where the Plebs League had been formed. This career was interrupted by the First World War, for he joined the South Lancashire regiment of the army, served in Gallipoli, Mesopotamia and France, and ended the war with the rank of major.

The end of the war saw the beginning of Attlee's rapid rise within the Labour Party. He joined the London School of Economics as a lecturer in social work, holding that position until 1923, and was also returned as a councillor for Stepney, becoming Mayor in 1919. In 1922 he won the Limehouse constituency which he represented in the Commons until it was reorganized in 1950, after which he represented West Walthamstow until 1955. Now an MP, Attlee rose quickly in the Labour ranks. He became Private Secretary to Ramsay MacDonald, the Labour Leader, and was Under-Secretary of State for War in the Labour government which MacDonald formed in 1924. Although soon out of government, with the collapse of the first Labour government at the end of 1924, he was placed upon the Simon Commission which was set up in 1927 to examine constitutional changes in India, becoming in the process an ardent supporter of gradual movement towards Indian self-government, a campaign which became one of Attlee's chief interests in the 1930s and 1940s. His involvement in this Commission prevented him from assuming office immediately on the formation of the second Labour government in 1929 but, in May 1930, he replaced Oswald Mosley as Chancellor of the Duchy of Lancaster. Attlee used this post, which entailed no departmental responsibilities, to develop an economic policy which appeared as a memorandum entitled 'The Problems of British Industry', but it was ignored. Attlee was also briefly Postmaster-General in this second Labour government.

The collapse of the second government in August 1931, followed by a disastrous general election result for Labour, projected his political career forward for he was one of only two Labour MPs with ministerial experience who were returned to the House of Commons, the other being Sir Stafford Cripps. At this time, the Labour Party had only 52 MPs, four of whom were associated with the increasingly troublesome Independent Labour Party. Despite Attlee's prominence, in the process of reshaping Labour policies in the 1930s he was a follower rather than a leader, which led Hugh Dalton to suggest that he was 'a small person with no personality, nor real standing in the Movement'. Small man or not, he acted as Deputy Leader of the Labour Party between 1931 and 1935, first to Arthur Henderson and then to George Lansbury. When Ernest Bevin, the great trade union leader, forced Lansbury to stand down as Leader, just before the November 1935 general election, it was Attlee who became 'interim' Leader. After the defeat of the Labour Party in the general election, although it improved markedly its parliamentary strength, Attlee defeated Herbert Morrison and Arthur Greenwood in the leadership contest and was to remain Labour Leader for the next twenty years, seeing off the occasional challenge from Herbert Morrison.

Attlee's style of leadership was one in which he preferred to accept collective decisions rather than to force through his own policies and initiatives. This meant that he did not shape events in the way Dalton did in moving Labour towards public ownership, nor did he shape attitudes towards the need for rearmament as an aspect of foreign policy, as did Ernest Bevin. Nevertheless, he edged the Labour Party towards the directions that both Dalton and Bevin had defined, and outlined the Labour Party's new strategy in his books *The Will and the*

Way to Socialism (1935) and *The Labour Party in Perspective* (1937).
Nevertheless, given that many trade unionists were Catholics and
concerned about the reported murders of Catholic priests in Spain,
Attlee followed a tight line by supporting non-intervention in the
Spanish Civil War in 1936 and early 1937 before gradually moving
towards support for the Spanish Republican government. By 1938 he
was determinedly opposed to the National Government's appeasement
policy towards Hitler and opposed the 1938 Munich Agreement,
which effectively abandoned Czechoslovakia to Germany. Attlee
could make decisions when necessary and, for the Labour Party, was
an ideal neutral force to balance the rival political claims of Herbert
Morrison, Hugh Dalton, Arthur Greenwood, Stafford Cripps and
Ernest Bevin.

Although Attlee was often seen as Labour's temporary Leader
before 1939, this attitude changed during the Second World War. He
decided that Labour would support Winston Churchill in his wartime
administration from May 1940 and informed the Labour Party
Conference of 1940 that 'the world that must emerge from this war
must be a world attuned to our ideals'. Thus he supported both
national unity and social change, although the latter issue became his
priority. According to some civil servants, it was he, rather than
Churchill, who made the clear and positive decisions in the War
Cabinet. Indeed, he forced Churchill to allow the publication of the
Beveridge Report on social insurance in December 1942, threatening
to withdraw from the Coalition if this was not done. On this, and most
issues, he was successful, and in the wartime Cabinet it was he who
was often the unflappable figure keeping it together, serving it as Lord
Privy Seal between 1940 and 1942, Secretary of State for Dominions
Affairs (1942–3), Lord President of the Council (1943–5) and,
officially from February 1942, as Deputy Prime Minister. Although
Attlee's Cabinet position gave rise to criticism from the Labour Left,
most obviously from Harold Laski and Aneurin Bevan, he managed to
retain the strong support of Ernest Bevin, who ensured that there was
no real wartime challenge to his position as Labour Leader.

The general election of July 1945 was Attlee's finest hour.
Appearing calm and responsible in the face of Churchill's infamous
radio broadcast which described the Labour Party's policies as those of
the Gestapo, Attlee presided over a Labour landslide victory which had
seemed possible since 1942. He accepted office immediately, ignoring
the Labour Party directive of the 1930s that such a decision should be
decided by the Party as a whole, and he fought off a last-minute
attempt by Morrison to push himself forward as Labour Leader and,

thus, Prime Minister. Attlee then, astutely, created a Cabinet of great talents, some of whom could not stand each other's company, by playing to their strengths. He neutralized the political opposition of Aneurin Bevan, making him Minister of Health, invoked the negotiating skills of Ernest Bevin by making him Foreign Secretary, appeased Dalton by making him Chancellor of the Exchequer, and called upon the organizational skills of Morrison by making him Lord President of the Council with responsibility for the introduction of a programme of public ownership. The end product is what Kenneth Morgan has called the most hyperactive peacetime government of the twentieth century. Indeed, it was, introducing a wide-ranging programme of public ownership, which included the coal industry and the railways, introducing the NHS based upon public control which Aneurin Bevan had envisaged, and introducing the modern welfare state based upon the insurance principles advocated by William Beveridge in 1942. He also gave some of the younger talents, such as Hugh Gaitskell and Harold Wilson, their first ministerial responsibilities in both junior and senior posts.

Obviously, the Attlee Labour governments achieved many successes and faced serious failures. The country was practically bankrupt as a result of the Second World War and had to borrow money from the United States. The conditions on which this was provided helped to create the economic crisis of 1947 which saw Sir Stafford Cripps attempt to engineer the removal of Attlee. There was a dollar-gap crisis in 1949 which saw the devaluation of the pound. Nevertheless, about 30 per cent of British industry and services was nationalized by 1948, exports increased enormously and the NHS and the social insurance system came into existence in the summer of 1948.

Attlee had little direct part to play in some of these achievements, although he dictated the environment in which they occurred. His only significant impact was in the field of foreign affairs, where he speeded up the process by which India was given independence on 15 August 1947 by replacing Archibald Wavell as Viceroy with Earl Mountbatten who was more committed to fixing the date for independence and attempting to keep India within the Common-wealth. He also supported Ernest Bevin in opposing the Soviet Union, bringing the Americans onto the world stage by creating NATO in 1949, building up the United Nations and deciding, in 1946, to build a British nuclear weapon.

Nonetheless, by 1949 the first Attlee government was facing serious difficulties. The weakness of the pound on the international money markets forced its devaluation; there was widespread trade union unrest, allegedly caused by Communist agitation; and the nationalization of the coal industry was creating a major political battle. Within government circles there was also conflict over the cost of the NHS, particularly between Bevan and Morrison. With his term of office almost at an end, Attlee called an election in March 1950, which Labour won narrowly with a majority of only fifteen seats. However, Attlee's second administration proved contentious. Although Bevan was moved to the post of Minister of Labour, he was unhappy at the prospect that prescription charges might be imposed upon NHS patients and he was also embroiled in further conflict with Hugh Gaitskell and Herbert Morrison over the succession to Attlee as Labour Leader. In the end Bevan, along with Harold Wilson and John Freeman, resigned from the government in April 1951. The turmoil within the Labour government was plain for all to see, and Labour's appeal was further diminished by the deaths of both Bevin and Cripps. Thus Attlee was forced to call a general election for October 1951, and though Labour gained the largest vote of any political party, it was the Conservative Party, with more seats, which formed a government.

Attlee was Labour Leader, and thus Leader of the Opposition, from 1951 to 1955. This was during a period of intense conflict between the fifty or sixty 'Bevanites', who supported Bevan in demanding that the Party implement more public ownership, and the 'Right' of the Party, led by Hugh Gaitskell and Anthony Crosland, who wished the Party to abandon public ownership. Such conflict weakened the Party, which lost the 1955 general election. Attlee moved to resign as Labour Leader at this point but was persuaded to stay on until December 1955, when he was replaced as Labour Leader by Hugh Gaitskell. He was given a peerage, becoming the first Earl Attlee of Prestwood and settled down to a political retirement in journalism. He died on 8 October 1967, was cremated and had his ashes interred in Westminster Abbey.

Attlee could rightly claim to be one of the greatest of twentieth-century British prime ministers. His first administration saw the granting of independence to India and the creation of the modern British welfare state, either of which would have marked him out as an exceptional talent. Recent opinion is, however, questioning about the extent to which the Second World War shaped his political thinking and actions. Indeed, John Swift has argued (p. 171) that Attlee's development of policies in the 1930s shaped the events of 1945 to 1951 rather more than did the events of the Second World War, which might well have encouraged the policy of universalism introduced by the modern British welfare state.

See also: Bevan, Bevin, Churchill

Further reading

Attlee, C., 1935, *The Will and the Way to Socialism*, London: Methuen & Co.
Beckett, F., 1997, *Clem Attlee: A Biography*, London: Richard Cohen Books.
Morgan, K., 1984, *Labour in Power, 1945–1951*, Oxford: Clarendon.
Pearce, R., 1997, *Attlee*, London: Longman.
Pimlott, B., 1986, *The Political Diary of Hugh Dalton 1918–40, 1945–60*, London: Cape in association with the London School of Economics and Political Science.
Swift, J., 2001, *Labour in Crisis: Clement Attlee and the Labour Party in Opposition, 1931–40*, Basingstoke: Palgrave.
Tiratsoo, N. (ed.), 1991, *The Attlee Years*, London: Pinter.

STANLEY BALDWIN 1867–1947

Despite being belittled by Winston Churchill, and other leading political figures, Stanley Baldwin was the dominant figure in British politics in the years between the two world wars. He led the Conservative Party from 1923 to 1937; was Prime Minister on three occasions, from 1923 to 1924, 1924 to 1929, and between 1935 and 1937; was closely associated with the defeat of the General Strike in 1926; and was involved in the early days of the 'appeasement' policy towards Hitler in the mid 1930s. Although frequently attacked by contemporaries for his lack of effort, and damned by Michael Foot, and others as one of 'the Guilty Men' of appeasement in 1940, he has, in more recent times, been resurrected as a great political leader who managed both to defeat Labour in the 1920s and to modernize the Conservative Party throughout the inter-war years during which time he identified it with 'one-nation' paternalist Conservatism. Indeed, it is now acknowledged that Winston Churchill, and other political figures, recognized him to be a most formidable opponent.

Baldwin was born on 3 August 1867, the only child of Alfred Baldwin, a Worcestershire ironmaster, and Louisa MacDonald. He was educated at Harrow and at Trinity College, Cambridge, and then worked in his father's business. He married Lucy Ridsdale in 1892 and appeared to be setting himself up for a career as an ironmaster. Indeed, since his father was an MP, it fell increasingly to him to run the family business. It was during these formative years that Baldwin developed many of the skills and attitudes that he was to employ in his later political life. He was a paternalistic employer and sought good relations between employers and workers; he had developed sound business acumen and, raised in semi-rural Worcestershire, he grew to love the English countryside, later turning this to his political advantage. The last of these interests he greatly developed, in the nostalgic society of the immediate post-First World War years, in his emphasis upon Englishness, which he associated with an idyllic rural and semi-rural society, a land of lost repose, where harmony and understanding resided. This theme was the subject of many of his lectures and some of his books. They emphasized the 'golden age of paternalism', the close relations between workers and employers, peace and industry, and a notion of 'Englishness'. Effectively he wanted to preserve the 'mythical' characteristic values of the past in the new industrial world and associated them with the Conservative Party.

Baldwin was returned to Parliament as the Conservative MP for Bewdley in 1908, in a by-election resulting from a vacancy left by the death of his father. He went on to represent the Bewdley seat until 1937, when he left the Commons and was ennobled as the first Earl Baldwin of Bewdley. At first he made no significant political impact; then in 1917 he was given the post of Joint Financial Secretary to the Treasury, holding it until 1921. He then became President of the Board of Trade. In 1922, however, he came into conflict with Lloyd George, whom he described as ' a dynamic force ... a very terrible thing' (Watts, 1996, p. 4), and expected that his political career would come to an end. However, at the Carlton Club of the Conservative Party it was decided that the Conservative Party would withdraw from the Lloyd George Coalition Government, and Austen Chamberlain, who opposed this move, resigned and was replaced by Andrew Bonar Law. In October 1922, Bonar Law became Prime Minister and he appointed Baldwin as Chancellor of the Exchequer. As a result of ill health, Bonar Law retired both as Conservative Party Leader and Prime Minister in May 1923 and Baldwin was appointed to the post, and so Prime Minister, in his place. Thus, within about two years Baldwin had risen from political obscurity to the highest political post in the land.

For many years it was fashionable to criticize Baldwin as an indolent figure who had risen to the highest office by good fortune. In the 1950s Charles Loch Mowat regarded him as one of the political pygmies of the age and G. Young, a biographer, was positively hostile to him. Yet these views can no longer be sustained, especially in the light of *Baldwin: A Biography*, a monumental work written by Keith Middlemas and John Barnes and published in 1969. This book posits an altogether tougher image of Baldwin. He is presented as a modernizer within the Conservative Party, and a powerful leader who always kept control by retaining the confidence of the majority of the Party's centre. Apparently, Baldwin was committed to capitalism, and sought to limit government commitments to subsidizing British industry. He was also committed to parliamentary politics, in a way in which Lord Curzon, the alternative candidate for Conservative Leader and Prime Minister in 1923, would not have been. Indeed, an undergraduate rhyme composed at Balliol College, Oxford, captures the superiority and lack of democratic appeal of Curzon:

My name is George Nathaniel Curzon,
I am a most superior person,
My cheek is pink, my hair is sleek,
I dine at Blenheim once a week
(Watts, 1996, p. 29)

Baldwin was at once faced with the need to reunite the Party in 1923 and to bring Austen Chamberlain and former supporters of Lloyd George back into the fold. There was also the need to tackle the serious economic problems of unemployment, which was still running at well over a million, and foreign protectionist tariffs. It thus made both political and economic sense to advocate protectionist measures, even more so since it was rumoured that Lloyd George was about to advocate protectionism. Therefore, in October and November 1923 he presented such measures in the build up to the 1923 general election, outlining his proposals in his famous Plymouth speech. However, the result of the election was inconclusive, although the Conservatives were the largest party in Parliament. Baldwin tried to form a government but the King's Speech was defeated on the issue of protectionism and thus, in 1924, the Labour Party was asked to form a minority government, with the support of the Liberals.

Such failure was short-lived and Baldwin returned to head a Conservative government after the general election of 1924. For just over four-and-a-half years, Baldwin's Conservative government attempted to transform the work and responsibilities of local government and to tackle the economic problems of the nation. However, there was little economic change. Unemployment remained above the 'intractable million' and the much-praised local government reforms were slower than anticipated. Yet Baldwin gained considerable kudos from his handling of the General Strike of 1926. This had occurred as a result of a wage and hours dispute in the coal industry which was only temporarily resolved in July 1925 by the provision of a nine-month coal subsidy from the government and by the formation of the Royal Commission on the Coal Industry. Nine months later, the dispute was unresolved, the coal dispute occurred and the Trades Union Congress supported the miners with a nine-day General Strike of vital workers. In the end, however, the TUC called the dispute off, unconditionally, and Baldwin was credited with being both firm and fair. He had struck a balance between protecting the constitution and offering conciliation and his 'Man of Peace' speech on the BBC on 8 May, in which he stated that 'I am a man of peace. I am longing and looking for peace. But I will not surrender the safety and security of the British Constitution', struck a chord with a significant sector of British society.

Nonetheless, by 1929 Baldwin's star was on the wane and his 'Safety First' slogan at the May general election did not deceive the public about the lack of ideas coming from the retiring Conservative government, any more than the gramophone record *Stanley Boy*, which was based upon the popular song *Sonny Boy* and included such lyrics as

England for the Free; Stanley Boy
You're the man for me; Stanley Boy!
You've no way of knowing,
But I've a way of showing,
What you mean to me; Stanley Boy!

Baldwin had attempted capture the middle ground of British politics but his detestation of Lloyd George prevented him from coming to terms with the Liberal Leader. Without Liberal support, Baldwin relinquished office to MacDonald and the second Labour government. This defeat, however, put Baldwin under pressure from the press barons, Lords Beaverbrook and Rothermere, who set up the Empire Party, in 1930, in direct opposition to the Conservative Party. Although the Empire Party was initially a major challenge, claiming to have attracted 170,000 members and winning two parliamentary by-elections in Conservative seats, it effectively ceased in March 1931. Indeed it was Baldwin who ended its activities in a famous speech on 17 March 1931 in support Duff Cooper, who was fighting the safe Conservative seat of St George's, Westminster, against a candidate of the Empire Party. Baldwin castigated the press barons, suggesting that 'They are engines of propaganda', using their newspapers, the *Daily Express* and the *Daily Mail* to promote their personal ends despite the concerns of the British public. He concluded his speech with the famous quote that 'What the proprietorship of these papers is aiming at is power, and power without responsibility – the prerogative of the harlot throughout the ages.' The last phrase was what hit the press, the words having been suggested by Rudyard Kipling, Baldwin's cousin.

In the financial crisis of August 1931, which brought an end to the second Labour government, Baldwin agreed to serve under Ramsay MacDonald in the National Government, reflecting that MacDonald had better sort out the mess he had created. After the October 1931 general election Baldwin led the largest political party in Parliament, which commanded about two-thirds of parliamentary seats. He could easily have replaced MacDonald, but was more intent upon maintaining the Coalition in the economic crisis. Otherwise he was concerned to develop the bipartisan line on India, which led to the implementation of Sir Samuel Hoare's 1935 Government of India Act.

In June 1935 Baldwin replaced MacDonald and become Prime Minister, for the third time, and then won a comfortable victory in the November 1935 general election. From then onwards he was concerned mainly with the threat of fascism from Europe and with the problem of the Abdication Crisis of Edward VIII. He was forced to sack Hoare as Foreign Secretary in December 1935 because of the public reaction against the Hoare–Laval Pact, an abortive effort by Britain and France to satisfy Italy's imperial ambitions in Africa by offering them half of Abyssinia. Public clamour forced the Cabinet to reject the pact and demand Hoare's resignation.

In 1936 Baldwin suffered a nervous breakdown but recovered sufficiently to deal with the abdication of Edward VIII. Neville Chamberlain became Acting Prime Minister for several months and Baldwin decided to resign at the coronation of George VI in May 1937. He was ennobled the same year, becoming the first Earl Baldwin of Bewdley. His prestige was dimmed somewhat when Michael Foot, and others, produced their book *The Guilty Men* in 1940, blaming Baldwin, amongst others, for fomenting the Second World War by failing to face up to Hitler and European fascism. The recent re-evaluation of the role of Neville Chamberlain in these events would now also call into question the accusation levelled against Baldwin. Baldwin died on 14 December 1947.

See also: Chamberlain (Neville), Churchill, Eden

Further reading

Baldwin, S., 1926, *On England, and other Addresses*, London: Allan & Co.

Ball, S., 1988, *Baldwin and the Conservative Party: The Crisis of 1929–1931*, New Haven and London: Yale University Press.

Hyde, H. Montgomery, 1973, *Baldwin. The Unexpected Prime Minister*, London: Hart-Davis MacGibbons.

Middlemas, K. and Barnes, J., 1969, *Baldwin: A Biography*, London: Weidenfeld & Nicolson.

Ramsden, J., 1978, *A History of the Conservative Party*, vol. 3, *The Age of Balfour and Baldwin 1902–1940*, London: Longman.

Watts, D., 1996, *Stanley Baldwin and the Search for Consensus*, London: Hodder & Stoughton.

Williamson, P., 1992, *National Crisis and National Government; British Politics, the Economy and Empire, 1926–1932*, Cambridge: Cambridge University Press.

Young, G. M., 1952, *Stanley Baldwin*, London: Rupert Hart-Davis.

ARTHUR JAMES BALFOUR 1848–1930

Arthur James Balfour was Conservative Prime Minister between July 1902 and December 1905, before he held any other of the very senior posts in government – a rare political occurrence in the nineteenth and twentieth centuries. Balfour's premiership was not particularly impressive and he is remembered more for his subsequent career and his immense pragmatism in a period of fundamental social and political change in the early twentieth century. Indeed, it was almost a quarter of a century after he left 10 Downing Street as Prime Minister that he left the Cabinet for the last time.

Balfour was born on 25 July 1848 at Whittingehame, East Lothian in Scotland, the eldest son of James Maitland Balfour, a Scottish landowner. His mother was Louise Blanche Cecil, the daughter of the second Marquess of Salisbury and the sister of the third Marquess, who became Prime Minister on three occasions. He was educated at Eton and Trinity College, Cambridge, where he studied moral sciences.

Balfour's political career began in 1874 when he became MP for Hertford, helped by the Cecil family from nearby Hatfield Hall. He represented the seat until he became MP for Manchester East in 1886. He held that seat until 1906 when he became MP for the City of London, representing that seat until 1922, at which point he was raised to the House of Lords as the first Earl Balfour. Yet this long political career began unimpressively. Indeed, despite his family's powerful political connections it was not until the 1880s that he began to make his political mark. At that point Balfour became a member of the 'Fourth Party', a group of Conservatives, led by Lord Randolph Churchill, who decided to attack Gladstone directly since Sir Stafford Northcote, the Conservative Leader, seemed unable to undertake this task. In the mid 1880s, however, Balfour transferred his loyalty to Lord Salisbury, his uncle, who became Prime Minister in June 1885. As a result, Balfour became President of the Local Government Board. In 1886, following Gladstone's short-lived third ministry, which toppled over the issue of Home Rule, Balfour became Secretary of State for Scotland. Within four months he had entered the Cabinet. Then, in March 1887, after the resignation of Sir Michael Hicks-Beach, he became Chief Secretary for Ireland, a role that earned him a reputation for toughness and gained him the respect of the loyalist, largely Protestant, community.

In October 1891, Balfour became the First Lord of the Treasury and Leader of the Commons, positions normally associated in the eighteenth and nineteenth centuries with the 'Prime' Minister. Balfour held these posts until 1892, when Salisbury's government fell, returning to them between 1895 and 1902 in Salisbury's subsequent government. In these posts, Balfour was effectively the Leader of the Conservative government in the Commons and without departmental responsibilities. As a result he occupied his time with Ireland and foreign policy. On Ireland he believed that the Catholic community would accept their existence within the United Kingdom as long as their economic and social conditions were improved; he therefore promoted the reforming Irish Local Government Act of 1898 and a series of land purchasing schemes, including the Wyndham Irish Land Act of 1903. On foreign policy he hoped to encourage alliances to shore up Britain's position as a great power but had failed to secure any such arrangements before the Boer War began in October 1899.

The Boer War divided political opinion in Britain but the Salisbury government was still able to win the general election of October 1900. When the Boers surrendered, unconditionally, in the summer of 1902 Salisbury resigned as Prime Minister and was replaced by Balfour, the only acceptable Conservative Leader given that his two rivals, the Duke of Devonshire and Joseph Chamberlain, were old Liberal Unionists who had split from Gladstone in the mid 1880s over the issue of Home Rule. Balfour inherited a Conservative and Unionist government which was deeply divided on the issues of education and free trade verses protectionism.

The 1902 Education Act, which owed a great deal to Balfour, proved contentious for whilst it removed 3500 school boards and re-placed them by 328 local education authorities (LEAs) and rationalized the education system the Act offended religious dissenters and non-conformists. David Lloyd George led resistance to the Act in 1902, advocating that opponents should refuse to pay that proportion of the education rate which would be paid by the LEAs to support Church of England schools. This was serious because it united the Liberals against the Act but there was also direct concern within the Conservative and Unionist Party. Joseph Chamberlain, a Unitarian, depended upon the dissenters' votes in his Birmingham constituency. This proved divisive within the Conservative and Unionist alliance but Chamberlain's advocacy of Imperial Preference and protection proved even more contentious.

In 1903 Joseph Chamberlain began his campaign to protect British industries from unfair competition, to extend social reform, and to build up a network of Imperial Preference. He was opposed by some Unionists, the 'Unionist Free-Fooders', and by Balfour who attempted to steer a middle course. Balfour's solution was to use the threat of protection to force protectionist countries to negotiate, and he outlined his views in his pamphlet *Insular Free Trade*. However, this did not solve his government's problems for Chamberlain resigned in order to advocate protectionism whilst C. T. Ritchie, Chancellor of the Exchequer, resigned because of his uncompromising free trade position. Other fiscal debates also created tensions within Balfour's government.

Nevertheless, despite these divisions Balfour's government could claim some political achievements. It passed the 1902 Education Act that formed the basis of the twentieth-century British education system. It also attempted to respond to the weakness of the British military machine, exposed by the Boer War, by moving to reform the navy and by creating a Committee of Imperial Defence. Britain's foreign relations were also improved when Lord Lansdowne, the Foreign Secretary, arranged the Anglo-Japanese Alliance and the Anglo-French Entente.

Yet, with an ailing government, Balfour resigned in December 1905 defying the divided Liberals to form a government. However, Campbell-Bannerman did precisely that and his government was confirmed in office at the subsequent general election, which saw the Unionists reduced to a mere 157 seats. In the process, Balfour lost his Manchester East seat, although was quickly returned for the City of London in a by-election in February 1906. From then until 1911, Balfour led the Conservative/Unionists in the House of Commons, organized the opposition to Lloyd George's 'People's Budget' and was prepared to form a minority government to allow George V to avoid having to accept the Liberal threat of the mass creation of new peers to ensure that the House of Lords would pass their reform legislation. In the end, in order to avoid the mass production of new peers, Balfour ordered his supporters in the Lords not to oppose the Liberal Party's Parliament Bill. The Unionist Party rebelled at Balfour's action, a 'BMG' (Balfour Must Go) campaign was mounted, and Balfour was replaced as Conservative and Unionist Leader by Andrew Bonar Law in November 1911.

Balfour, now 64 years of age, continued in political life and was invited by Herbert Asquith, the Liberal Prime Minister, to be a member of the Committee of Imperial Defence. In the wartime Coalition Government, formed in May 1915, he became the First Lord of the Admiralty and, in December 1916, he became Foreign Secretary in David Lloyd George's wartime administration, holding the post until 1919. At the Paris Peace Conference in 1919, he played second fiddle to Lloyd George. Nonetheless, the most famous event of this period, the 'Balfour Declaration', was entirely his own doing. On his personal initiative he announced, in November 1917, that the Jews would be promised a 'national homeland'. The question of Jewish settlement in Palestine came to dominate the next three decades.

In October 1919 Balfour became Lord President of the Council and was deeply involved in negotiations with Japan and the United States in connection with the Washington Naval Treaty of 1922. In May 1922 he became the first Earl Balfour and entered the House of Lords. Convinced of the need for a Coalition Government he left office when Lloyd George was replaced as Prime Minister by Andrew Bonar Law, not returning again until April 1925 when he was offered the post of Lord President of the Council by Stanley Baldwin. In this office he was involved in discussion about the relationship of the United Kingdom to its Dominions and also encouraged scientific research through the Medical Research Council and several other similar bodies. He eventually stood down from political office in June 1929, dying less than a year later, a few months short of his eighty-second birthday, on 19 March 1930.

Balfour was always an aloof and distant politician whose political opportunities arose partly as a result of his connection with the Cecil family and the patronage of his uncle, Lord Salisbury. Nevertheless, he was a politician who recognized that the political climate was changing and that the implication of the extension of democratic voting to the working classes was that aristocratic rule could not survive. His premiership was without any major success, other than the controversial 1902 Education Act, but his later political career was a study in pragmatic politics. In 1911 he recognized that the House of Lords could not continue to block Lloyd George's 'People's Budget', the means of financing many of the Liberal social reforms. In the First

World War he recognized that there was a need for a David Lloyd George to move Britain towards democratic government. He also recognized that there would be an overwhelming need for a Jewish state. In the end, Balfour, who never won a general election, was possibly the first Conservative Prime Minister and Party Leader who was driven more by political pragmatism than by political principle. Nonetheless, he is often remembered for the Balfour Declaration and his fathering of the idea of a Jewish state in Palestine.

See also: Asquith, Chamberlain (Joseph), Lloyd George

Further reading

Egremont, M., 1980, Balfour, London: Collins.
Mackay, R. F., 1985, Balfour. Intellectual Statesman, Oxford: Oxford University Press.
Ramsden, J., 1978, A History of the Conservative Party, vol. 3, The Age of Balfour and Baldwin 1902–1940, London: Longman.
Searle, G. R., 1990, The Quest for National Efficiency. A Study in British Politics and Political Thought, 1899–1914, London: Ashfield Press.
Shannon, C., 1988, Arthur James Balfour and Ireland, 1874–1922, Washington, DC: Catholic University of America Press.
Zebel, S., 1973, Balfour: A Political Biography, Cambridge: Cambridge University Press.

LORD BEAVERBROOK (WILLIAM MAXWELL AITKEN) 1879–1964

Lord Beaverbrook is rightly known as the most influential 'press baron' of the twentieth century, although his personal campaign against Stanley Baldwin was remarkably unsuccessful in the 1920s and 1930s. Nevertheless, he also acted as a government minister in both World Wars, being particularly effective as Minister of Aircraft Production in 1940–1.

Beaverbrook was born William Maxwell Aitken in Canada in 1879. He acquired a fortune there before moving to Britain in 1910. An ardent believer in the tariff reform policies of Joseph Chamberlain, he was elected as Conservative MP in December 1910. This was largely as a result of his friendship with fellow Canadian Andrew Bonar Law who was at that time becoming the leading force within the Conservative and Unionist Party. Indeed, the relationship became symbiotic and whilst Aitken was not a very effective MP he was considered a more than capable manipulator in politics and was one of those who encouraged Bonar Law to become Conservative Leader in November 1911.

Aitken's close association with Bonar Law gave him a power base within the Conservative Party. In this respect he was influential in bringing together Bonar Law and Lloyd George in December 1916 to force Asquith's resignation and to replace him as Prime Minister. Although a close friend of Lloyd George, he was also influential in the Conservative Party's Carlton Club meeting in October 1922 which opposed the continuation of the post-war Coalition Government under Lloyd George, encouraged Austen Chamberlain to resign the leadership of the Conservative and Unionist Party, and paved the way for the return of Bonar Law as Conservative Leader and Prime Minister. He began to earn a reputation as a political 'kingmaker' but lost some of his power base when Bonar Law resigned as Prime Minister, as a result of ill health, dying in 1923. Nevertheless Aitken's political importance had been quickly recognized and he had been created the first Baron Beaverbrook in 1917.

It is primarily as a newspaper baron that Beaverbrook is best known. He had acquired control of the *Daily Express* in 1916 and founded the *Sunday Express* in 1918. In 1923 he added to his newspaper empire by purchasing the *Evening Standard*, the London afternoon paper. He constantly monitored the style and content of these papers and his influential position in the newspaper world accounts for the fact that Lloyd George appointed him as his Minister of Information between 1918 and 1919. It was believed that he, along with other newspaper barons such as Lords Northcliffe and Rothermere, wielded enormous political power during the inter-war years. Indeed, Beaverbrook and Rothermere, the owner of the *Daily Mail*, put that to the test in the early 1930s. Alarmed at what they saw as the political ineptitude of Stanley Baldwin, who had lost the May 1929 general election, they moved to press forward the policies of protectionism onto the Conservative Party and to replace Baldwin as its Leader. Indeed, they set up an Empire Party in 1930 and conducted an 'Empire Crusade', committed to protectionism and the creation of a free-trade area within the British Empire. This new Party contested parliamentary by-elections in which Conservative candidates were defeated. Yet, in the end, the campaign was defeated by a more-than-wily Baldwin, who conceded the need for protectionism in October 1930, reviving the policy he had first put forward at the 1923 general election. In the spring of 1931 Baldwin also launched his bitter attack against the press barons, concluding that their role was that 'of the harlot' aiming at 'power without responsibility'. It is rumoured that one the platform audience jokingly added that 'He's lost us the harlot's vote'. The Empire Party's political demands were further undermined when Baldwin, effectively Deputy Prime Minister in the National Government of James Ramsay MacDonald, pushed forward with protectionist measures in 1931 and 1932 and secured an element of Empire Free Trade, through bilateral arrangements, at the Ottawa Conference in the summer of 1932.

Thwarted within the Conservative Party, Beaverbrook and Rothermere quickly transferred their political support to the emerging British Union of Fascists which had been formed in 1932 under the leadership of Oswald Mosley. This was a short-lived affair, conducted more by Rothermere than Beaverbrook, and did not survive the violence associated with the big fascist meeting at Olympia in June 1934.

With the outbreak of the Second World War Beaverbrook developed a close friendship with Winston Churchill, who became Prime Minister of a wartime government in May 1940. He was a successful Minister of Aircraft Production between May 1940 and May 1941. He was Minister of Supply between 1941 and 1942, left the government for eighteen months to campaign for the opening of the second front in Europe to relieve the Russians from the full military might of the Germans, and then returned to become Lord Privy Seal between 1943 and 1945. He was regarded as a mischievous force in this role and, perhaps unjustifiably, was blamed for the Conservative Party's defeat in the general election of 1945.

After 1945 Beaverbrook played a less prominent role in British politics, and was greatly involved in writing up his own account of the political events of his lifetime. He died in 1968, and was remembered as possibly the most influential press baron in British history, although it is clear that his influence was not as great as has sometimes been claimed. Whilst he was considered a 'kingmaker', who could influence the public mood, he was often outmanoeuvred on the major political issues of the day.

See also: Baldwin, Chamberlain, Churchill

Further reading

Ball, S., 1988, *Baldwin and the Conservative Party: The Crisis of 1929–1931*, New Haven and London: Yale University Press.

Beaverbrook, Lord, 1960, 2nd edition, *Politicians and the War, 1914–1916*, London: Oldbourne Book Co.

Beaverbrook, Lord, 1963, *The Decline and Fall of Lloyd George. And Great was the Fall Thereof*, London: Collins.

Chisholm, A. and Davie, M., 1992, *Lord Beaverbrook: A Life*, London: Hutchinson.
Taylor, A. J. P., 1972, *Beaverbrook*, London: Hamilton.

ANEURIN (NYE) BEVAN 1897–1960

Aneurin Bevan was one of the key figures in Clement Attlee's post-war Labour governments of 1945 to 1951, being largely responsible for the free National Health Service (NHS) which came into existence in July 1948. His opposition to the attempts of Herbert Morrison and Hugh Gaitskell to impose prescription charges led him to resign from the government in April 1951 and to act as the centre for a loose grouping of the socialist Left within the Labour Party that became known as the Bevanites. Nevertheless, he returned to the centre of Labour Party politics in the late 1950s and eventually became the Deputy Labour Leader to Hugh Gaitskell, a man who he had despised in his earlier years.

Bevan was born in Tredegar, South Wales, on 15 November 1897 and had an elementary education. He became a miner but won a scholarship to the Central Labour College, London in 1919. Returning to Tredegar in 1921 he became involved in trade union affairs, acting as Chairman of the Tredegar Council during the General Strike of 1926. Yet Bevan was very much a political animal. He became MP for Ebbw Vale in 1929, a constituency he represented until his death in 1960.

In Parliament, Bevan campaigned tirelessly in the interests of both the employed and unemployed members of the working class. He briefly supported Oswald Mosley's New Party in 1931, because Mosley seemed to offer policies to tackle unemployment, but soon became disillusioned with Mosley's movement especially once he supported the Anomalies Bill of 1931, which was designed to deprive married women of unemployment benefit on the grounds that they could not be 'genuinely seeking work'. He opposed the Household Means Test throughout the early 1930s and operated through the left-wing journal *Tribune*, formed in 1937, to attack the Labour leadership. It was in these years, in 1934 indeed, that he married Jennie Lee who, in her own right, became an influential force within the Labour Left. During the Second World War Bevan, rejected the political truce between the main political parties and fought the war on two fronts – against the Tory Party and the Fascists – and was unflinching in his attack upon Winston Churchill. It was during these years that he gained a reputation for being an orator reminiscent of his fellow Welshman David Lloyd George.

Yet Bevan's finest hour arrived when he was appointed Minister of Health and Housing in Attlee's Labour government of 1945. In that role he cajoled the private doctors and the British Medical Association (BMA), who referred to him as a 'squalid nuisance', the 'Minister of Disease' and a 'Tito from Tonypandy', into working with the NHS, even though the BMA organized votes of its members against entering the new service because of the dangers it posed in restricting their freedom and making them civil servants. They also objected to being forced into 'under-doctored' areas and the restrictions they might find in selling their practices. Bevan's remark that his Tory opponents were 'lower than vermin' caused great controversy at the time and led many Conservatives to form themselves into 'vermin clubs'. Bevan's NHS went further than the wartime health reforms, and much further than the Labour Party had outlined in its 1945 election manifesto, by effectively nationalizing the hospitals, creating a public general-practitioner service, and making the treatment of illness and provision of medical treatment entirely free. In his book *In Place of Fear* (1952) he explained that it was ludicrous to expect patients to await a vital operation because they lacked the right number of self-contributions. But the NHS proved to be expensive and both Attlee and Morrison sought to curb expenditure and introduce prescription charges. Bevan fought off these attempts at the 1950 general election but then, on 17 January 1951, was moved to the post of Minister of Labour and National Service. The move coincided with the decision of Gaitskell, Chancellor of the Exchequer, to impose health charges. This provoked Bevan to resign from the government on 24 April 1951, along with Harold Wilson and John Freeman.

Between 1951 and 1955 Bevan was the figurehead of a loosely organized group of left-wing Labour MPs, based upon the Keep Left Group, who became known as the Bevanites. Keep Left included Richard Crossman and Barbara Castle, and saw itself as the left-wing alternative to the right-wing revisionist group emerging around Hugh Gaitskell and Anthony Crosland. The Bevanites advocated unilateral nuclear disarmament and Bevan's decision to oppose the Parliamentary Labour Party line of supporting manufacture of the hydrogen bomb almost got him expelled from the Party in 1955. At this point, however, Bevan's position changed. Having been defeated by Gaitskell in the leadership contest of December 1955 he appears to have come to an understanding with the new Leader, who made him Shadow Colonial Secretary. From then on, he was patriotic over the Suez Crisis and was Treasurer of the Party between 1956 and 1960. He effectively divested himself of the title 'Leader of the Left' when, in

1957, he attacked unilateral disarmament at the 1957 Labour Party Conference, asking delegates not to send a future Labour Foreign Secretary 'naked into the Conference chamber'. In other words, he preferred to negotiate away nuclear weapons than abandon them. In 1959 he became Labour's Deputy Leader and adorned Labour's election poster alongside Hugh Gaitskell and Barbara Castle in a forceful demonstration of the Party's new-found unity. However, all was to no avail and Labour was defeated once again. Shortly afterwards, in 1960, Nye died of cancer. So ended one of the finest political careers of any British politician.

Bevan never gained the really big offices of state and, indeed, would probably have been temperamentally unsuited to being Prime Minister, Chancellor of the Exchequer or Foreign Secretary. Nevertheless, he was an excellent Minister of Health and Housing and a more than passable Minister of Labour. His precise political leanings have been the subject of controversy however, with Michael Foot emphasizing Bevan's traditional Labour credentials and John Campbell referring to Bevan's Communist/Marxist roots. Nevertheless, Bevan's great claim to fame is that he created the NHS, which stemmed more from his own ideas than those of William Beveridge and the wartime social reformers. Also, according to Harold Macmillan in his television discussion of the past political masters and politicians, Bevan ranked alongside Lloyd George and Churchill as one of the great parliamentary orators of his generation, using his famous stutter to great effect. His speaking ability might well have passed from the popular memory but his main legacy, the NHS, is still with us.

See also: Attlee, Castle, Churchill, Crosland, Gaitskell

Further reading

Campbell, J., 1987, *Aneurin Bevan and the Mirage of British Socialism*, London: Weidenfeld & Nicolson.

Foot, M., 1962, *Aneurin Bevan. A Biography. Vol. 1: 1897–1945*, London: Granada.

Foot, M., 1973, *Anerurin Bevan. A Biography. Vol. 2: 1945–1960*, London: Davis-Poynter.

WILLIAM (HENRY) BEVERIDGE 1876–1963

William Henry Beveridge's name is closely associated with the emergence of the British welfare state. Indeed, the Beveridge Report of 1942, which focused upon the future needs of society and laid down the extension of the insurance principle, greatly shaped the general approach of the post-war Attlee governments to welfare provision, with the exception of its strategy towards the formation of the National Health Service. Whilst he has often enjoyed a high reputation for his work within Liberal and socialist circles since the 1970s Beveridge has come under substantial criticism for his actions, especially from right-wing critics such as Correlli Barnett who saw his 1942 report as imposing a financial burden upon Britain which significantly contributed to Britain's post-war decline.

Beveridge was born in 1879 into an upper-middle-class English family stationed in India. He was educated at Charterhouse and Oxford University. However, at Oxford became interested in social reform, influenced greatly by Edward Caird, the then Master of Balliol College, Oxford. After leaving Oxford he took a post as leader-writer for the Conservative newspaper the *Morning Post* but also lived in at Toynbee Hall, a university settlement in the East End of London.

Beveridge spent the years 1903–7 as a sub-warden of Toynbee Hall, where university graduates worked amongst the poor in their spare time. He felt that whilst the settlement movement exerted little impact upon unemployment and poverty it did provide opportunities for research. His work at Toynbee Hall put him into contact with the Webbs, George Lansbury and many others who were equally concerned about unemployment. His voluminous correspondence in the British Library of Political and Economic Science bears witness to the value of his researches and contacts.

During 1906 and 1907 Beveridge, along with George Lansbury, a prominent Labour Leader, was a member of the Colonies Committee, a voluntary body concerned about unemployment. Whilst on good personal terms with Lansbury, Beveridge found that there was a fundamental disagreement between them. Lansbury felt that Beveridge's ideas on labour exchanges simply emptied the reservoir of unemployed on a temporary basis, and he wrote that:

> I cannot see how your system is going to prevent the creation of the unemployed. You seem to imagine that the unemployed are where they are for reasons other than the real ones. The unemployed are unemployed simply because there is not enough employment to go round.[...]
> In conclusion remember that my difference with you is this: you think that once you have got the problem stated and set out in an understanding manner there will be left a multitude of people who emigration or colonies must deal

with and that so far, the problem has been settled. On the other hand, I contend that while production is carried on for profit, there must be and will be a margin of unemployed labour on which the employer can draw whenever he pleases, and which will enable him to determine wages....

As I have already said, there is no way out of this except in State organisation of industry....

(W. H. Beveridge papers, British Library of Political and Economic Science, personal papers Ib 6, letter from George Lansbury to Beveridge, 1 February 1907)

Beveridge was also closely involved with Beatrice Webb, who attempted to draw upon his expertise to counter the Charity Organization Society's negative attitude whilst dealing with the able-bodied unemployed on the Royal Commission on the Poor Laws (Beveridge Ib 6, letter from Beatrice Webb to Beveridge, 4 May 1907). He was also concerned with efforts to finance the Outer London Inquiry into poverty mounted by Canon Barnett, a founder of Toynbee Hall, and Frances W. Buxton. The Inquiry sought to raise £600–700 in order to examine 'Life and Labour in Extra-Metropolitan areas', particularly West Ham which had a population of 300,000, the great majority of them being poor. Effectively, this was to be a survey of the poor and casual labour.

Drawn into the study of poverty and unemployment at many levels, Beveridge quickly became the expert on unemployment and directed and influenced affairs. His ideas greatly influenced both the Majority and Minority Reports of the Royal Commission on the Poor Laws, both of which accepted that there were differences between temporary unemployment of skilled workers in periods of depression and the permanent under-employment of the unskilled or semiskilled in an overstocked labour market. Both reports proposed the establishment of national labour exchanges at which all unemployed workmen would be registered and where all vacancies would be notified; the Minority Report suggested programmes of public works while the Majority Report accepted such measures as necessary only in times of depression. Industrial retraining in the colonies was recommended by the Minority Report for those who refused to work but was less enthusiastically accepted by the Majority Report, which advocated unemployment insurance whilst the Minority Report sought non-contributory benefits.

Beveridge influenced the Poor Laws Commission but Winston Churchill, who was to become President of the Board of Trade in 1908, was already contemplating a package of changes, including labour exchanges. Beveridge's influence was plainly visible here for Churchill recruited him to the Board of Trade in July 1908 with responsibility for instituting these proposals. The Commons approved the formation of labour exchanges and by June 1909 they had become a reality. There were 423 such exchanges by February 1914 with appointed management boards containing worker representatives.

It is debatable how successful the exchanges were. By 1914 they were registering over two million workers per year and finding 3000 jobs per day. Nevertheless, three-quarters of the registered did not get jobs through the exchanges and there was always a lurking suspicion among the trade unions that the labour exchanges could be used for strike breaking. It is certainly questionable whether or not they achieved the 'organized fluidity of labour' claimed by Beveridge in his book *Unemployment: A Problem of Industry* (1909).

In 1909 Churchill introduced the Trades Boards Act, establishing boards of employers and employees to fix minimum wages in the unionized 'sweated trades'. Again, the effectiveness of this legislation is debatable. Less so was the introduction of unemployment insurance, which became Part II of the 1911 National Insurance Act. Once again the idea came from Beveridge, who felt that unemployment insurance could be provided for most workers, if not for the chronically unemployed. Aided by H. Llewellyn Smith, Beveridge developed the idea that certain trades should be covered by a compulsory system of contributory insurance. Churchill presented their ideas to the House of Commons on 19 May 1909, they were implemented in the 1911 National Insurance Act and so became embodied in British legislation – the commitment of both state and the individual to providing cover against the risks befalling workers in the life cycle.

During the First World War, Beveridge worked for the Ministries of Munitions and of Food. After the war, in 1919, he gained a knighthood and was appointed Director of the London School of Economics, where he attempted to implement schemes supplementing the incomes of those members of staff with families. He held this post until he became Master of University College, Oxford, in 1937. He was also involved in various government work from time to time. Most notably he was a member of the Samuel Commission which investigated conditions in the coal industry in 1925 and 1926, concluding that miners' wages should be reduced whilst the industry was rationalized by the employers. He was also Chairman of the Insurance Statutory Committee between 1934 and 1944, which presided over the funds gathered from those who paid insurance and the payment of insurance benefits.

Beveridge was an intelligent man but was also considered to be vain and rude. This partly explains why it was not until 1940 and the Second World War that he was drawn into the administration of government, and then only put in charge of the relatively insignificant Ministry of Labour manpower survey. Ernest Bevin, the Minister of Labour, released him and permitted him to become Chairman of a proposed inquiry into the reorganization of social, insurance and allied services that was to form part of a plan for post-war reconstruction. He was actually appointed to this new post in June 1941 by Arthur Greenwood, Minister without Portfolio, who was responsible for post-war reconstruction. Beveridge's brief was to undertake, with special reference to the possibilities for inter-relation, a survey of the existing national schemes of social insurance and allied services, including workmen's compensation, and to make recommendations.

When the controversial nature of the report emerged it was decided that Beveridge would sign the report himself and that the civil servants would be regarded as his advisers. For more than a year he drew ideas and papers together to produce his solution to poverty, permitted by the last four words of his brief – 'and to make recommendations'.

The report *Social Insurance and Allied Services* was published in December 1942, just after the British success at El Alamein and a time when public confidence and spirit was high. Indeed, the Beveridge papers contain numerous letters, from the full range of the political spectrum, supporting all parts of the report. It was an immediate bestseller and established upon the minds of the British public three major guiding principles. First, it claimed to be a break from the past, although in fact it relied very much on the contributory system put forward by the Liberals before the First World War: Beveridge wrote that 'I am sure that it is good Liberal doctrine'. Second, social insurance was directed at tackling 'Want', although the report assumed that it would be a part of an attack upon the 'five giant problems of Want, Disease, Ignorance, Squalor and Idleness'. Third, it wished to combine state and personal initiative. Beveridge also assumed that any government would also wish to establish a family allowance system (as he had done at the London School of Economics), create a comprehensive health service, and establish full employment. With these in place he argued that his attack upon Want would work.

The Beveridge scheme was not particularly revolutionary or extreme. It simply suggested that in return for a single and uniform weekly contribution a qualified individual would have the right to the standard benefits for sickness, unemployment, widows, orphans, old age, maternity, industrial injuries and funerals. The system would be universal and would provide subsistence benefits for all on the six principles of: flat-rate subsistence benefits; flat-rate contributions; the unification of administrative responsibilities; the adequacy of benefits; comprehensiveness; and classification (adjustment to the needs of differing circumstances).

Nevertheless, it was a vitally important document for it built up a scheme based upon proven past experience and applied it to the whole nation. What was distinctive about it is that it was to be universal rather than selective and that dependants would also be covered by the new arrangements. Even more significant was the fact that this attempt to tackle Want was linked to the other four giants that had to be called to order to properly tackle poverty from all its angles. As Derek Fraser suggests, 'Here, in the totality of vision, was the revolutionary element in the Beveridge Report' [1973, p. 216]. It would work if unemployment was no more than 3.5 per cent and assuming that the governments maintained a commitment to full employment, by which he meant a level of about 3 per cent.

Rodney Lowe is not so convinced of the revolutionary nature or effectiveness of the Beveridge Report. He regards the report as being a flawed and illogical document. Its universalism led to vast and unnecessary expenditure; it did not eliminate the means test, which still survived for pensioners who might be expected to contribute to their rents; and it failed to consider the need to merge the tax and benefits system. Above all, it did not eliminate poverty. These criticisms are, with hindsight, obviously justified. Yet these are clearly issues that have not been resolved to this day. The recent more selective approach to benefits has not eliminated poverty and the major political parties are still examining, with little progress, how to merge the tax and benefit system.

Whatever the current criticisms, it is clear that within the context of the Second World War, and in the euphoria of a recent military victory, the Beveridge Report was seen as Utopia by many contemporaries. However, this was not a view held by Churchill and some of his colleagues. He was suspicious about where such demands might lead and was already on record as having noted that 'Reconstruction was in the air' and that there was 'a dangerous optimism ... growing about post-war conditions'. The Beveridge Report confirmed him in his suspicions. Indeed, his government refused to implement this policy straight away, and this hesitancy was compounded by the fact that the Army Bureau of Current Affairs had its published survey of the Beveridge Report withdrawn within two days on the orders of the War Office. Such actions provoked the only major anti-government revolt by the Parliamentary Labour Party during the Second World War.

In interviews Attlee had suggested that social security was effectively socialism: 'Socialism does not admit to an alternative, Social Security to us can only mean Socialism' (Harris, 1982, p. 220). For he and his supporters it was vital that the Beveridge Report should be accepted quickly as an essential commitment by the government. But it was quite clear that Churchill intended to delay its publication, and Attlee even felt that it might be saved until the end of the war to form part of the Conservative programme. He was also hostile to the Churchill memorandum sent round government circles in which it was suggested that the economics of life might be such as to force a choice between 'social insurance and other urgent claims on limited resources'. Attlee sent a counter-memorandum to the government urging that 'decisions must be taken and implemented in the field of post-war reconstruction *before* the end of the war'. Churchill relented and the government accepted most of the report but gave the impression that it was committed to nothing. A Labour resolution that the government should support the Beveridge Report and implement it was defeated on 18 February 1943, by 335 votes to 119, but 97 Labour MPs had voted against the government – 22 of whom were government ministers.

Churchill's reluctance stemmed partly from the fact that the Treasury felt that the post-war economic revival would be damaged if industry were burdened with high costs. He was also advised by a secret report to the Conservative Party that the Beveridge Scheme was unsustainable and there were other criticisms that the Children's Allowance would depress wages and that fairness could not be achieved by flat-rate benefits.

It is clear that the Beveridge Report became a sensitive issue, especially after the midsummer Gallup polls in 1943 when Labour registered a lead of 11 per cent over the Conservatives and when James Griffiths, a prominent Labour politician, reflected that the parliamentary vote on the Beveridge Report made Labour's return at the next general election almost inevitable. In the end the government was forced to set up a Reconstruction Committee towards the close of 1943. This saw the publication of a White Paper, *A National Health Service*, which advocated the creation of a comprehensive health service. The Committee also inherited R. A. Butler's 1943 White Paper on *Educational Reconstruction*, which anticipated the passing of the 1944 Education Act with its commitment to raising the school-leaving age to 15, and its creation of the primary, secondary and further education divide along the lines of the Hadow and Spens reports produced during the inter-war years. In 1944 the Reconstruction Committee also put forward the White Paper on *Employment Policy*, which accepted Keynes's policies about using public expenditure to manage the economy if unemployment rose to high levels. However, this was rather modest in comparison to Beveridge's *Full Employment in a Free Society*, published privately, which offered much the same approach although, as Beveridge noted, the government paper was essentially a 'policy of public works planned five years at a time and kept on tap to mitigate fluctuations', whilst his scheme was a 'Policy for Full Employment, defined as meaning always more vacant jobs than idle men' and was to be part of the wider scheme that he had envisaged in his 1942 report. It would include policies on housing, health, children's allowances, the extension of government control of industry, mobility of labour and the creation of a battery of policies including the vital elements of multilateral trade: full employment, balancing international accounts, and stability of economic policy. In other words, the White Paper was an 'anti-cycle policy, not a policy for full employment', whilst Beveridge offered a policy for full employment. (Beveridge, 1944, pp. 272–3.)

Beveridge's publication did not appear until November 1944, by which time he had been returned to the House of Commons as MP for Berwick-on-Tweed and Parliament had adopted the White Paper. Indeed, Ernest Bevin had moved for its adoption by Parliament in June 1944 but found himself opposed from within his own Party by Aneurin Bevan, who felt that it was simply a device for propping up capitalism and that socialism alone was the cure for unemployment.

The 'Paper Chase' was completed by the publication of the White Paper on *Social Insurance* in September 1944, which accepted many aspects of the 1942 Beveridge Report. The major difference was that it did not accept subsistence benefits and it became the model of the Labour government's 1946 Insurance Act.

Contemporary Labour politicians, such as Hugh Dalton, expressed some concerns about the Beveridge Report, whilst accepting that it was a fine document. Yet these were nothing when compared with the reactions of recent right-wing writers such as Max Beloff and Correlli Barnett (Beloff, 1982; Barnet, 1986). Just as Mrs Thatcher's early traumas in office were blamed upon the social policies forced upon Britain by the Beveridge Report and wartime radicalism. To Barnett it was the Beveridge Report that provided the battlefield on which the decisive struggle to win a national commitment to New Jerusalem was waged and won. It was Beveridge who was the main architect of the report and the post-war welfare state:

> As appropriate for a prophet and a brilliant Oxford intellect, Beveridge thought a lot of himself, so that righteousness went hand in hand with authoritarian arrogance and skill at manipulating the press to make him the Field Marshal Montgomery of social welfare.
>
> (Barnett, 1986, p. 26)

According to Barnett, the War Cabinet was misled by its advisers, most notably Beveridge, into building a comprehensive welfare state system, the 'New Jerusalem', which Britain's industrial economy has been unable to support.

Whatever current and contemporary criticisms occurred it is clear that, apart from the creation of the NHS, which created a nationalized health provision never envisaged by Beveridge, most of the other legislation introduced by Attlee's post-war Labour governments reflected Beveridge policies. This was evident in the 1945 Family Allowance Act, the 1946 National Insurance Act and the 1948 National Assistance Act.

In the post-war years Beveridge was given a peerage, having lost his Berwick-on-Tweed seat in the 1945 general election. He continued in public life, chairing and acting on various commissions until his death in 1963. When he died there was immense respect for the founder of the modern British welfare state, although since then his role and its value have been subjected to an academic and political buffeting.

See also: Asquith, Churchill, Lloyd George

Further reading

Barnett, C., 1986, *The Audit of War: The Illusion and Reality of Britain as a Great Nation*, London: Macmillan.

Beloff, M., 1984, *Wars and Warfare*, London: Edward Arnold.

Beveridge, Lord, 1953, *Power and Influence*, London: Hodder & Stoughton.

Beveridge, W., 1944, *Full Employment in a Free Society*, London: Allen & Unwin.

Fraser, D., 1973, *The Evolution of the British Welfare State*, London: Macmillan.

Harris, J., 1977, *William Beveridge. A Biography*, Oxford: Clarendon.

Social Insurance and Allied Services, 1942 (Beveridge Report) Cmnd 6404, London.

Williams, K. and Williams, J. (eds), 1987, *A Beveridge Reader*, London: Allen & Unwin.

ERNEST BEVIN 1881–1951

Ernest Bevin was probably the greatest British trade union leader of the twentieth century. He was also a prominent member of the Trades Union Congress at the time of the General Strike in 1926 and an influential figure in the reshaping of Labour Party policy during the 1930s. Yet his greatest claim to fame is that he was Minister of Labour between 1940 and 1945, overseeing the organization of labour resources in Winston Churchill's wartime government, and was Foreign Secretary in Clement Attlee's Labour governments of 1945–50. It was in this last role that he was instrumental in forcing through the formation of the North Atlantic Treaty Organization (NATO) in 1949, thus helping to shape international politics for the next fifty years.

Ernest Bevin was born at Winsford, in Somerset, on 7 March 1881, although some sources suggest it was 9 March. He was the illegitimate son of an agricultural labourer, raised by his mother until he was eight when, upon her death, he was raised by his half-sister in Devon. He received little formal education, and began working on a farm at the age of eleven. Then, at the age of thirteen, he moved to Bristol to live with his half-brother and became a soft rounds drinksman (a mineral water deliveryman). He became an active lay preacher in the Baptist Church where he gained experience in public speaking, but was soon attracted to the Bristol Socialist Society. It was about this time that he married Florence Townley, and they had one child, Queenie, who was born in 1914.

Bristol, with its outlying docks, was still an important seaport at this time and Bevin was drawn into helping organize the dockers and carters as a result of his concern for the unemployed and his work on Ramsay MacDonald's 'Right to Work' Movement in 1908. Indeed, in 1910 he was asked to organize the carters for the Dock, Wharf, Riverside, and General Labourers' Union, better known as the Dockers' Union. He increased local membership significantly and by 1914 had risen to become one of the three national organizers of the Union, working closely with Ben Tillett, the famous leader of the London Dock Strike of 1889. Seeing that employers' organizations were uniting, and growing much stronger, Bevin became convinced that trade unions needed to organize together more effectively. In this respect, he advocated the formation of the General Council of the Trades Union Congress (TUC) in 1920, to give more centralized industrial direction to the trade union movement, and pushed forward with the amalgamation of fourteen different unions into the Transport and General Workers' Union in January 1922.

Throughout the inter-war years, Bevin was the dominant British trade union leader. He organized the General Strike, which lasted for nine days in May 1926, ensuring that there was some semblance of discipline in the last-minute arrangements of the TUC to support the miners who had been locked out by the coal owners. In the role, he earned the criticism of the Communist Party of Great Britain which could not accept the calling off of the General Strike, a level of obloquy which saw Bevin in conflict with communists throughout the 1930s.

He attempted to influence the economic policy of Ramsay MacDonald's second Labour government of 1929 to 1931 by acting on the Economic Advisory Committee and the Macmillan Committee, but found that his influence was limited. In the end he published his own expansionist policies for tackling unemployment in his pamphlet *My Plan for 2,000,000 Unemployed* (1932). This advocated raising the school-leaving age and lowering the retirement age as well as policies to generate immediate work. He had more success with the Labour Party. The National Council of Labour (formerly the Joint Council of Labour) brought the executives of the Parliamentary Labour Party, the Labour Party and the TUC together to attempt to co-ordinate the policies of the British Labour movement. Bevin steered this organization into discussing the need for public ownership, or the 'socialization of industry', in the 1930s and to direct Labour's foreign policy. In the case of rearmament, in order to deal with the threat of European fascism, Bevin first opposed it but then, in 1937, pushed staunchly for it in the wake of the Spanish Civil War and the powerful demonstration of air power by the German air force when it bombed Guernica, in Spain. He was also a formative influence on the Amulree Committee (Committee on Holidays with Pay), which, in 1938, recommended that workers should receive at least one week's annual holiday with pay. Indeed, he had helped to organize the Trades Union Congress's 'seaside drive' campaign to win support for paid holidays throughout seaside resorts in Britain in 1937.

Bevin saw himself as a trade union leader and not as a political figure. He felt that politicians, and particularly intellectual middle-class politicians, were people 'who stabbed you in the back'. As a result he was not crestfallen at his failure to secure a parliamentary seat in both the 1918 and the 1931 general elections. However, with the formation of Winston Churchill's wartime Coalition Government in May 1940, Bevin was offered the post of Minister of Labour and National Service. In fact the MP for Central Wandsworth stood down and Bevin was returned for that seat, retaining it until 1951, although it was known as East Wandsworth from 1950. In his new role, Bevin attempted to organize the whole country behind the war effort. His scheme to increase the number of coal miners in the country by directing young men, some of them public school boys, to the mines gave rise to the term 'Bevin's Boys'.

Towards the end of the Second World War, when victory in Europe had been achieved, the Labour Party won the 1945 general election. Bevin supported Attlee against the rival claims of Herbert Morrison for the position of Labour's Leader, and thus Prime Minister, and was rewarded with the post of Foreign Secretary in Attlee's post-war Labour governments. He was a much-respected Foreign Secretary, particularly within the Foreign Office which now found itself with an increased role in world affairs. He gave it an increased importance through his support of the Marshall Plan of 1947, whereby financial assistance was given to Western Europe, and through his pressure to secure the formation of NATO in 1949. Indeed, in this role he sought to preserve Britain's status as a world power, to work with the United States, and to oppose the threat to both Eastern Europe and Western Europe posed by the Soviet Union. In particular, he worked hard to defeat the Soviet Union's air blockade of Berlin in June 1948.

Bevin was seriously ill in his later years and decided to resign as Foreign Secretary on 19 February 1951 to become Lord Privy Seal, which involved no departmental responsibilities. He left government less than a month later, on his seventieth birthday, and died on 14 April 1951.

Bevin was one of the great British trade union leaders, an impressive Minister of Labour and a highly-respected Foreign Secretary, although this aspect of his career has suffered much criticism from the Labour Left in the last fifty years. Whatever the assessment may be, there is no doubt that he was a profoundly influential Foreign Secretary, who left an important legacy for twentieth-century British governments.

See also: Attlee, Baldwin, Churchill, MacDonald

Further reading

Bullock, A., 1960 and 1967, *The Life and Times of Ernest Bevin*, 2 vols, London: Heinemann.

Bullock, A., 1983, *Ernest Bevin: Foreign Secretary 1945–1951*, London: Heinemann.

Weiler, P., 1993, *Ernest Bevin*, Manchester: Manchester University Press.

(ANTHONY) TONY (CHARLES LYNTON) BLAIR 1953–

Tony Blair became Leader of the Labour Party on 21 July 1994 and then Labour's new Prime Minister on 1 May 1997, ending an eighteen-year period of Conservative rule during which the Labour Party despaired of ever forming another administration. He was also successful in the general election of 7 June 2001, securing a second term of office. Since becoming Labour Leader he has pursued his 'New Labour' policy of the 'Third Way', that is, of using both public and private bodies in the tackling of economic growth and social welfare. In effect, he has abandoned Labour's traditional commitments to public ownership, full employment and a close association with the trade unions.

Anthony Charles Lynton Blair was born on 6 May 1953 into a Conservative family. His father, Leo, was a law lecturer and a Conservative activist in the north-east of England, and his mother was Hazel Corscaden. The young Tony was educated at Fettes College, a leading Scottish public school, in Edinburgh, and read Law at St John's College, Oxford. Whilst at Oxford he became both a confirmed member of the Church of England and an adherent to the views of Christian ethical socialists, such as R. H. Tawney. He graduated from Oxford in 1975 and, in 1976, was called to the Bar at Lincoln's Inn, practising as a barrister until 1983 and specializing in employment and industrial law. He worked in the Chambers of Alexander Irvine, later Lord Chancellor in Blair's first Cabinet, where he met Cherie Booth. He married Cherie, who is now a barrister at Queen's Counsel and Judge, in 1980 and they have three sons and a daughter, the last being Leo who was born on 20 May 2000, giving Blair the distinction of being the first Prime Minister for 150 years to have a child born whilst in office.

Blair first entered Parliament in June 1983, at the age of thirty, as MP for Sedgefield. He had previously lost his deposit in contesting the Beaconsfield seat in a parliamentary by-election in 1982. He revealed an interest in financial and economic matters and was promoted to the Opposition Treasury front bench team in 1985 and, in 1987, he became spokesperson on trade and industry with special responsibility for consumer affairs and the City. He was elected to the Shadow Cabinet in 1988, and was appointed Shadow Secretary of State for Energy. In the following year he was made Shadow Secretary of State for Employment, and forged a new industrial relations policy which ended Labour's support for the closed shop and backed the retention of Conservative legislation on strike ballots and secondary action. He also supported Neil Kinnock's other reformist policies, most obviously his commitment to Europe, the advocacy of multilateral rather than unilateral nuclear disarmament, and the demand for wider democratic involvement in the Labour Party at the expense of the trade unions.

Following the general election defeat in 1992, Blair was appointed Shadow Home Secretary by John Smith, Labour's new Leader. In this role, he successfully wrested the law and order issue from the Conservatives, his slogan being 'Tough on crime, tough on the causes of crime'. In September 1992 he was also elected to Labour's National Executive Committee, the ruling body of the Labour Party. He was elected Labour Leader on 21 July 1994, following the sudden death of John Smith in May.

Tony Blair, perhaps more than any other Labour Leader, has been the modernizer who has not had to look to the past. Following through the ideas of his mentor Neil Kinnock, he was determined not to be constricted by the old Labour culture and felt that change was now more necessary than ever since the traditional mass industrial techniques had given way to a lighter more service-oriented style of industry. The traditional working-class workforce had changed enormously and declined. Blair maintained that the Conservative Party had been successful because it was seen as the Party that opposed state control while Labour was seen as the Party linked with trade unionism, the state, and ethnic minorities and social security claimants. He felt that such perceptions, whether real or exaggerated, had to be changed. The 'New Labour' Party he was to lead needed to cultivate the moderate image for which Kinnock had been pressing in the 1980s and the early 1990s. It needed to accept some of the changes that the Conservatives had introduced and to convince voters that it would not raise taxes, favour the trade unions, overspend and build up debts. In other words, it had to remove the demons of 'Old Labour'.

The symbol of this change from 'Old Labour' to 'New Labour' was the removal of the traditional Clause Four of the Labour Party Constitution, which committed Labour to common ownership of the means of production. Blair announced his intention to reject the existing Clause Four at the 1994 Labour Party Conference, also praising the successes of capitalism. Soon afterwards, he presented his alternative Clause Four. It committed Labour 'to work for a dynamic economy, serving the public interest, in which the enterprise of the market and the rigour of competition are joined with the forces of partnership and co-operation ... with a thriving sector and high quality public services....' In addition, there were vague references to a just society, security against fear, equality of opportunity and other related issues. This new Clause Four was to replace the existing one which formed the basis of Labour's commitment to social justice, equality and full employment. Effectively, the idea of redistribution of wealth and income within British society was being rejected. The race was on to get this accepted by the Party as a whole.

At first it appeared that constituencies and trade unions would be against the change, and so, at the end of 1994, Blair held an intensive round of meetings where he personally appealed to 30,000 Party members to support his new Clause Four. There was strong trade-union opposition to the new version, particularly from the Transport and General Workers' Union, but with more than two-thirds of the constituency Labour parties deciding to ballot their members, it was clear that about 85 per cent of their members would support Blair's new Clause.

At a special Conference of the Labour Party held on 29 April 1995, which was seen by the press as a test of Blair's ability to deal effectively with the trade unions, he won support for his new Clause Four by just under two-thirds of the vote. This revealed that over half (54.6 per cent) of the 70 per cent union vote and about 90 per cent of the 30 per cent constituency vote had supported Blair. Effectively, Blair had won support for his reforming leadership of the Labour Party, and the press and media recognized that this had been his personal triumph. He had tackled and tamed trade union opposition, buoyed up by the recognition that he and the Labour Party would not be taken seriously by the public if the proposal had been defeated. In the end, the majority of trade unions and constituency parties dared not vote against Blair if they wished the Party to have a significant political future.

'New Labour' has rejected the Keynesian social democracy of the 'Old', which had suggested that the state could intervene to promote growth and thus ensure economic growth and employment. Instead, it was now committed to the pursuit of low inflation, through the increased powers of the Bank of England, and was prepared to use interest rates in the same fashion as the Thatcher and Major governments had done. This meant that progressive taxation was ruled out and that Labour's past commitment to redistributing income and wealth was at an end.

These views were confirmed in a book written by Peter Mandelson and Roger Liddle, two of Blair's spin doctors, which was entitled *The Blair Revolution: Can New Labour Deliver?*, written in 1996. This suggested that Labour was standing on the brink of power and outlined the type of society that New Labour wished to create. They suggested that

> New Labour has set itself a bold task: to modernize Britain socially, economically and politically. In doing so it aims to build on Britain's strengths. Its mission is to create not destroy. Its strategy is to move forward from where Margaret Thatcher left off, rather than to dismantle every single thing she did.

They further suggested that New Labour's approach was based upon five insights: the need for people to feel secure; investment, partnership and top-quality education for all; recognition of the potential of government; 'One Nation socialism' going beyond the battles of the past between private and public interests; and the need to unite public and private activities in the ideal of social co-operation. Put more explicitly:

> New Labour believes that it is possible to combine a free market economy with social justice; liberty of the individual with wider opportunities for all; One Nation security with efficiency and competitiveness; rights with responsibilities, personal self-fulfilment with strengthening the family; effective government and decisive political leadership with a new constitutional settlement and a new relationship of trust between politicians and the people; a love of Britain with a recognition that Britain's future has to lie in Europe.

The commitment to partnership between public and private sectors, or the 'Third Way', has been the fundamental characteristic of New Labour's general strategy. Despite repeated indications of this in policy, and Blair's willingness to cut across political barriers to gain advice and help, it would appear however that this was not immediately evident. To the media and the public, Blair was more the man who had stood up to the unions and abandoned nationalization. The more subtle points of his policy, most obviously the rejection of Keynesian economic, large-scale government intervention and the maintenance of full employment, were not immediately detected. Instead, Blair's personality, charm and communication skills quickly endeared him to the British electorate and the Labour Party. Indeed, his draft manifesto *New Labour. New Life for*

Britain was overwhelmingly endorsed by the Labour Party Conference in October 1996.

On 1 May 1997 Tony Blair headed a sweeping victory for the Labour Party at the general election, winning 44.4 per cent of the vote, 419 seats, and gaining a majority of 179 seats. He had successfully presented the modernization of the Labour Party as the precursor of the modernization of Britain: 'New Labour, New Britain'. Once in office, Blair moved quickly to establish his New Labour credentials. From the start, he decided to strengthen the centre of government. Peter Mandelson was appointed Minister without Portfolio inside the Cabinet Office to co-ordinate the work of government departments, and a strategy committee of the Cabinet was set up under Blair's own chairmanship. The Labour government also introduced a new ministerial code requiring that all media contacts and policy initiatives by ministers should be cleared in advance by Downing Street.

In order to strengthen control further, Blair pressed the Labour Party Conference of 1997 to adopt *Partnership into Power*, a document which set out a radical programme to reform the Party's decision-making processes. By this, the Party Conference lost its control over Party policy to a 175-strong National Party Forum, which would discuss policies in a two-year rolling cycle, and the National Executive Committee (NEC) of the Party was altered. The women's section of the NEC was to be abolished and trade union representatives reduced from 17 to 12, although 6 were to be women. Three places were to be reserved for members of the Labour government (or Party), appointed by Tony Blair (Party Leader/Prime Minister), and one place for the Leader of the Labour Group in the European Parliament. Six were to be set aside for representatives elected by postal ballot of all members. These changes weakened the Labour Party Conference, reduced the power of the trade unions, and strengthened the hand of Tony Blair, as Labour Leader.

Riding high upon huge popular support, Blair responded by beginning a variety of initiatives. In May, Robin Cook, the new Foreign Secretary announced that the United Kingdom would sign up to the European Social Charter, Blair offered Sinn Fein a meeting with officials on the Northern Ireland peace process without the pre-conditions of a renewed cease-fire, and, in the Queen's Speech to Parliament, the new Labour government set out the commitments to a minimum wage and to constitutional reform. Gordon Brown, the new Chancellor of the Exchequer, also announced that the Bank of England, rather than the government, would take responsibility for setting interest rates through a new monetary policy committee. In

June 1997, task forces were established on NHS efficiency and youth justice.

Blair's 'New Labour' Party, in applying its philosophy, has focused on five main areas. First, it has sought to communicate with the public and to present a better image of Labour policies than has previously occurred. It has also emphasized that there would be a greater openness in government. Second, it has sought to apply market-led forces to its economic and social strategies, with an emphasis being placed upon the state acting as an enabler rather than simply as a provider. Third, its emphasis is essentially pro-European and pro-American. Fourth, it is committed to brokering a peace in Northern Ireland. Fifth, it has stressed the need for constitutional reform in such areas as the electoral system, the devolution of government, and changes in the House of Lords.

Ostensibly, New Labour is about communication and more open government. Blair has emerged as the great communicator and as a populist leader. This was most evident on 31 August 1997 with the death of Diana, Princess of Wales. His style tapped into the popular mood of remorse throughout the nation at that time. In other areas, however, there has been less transparency than initially suggested. Indeed, David Clark was given the Cabinet post of Chancellor of the Duchy of Lancaster, with responsibility for brokering a Freedom of Information Act. A White Paper was published in December 1997, indicating government thinking on the proposed Act, dealing with national and local government, quangos (non-elected bodies dealing with the distribution of government money), the NHS, and privatized utilities. Nonetheless, since David Clark's removal from office in the ministerial reshuffle of July 1998, the development of such an Act has slowed down as exceptions to it have been discussed.

The market-led nature of New Labour's approach, the second feature of Labour policy, was, of course, blatantly obvious in Brown's 1997 Budget, particularly in the explicitly titled programme of 'Welfare to Work'. It was also evident in the statement of November 1998 that pledged that there would be a fundamental reform of the welfare state and which proposed a tax credit scheme for poor working families. In December, as part of that strategy, the government pressed forward with a reduction in benefits for lone parents, which led 47 Labour MPs to vote against the action, on a three-line whip, and for 14 to abstain. The Labour government in fact won by 457 votes to 107, with the support of the Conservatives.

Nevertheless, in January 1998 the Blair government did announce a New Deal for unemployed 18-to-24-year olds. The deal offered work with subsidized private employers, education or training, self-employment or a variety of other alternatives in its strategy to eliminate unemployment by the twenty-first century. And in March 1998, Brown announced a redistributive Budget strategy which included the introduction of a Working Family Tax Credit, from October 1999, a Disabled Persons Tax Credit, increases in child benefit, subsidies for employers taking on the long-term unemployed and extra spending in many other areas. It has not been entirely clear that New Labour has played down the redistribution of income element, although its great adherence to market forces suggests that social differences may be widened rather than narrowed.

The philosophy behind New Labour seems to be to reduce social need through an alliance between the state and the private sector. This was outlined by Tony Blair on 18 March 1999. The context was a government pledge to a 20-year programme to eradicate child poverty. Committing £6,000 million to help tackle child poverty in the course of the current Parliament, 'the quiet revolution', Blair suggested that a modern welfare state should be 'active, not passive, genuinely providing people with a hand-up, not a hand-out'. Indeed,

> The third way in welfare is clear: not to dismantle it or to protect it unchanged but to reform it radically, taking its core values and applying them afresh to the modern world. [...] Poverty should not be a birthright. Being poor should not be a life sentence. We need to break the cycle of disadvantage so that children born into poverty are not condemned to social exclusion and deprivation. [...] There will always be a mixture of universal and targeted help. But one is not superior or more principled than the other.

In effect, Blair's statement stressed that the state under New Labour would become an enabler as well as provider, helping people into jobs as well as ensuring that their interests are protected. It was now in partnership with, not hostile to, private industry.

The third feature is that New Labour is committed to Europe. In government it has followed through that commitment, recognizing that the European Economic Community is responsible for half of British exports and is responsible for guaranteeing around three million jobs in Britain. Indeed, in October 1997, Gordon Brown announced that the government favoured eventual entry into the European Monetary Union (EMU), but not in the lifetime of Blair's first Parliament and only if agreed in a referendum.

The British political and military alliance with the United States is obvious. It is particularly evident in Blair's constant support for Bill Clinton and George Bush, successive presidents of the United States, in containing Saddam Hussein and Iraq from military expansion, and in the close relationship developed between Britain and the United States in dealing with the Yugoslavian government and the Kosovan refugee crisis throughout 1999. Indeed, in the Kosovan crisis Blair took the lead in the NATO action against the Serbian-dominated Yugoslavian state. In the case of Kosova, in particular, Blair seems to have carved out for himself the reputation of being a major political player on the world stage.

On Ireland, the fourth area of activity, in May 1997 the Blair government offered Sinn Fein, the Irish Republican political party, a meeting with officials to discuss the preconditions for a renewed cease-fire. By July 1997 the Irish Republican Army (IRA) had declared a cease-fire and Sinn Fein representatives were allowed to enter Stormont, although they were not allowed to be involved in the peace-process discussions. In October 1997, Blair met Gerry Adams, the Sinn Fein Leader, and full-scale negotiations began. After many political twists, Blair focused the minds of all and gained an agreement on the Irish peace process, including provision for a Northern Ireland Assembly and, a North–South Ministerial Council of the Isles. There remains, however, the issue of implementing the agreement and the problem of decommissioning of arms, which the IRA seems reluctant to deliver but which is a vital part of the 'Good Friday Agreement' of 1998.

The fifth major commitment of New Labour has been to constitutional and electoral reform. Such a commitment was first announced in the Queen's Speech in May 1997. In June 1997 it was announced that the Liberal Democrats were being invited to take seats on the Cabinet Committee to discuss constitutional reform and other mutual interests. In December 1998 the Electoral Reform Commission was set up under Lord Jenkins, the former Labour Minister and co-founder of the SDP. Lord Jenkins was set the task of devising a system of proportional representation for the Westminster elections in preparation for a referendum on the issue. In October 1998, Blair accepted its recommendation of an Alternative Vote Top-Up System of proportional representation for parliamentary elections and in June 1999 the elections for European MPs was based upon a system of proportional representation, with electors voting for parties not individuals.

Blair's Labour government also moved in 1999 to create both a Scottish and Welsh Assembly, which would allow for greater representation of national minority interests groups thus undermining demands for political independence in both Scotland and Wales. And, in addition, there have been moves to modernize the monarchy and discussions about replacing the House of Lords with an assembly largely made up of lifetime peers and a much-reduced number of hereditary peers.

The Blair government has certainly been hyperactive. Indeed, it is fair to argue that Blair has largely achieved the objective he set himself, at the 1997 Labour Party Conference, of making his administration 'one of the great reforming governments in British history'. Certainly, there have been constitutional, economic and welfare reforms in abundance. Most certainly, the direction of British politics has changed. Nevertheless, one might question the direction of some of these reforms.

The main opposing voice has been Roy Hattersley, the former Deputy Leader of the Labour Party, who, as early as July 1997, was declaring his lack of commitment to New Labour because of its desertion of policies to deal with the poor and its blatant ignoring of the need to redistribute wealth in order to move toward equality. The market-forces approach of both state and private enterprise will not, and has not, redistribute wealth or create a fairer society, although Hattersley's concerns on this were probably partly allayed by Blair's commitment to eradicating child poverty. Also, since the general election of June 2001 when Blair's Labour government secured a majority only slightly down on the 1997 general election, there has been growing opposition to the public and private approach by many Labour MPs and activists. However, the TUC's opposition to such developments was sidetracked in the autumn of 2001 when, on 11 September, the attacks upon the World Trade Center in New York and the Pentagon brought both Britain and the United States onto a war footing against terrorism.

＊As Britain enters the twenty-first century it is led by a Labour government with a strong reforming zeal, and has a Labour Leader, in Tony Blair, who is becoming the great communicator and a populist figure. Labour is offering a wider participation in politics, more regional and local decision-making, closer links with Europe, a modern political society and, above all, the Third Way in British politics – uniting the state and private industry in tackling the social and economic problems of the nation. The Blair Labour government is thus far removed from its predecessors, with less dependence upon the trade unions and less emphasis upon state intervention in the economy to ensure full employment. In capturing 'middle England'

and the middle classes, Labour under Blair has freed itself from its old traditional roots. Labour is no longer the class-based party of 1918, nor even the more loosely based trade union party of 1983.

See also: Kinnock, Major, Thatcher

Further reading

Anderson, P. and Mann, N., 1997, *Safety First: The Making of New Labour*, London: Granta.

Blair, T., 1996, *New Britain. My Vision of a Young Country*, London: Fourth Estate.

Draper, D., 1997, *Blair's Hundred Days*, London: Faber & Faber.

Laybourn, K., 2000, *A Century of Labour. A History of the Labour Party*, Stroud: Sutton.

Mandelson, P. and Liddle, R., 1996, *The Blair Revolution. Can New Labour Deliver?*, London: Faber & Faber.

Panitch, L. and Leys, C., 2001, *The End of Parliamentary Socialism*, 2nd edn, London: Verso.

Rentoul, J., 1996, *Tony Blair*, London: Warner.

RICHARD AUSTEN BUTLER (LORD BUTLER OF SAFFRON WALDEN) 1902–1982

Richard Austen Butler, often known by the acronym 'RAB', was the nearly man of British politics, a Conservative politician who filled all the major offices of government save one – that of Prime Minister. Nevertheless, he became almost a household name, giving his name to the phrase 'Butskellism', a belief and commitment to a post-war economic and political consensus which many claim dominated British politics until 1979 and the 'Thatcher' era.

Butler was born in Attock, Serie, in the Punjab, India in 1902 into a family which had connections both with the Imperial Service and with the University of Cambridge. His father was the distinguished administrator Sir Montague Butler. Butler was educated at Marlborough College and the University of Cambridge, where he became President of the University Union in 1924 and Fellow of Corpus Christi College between 1925 and 1929. In 1926 he married Sydney Courtauld, heiress to the fortunes of the famous family which dominated the British chemical industry, and thus obtained a financial settlement which guaranteed £5,000 a year for life tax free. The financial security he derived from this marriage encouraged him to enter into a political career and he became Conservative MP for Saffron Walden in 1929, holding the seat until his retirement from the House of Commons in 1965.

Butler gained an early boost up the political ladder. In the National Governments of 1931 to 1940 he became Under-Secretary for India (1932–7), Parliamentary Secretary to the Minister of Labour (1937–8) and then Under-Secretary for Foreign Affairs (1937–41), the last office continuing into the wartime government of Winston Churchill. Since Lord Halifax, the Foreign Secretary on the eve of the Second World War, was in the House of Lords, Butler became the principal spokesman on foreign affairs in the House of Commons and gained an influential position in politics. In this respect he was associated with the policy of appeasement advocated by Neville Chamberlain and Lord Halifax, and was identified as one of those politicians who were prepared to hand over Czechoslovakia to Hitler under the Munich Agreement of 1938. He was closely associated with 'the Guilty Men' in 1940, identified by Michael Foot, and others, as the 'appeasers'.

On leaving the Foreign Office in 1941 Butler became President of the Board of Education (1941–4) and then Minister of Education (1944–5) in Churchill's wartime administrations. In these roles he was responsible for the introduction of the 1944 Education Act which lay down the post-war system of education in England and Wales, raising the school-leaving age to 15 and formalizing the tripartite system of secondary education – grammar schools, central schools and secondary modern schools – and free secondary education for all. In 1945 he was also, rather briefly, Minister of Labour in Churchill's outgoing government.

The 1945 general election brought about a landslide victory for the Labour Party. In opposition, Butler was Chairman of the Conservative Research Department between 1945 and 1951, and helped to change the Conservative Party from a monetarist into a Keynesian interventionist party. In 1947 he chaired the Conservative Committee which drafted the Industrial Charter of 1947, committing a reluctant Churchill and the Party to the need for economic intervention in the economy and support for most aspects of the Labour Party's welfare state. In this sense, he helped to create the political consensus that seems to have dominated both Labour and Conservative governments on such issues for the next thirty years. With the formation of another Churchill administration, following the general election of 1951, Butler became Chancellor of the Exchequer.

As Chancellor, between 1951 and 1955, Butler was able to consolidate the development of this political consensus. His first two Budgets were popular ones. However, he found that there were problems both in allowing high wage increases in the economy and seeking to build the 300,000 houses per year that the Conservative government had offered in its manifesto. By 1955 he was facing serious difficulties, which forced him to raise interest rates, but nevertheless he reduced income tax by 6d (2.4p) in the pound in the electioneering 1955 Budget. It helped to win the general election for Sir Anthony Eden but Butler had to bring in another revised Budget at the end of the year to control expenditure and staunch the run on the pound. This persuaded Eden to remove Butler as Chancellor and to make him both Leader of the House of Commons (1955–61) and Lord Privy Seal (1955–9). He continued in those posts when Eden was replaced by Harold Macmillan following the 1956 Suez Crisis in which the United States forced both British and French troops to withdraw from the Suez Canal. Although he played little part in the Suez affair he had advocated that British, French and Israeli forces should attack Egypt as a whole rather than merely occupy the Canal Zone, a plan of action that was not accepted.

Butler did not enjoy the best of relations with Macmillan, the next Conservative Prime Minister, having hoped that he himself would have attained the position in 1957. Nevertheless, Macmillan did add to Butler's duties by making him Home Secretary, a post he filled with distinction from January 1957 to July 1962, as well as Chairman of the Conservative Party from 1959 to 1961 and Deputy Leader of the Conservative Party between 1962 and 1963. He was also First Secretary of State and Minister in Charge of the Central African Office between 1962 and 1963. He was removed from this last post in 1963 but in October of that year was appointed Foreign Secretary, holding the post until October 1964 and the government of Sir Alec Douglas Home, the man who replaced him as the obvious successor to Macmillan. In 1963 Butler had taken over responsibility for running the government from Macmillan who was having an operation for prostate cancer. However, this was as near to being Prime Minister as he ever came, having failed in 1957 and again in 1960 during a difficult time for Macmillan.

Once the Labour government was formed under Harold Wilson in October 1964 Butler decided that his political career was at an end. He left the Commons in 1965 and was raised to the House of Lords as Lord Butler of Saffron Walden. From that point onwards he contented himself with an academic career, acting as Master of Trinity College, Cambridge, between 1965 and 1978. He died on 8 March 1982.

Contemporaries have suggested that Butler was always a good second-in-command, Macmillan suggesting that 'he lacked the last six inches of steel' necessary for leadership. Indeed, this judgement seems fair given that he was rarely a spectacular success as a minister.

Nevertheless, his ushering in of the Education Act of 1944 and his advocacy of economic and political consensus ('Butskellism') ensure that he has a political reputation that extends beyond mere partisan politics. Indeed, once described as 'both irrepressible and unapproachable', he was always one of the most progressive of Conservative leaders.

See also: Chamberlain (Neville), Churchill, Home, Macmillan

Further reading

Butler, Lord, 1971, *The Art of the Possible*, London: Hamilton.
Cosgrave, P., 1981, *R. A. Butler: An English Life*, London: Quartet Books.
Howard, A., 1987, *RAB: The Life of R. A. Butler*, London: Cape.
Thorpe, D. R., 1980, *Uncrowned Prime Ministers*, London: Darkhorse Publishing Co. Ltd.

(LEONARD) JAMES CALLAGHAN (LORD CALLAGHAN OF CARDIFF) 1912–

James Callaghan is the only twentieth-century politician to have filled all the four major offices of state, and given his unique position in British politics he cannot be seen as the political lightweight he is sometimes portrayed as being. Although his three years as Labour Prime Minister, between 5 April 1976 and 5 May 1979, left the Labour Party weaker than it had been for a generation he was, according to Denis Healey, second only to Clement Attlee in the pantheon of Labour prime ministers for keeping the Labour government in office that long. Indeed, it may well be argued that whilst he is often represented as Old Labour – with its emphasis upon trade unionism, working-class politics, nationalization and expansionary Keynesian economics – he was in fact in many ways a pioneer of Tony Blair's 'New Labour/Third Way' approach which has abandoned public ownership and sought a closer relationship between the private and public sectors of British society. Perhaps, also, his premiership was not the disaster it was presented as being in the 1980s.

James Callaghan was born on 27 March 1912, the youngest child of James Callaghan and Charlotte Cundy. He was bought up in a working-class district of Portsmouth during and just after the First World War and was educated at Portsmouth Northern Secondary School. His father, a coastguard, died in 1921 and the family faced difficult financial circumstances. Nevertheless, he did well at school and gained entry into the civil service. Although he was raised in poverty his mother ensured a strict puritanical upbringing by sending him to the local Baptist church. He moved from that to socialism in later life. Raised in Portsmouth, with its strong naval tradition, he spent his early years in a highly charged patriotic atmosphere.

On leaving school Callaghan rose quickly in the Inland Revenue section of the civil service. He soon became a prominent member of the tax officers' union and, at the age of 24, was an assistant secretary in the Inland Revenue Tax Federation. He had already joined the Labour Party in 1931. In 1936 his Labour Party membership and his commitment to trade unionism spurred him on to raise money for the Republican side in the Spanish Civil War. In 1938 he married Audrey Moulton. During the Second World War he prepared a pamphlet on Japan for the Royal Navy, and then served on a aircraft carrier in the Far East, but he did not see enemy action. Also during the war he became a staunch supporter of the social change many expected to arise from what was described as the 'People's War'.

By 1945 Callaghan was a strong believer in trade unionism, an area with which he was always closely associated until the 1960s, an experienced negotiator, a member of the Labour Party, and committed to the social reform emerging during the war years. In the 1945 general election he won the Cardiff South seat for Labour and represented the seat in its other forms (Cardiff South East, 1950–83, Cardiff South and Penarth 1983–7) until his retirement from the House of Commons in 1987, when he became Lord Callaghan of Cardiff and entered the House of Lords.

By any standards Callaghan had a distinguished political career. However, his early career as a backbencher and junior minister did not suggest that he would be a future Labour Leader. At first he was a rather troublesome backbencher, attacking Ernest Bevin's anti-Soviet foreign policy and, in 1947, he became involved in the backbench rebellion that forced the proposed period for national service to be reduced. He became a junior minister in the Ministry of Transport in October 1947 and acted as Parliamentary and Financial Secretary of the Admiralty between 1950 and 1951. It was at this point that he revealed himself to be both a popular and able politician, one who, although prone to hasty comments, always followed the government line in the end. Somehow, he always found a middle course between the extremities of views within the Labour Party. Indeed, this was evident in the 1950s when he steered a middle course between Hugh Gaitskell's reformism and Nye Bevan's more immediate demands for socialism and public ownership. Yet, in truth, he steered his own course. He was identified with the trade unions, who rejected

Gaitskell's attempt to get the Labour Party Conference to abandon public ownership; he opposed the Campaign for Nuclear Disarmament; and he was a convinced supporter of the North Atlantic Treaty Organization (NATO). Nevertheless, recognizing Callaghan's abilities, Gaitskell, Labour Leader from 1955, gave him the post of Shadow Colonial Affairs spokesman in December, a post he filled until 1961. In this role he had deal with the issue of conflict in Cyprus and the Mau Mau guerrilla activities in Kenya, earning the respect of many of those African leaders, such as Kenneth Kaunda and Julius Nyerere, who were later to become leaders of their own countries. The fact is that Callaghan attempted to encourage a coherent policy of progressive and constitutional change in Britain's African Commonwealth nations. In 1961 he was promoted to Labour's Shadow Chancellor (of the Exchequer). This projected him forward to such an extent that when Gaitskell died in 1963 Callaghan was third in the Labour hierarchy behind only Harold Wilson and George Brown. Wilson became Labour Leader and won the 1964 general election, and Callaghan was appointed Chancellor of the Exchequer, a position he filled from 1964 until 1967.

Callaghan was not the most fortunate of Chancellors. He inherited a large balance of payments deficit of about £800 million from Reginald Maudling, the previous Conservative Chancellor. In this situation it was felt by some in the Cabinet that Britain should have devalued the pound. However, Callaghan felt that if industrial productivity increased and wage levels were controlled devaluation could be avoided, and he was supported in this contention by Wilson, the Prime Minister. In addition, Callaghan introduced an import surcharge of 15 per cent on non-food items in an attempt to curb imports and reduce the balance-of-payments deficit. With George Brown, Callaghan also helped to develop the prices and incomes policy, which was rather less effective than the Labour government hoped.

In this poor economic situation Callaghan had to introduce deflationary Budgets to correct the deficit, and when this did not work faced a massive balance-of-payments crisis in July 1966. The situation did not improve, especially in 1967 when the Arab–Israeli War caused an oil crisis and there was the seamen's strike. After it became evident that the deflationary measures to curtail imports were failing, the Labour government finally decided, on 16 November 1967, to devalue the pound from $2.80 to $2.40, implementing the change on 18 November. At this point, Callaghan resigned in favour of Roy Jenkins, and replaced Jenkins as Home Secretary. Although damaged by devaluation, Callaghan remained a major figure within the Labour

Party, having been elected Treasurer the previous month as a result of votes from the mining, engineering and transport unions.

Home Secretary from 1967 to 1970, Callaghan was not at first considered a great success, although he was later to handle anti-Vietnam protests, and policing in general, with some success. However, he made his mark in government in two matters at this time. The first was by resisting, on behalf of the unions, the intention of Harold Wilson and Barbara Castle to apply the White Paper *In Place of Strife* to British industrial relations. The proposal was eventually withdrawn but if applied would have imposed penal sanctions to restrict strike action. The second was in handling the situation in Northern Ireland. Reacting to the violence in Londonderry's Bogside and Belfast's Falls Road areas in 1968 and 1969, Callaghan set out a programme of civil rights measures in the 'Downing Street' declaration. He also abolished the paramilitary B specials and reformed the traditionally Protestant-dominated Royal Ulster Constabulary.

Labour's defeat in the June 1970 general election meant that Callaghan was faced with four years in opposition. At 58 years of age it might have appeared that his political career at the summit of British politics was at an end. However, with Roy Jenkins, the Deputy Labour Leader, resigning because of his pro-European views and with George Brown losing his seat, it was clear that he was still the most likely alternative to Wilson as Labour Leader. He also allied himself with the trade unions in opposing Edward Heath's move to impose legal sanctions on them and their strike activities, and adopted the anti-European attitudes of many trade unionists. When Labour was returned to office in March 1974, he was awarded the position of Foreign Secretary.

Callaghan was a determinedly 'hands-on' political Foreign Secretary, holding almost daily meetings on the government's position with Harold Wilson, and he performed well on most occasions. He played an important part in the Helsinki Accord with the Soviet Union and was friendly with the American Secretary of State, Henry Kissinger, and with the German Chancellor, Helmut Schmidt. On membership of the European Economic Community (EEC), which Britain had entered under Edward Heath, Callaghan took up the task of re-negotiating Britain's membership. Personally, he had always doubted the economic arguments for joining the EEC and on political grounds favoured NATO and the Commonwealth. Nevertheless, he gained some trading concessions for the Commonwealth countries and the pegging of the United Kingdom's budgetary contribution to the EEC. This saw the Labour government through the referendum in

1975 in which there was a two-to-one vote in favour of continued membership of the EEC.

Such successes pushed Callaghan forward as the natural successor to Wilson, who resigned as Labour Leader and Prime Minister in March 1976. Roy Jenkins soon withdrew from the subsequent Leadership contest and Michael Foot had insufficient support to merit being a genuine contender. Thus on 5 April 1976 Callaghan became the fourth Labour Prime Minister. He inherited a minority government which lost its majority on the same day with the defection of John Stonehouse. The most remarkable thing was that the government lasted for three years.

Callaghan ran his Cabinet in an open fashion, involving all its members in policy making, thus avoiding the 'kitchen cabinet' arrangement with which Wilson had steered government policy. Nevertheless, he faced great difficulties from the start. He worked with a minority government and was therefore forced in 1977 to make a pact with the Liberal Party, led by David Steel, in order to ensure a working parliamentary majority. His government, through Denis Healey, was also involved in securing a loan of £3,900 million from the International Monetary Fund in 1976, although the decision was actually made in December 1975, in return for imposing cuts on government spending. In the end the cuts were not so severe and the economy recovered quickly from the crisis it had faced through 1976 and 1977. Government reserves improved and the economy was buoyant by the summer of 1978. Yet there was to be no going back to the spending policies that had been used to tackle unemployment in the past. Indeed, Callaghan had already informed the Labour Party Conference of October 1976 that Britain could no longer spend its way out of a recession. He stated that:

> We used to think you could spend your way out of recession and increase employment by cutting taxes and boosting Government spending. I will tell you with candour that that option no longer exists and that insofar as it ever did exist, it only worked on each recession since the war by injecting a bigger degree of inflation into the economy, followed by a higher level of unemployment as the next step.
>
> (Callaghan, 1987, p. 426)

It was at this point that matters began to go wrong for the government. Callaghan began to alienate his traditional trade union support by suggesting that pay increases should be pegged at about

5 per cent. This provoked many trade unions, particularly in the service sector but also in road haulage, into strike action in the winter of 1978 and 1979, a situation not helped by Callaghan's reported statement, on returning from an international conference in Guadeloupe, 'Crisis, what crisis?'. There were also other disasters. For instance, on 1 March 1979 the referenda on devolution in Wales and Scotland went badly – devolution was overwhelmingly rejected in Wales and only narrowly accepted in Scotland. The Liberals also deserted the Labour government and on 29 March the government was defeated in the Commons by one vote. Callaghan's government was then defeated at the general election of May 1979, to be replaced by a Conservative government under Margaret Thatcher. Callaghan remained Labour Party Leader until 1980 when he resigned, to be replaced by Michael Foot. He remained in the House of Commons until 1987, from 1983 as the longest-serving MP and 'Father of the House'. In 1987 he was raised to the House of Lords.

Although often described as a traditional Labour figure, representing the interests of Old Labour and the trade unions, Callaghan was far from being so. He was a pragmatic politician who was prepared to move with the times and his speech to the Labour Party Conference in October 1976 almost anticipated the New Labour approach of Tony Blair. Indeed, he kept the Labour government together in the late 1970s in a very difficult situation. His one major mistake was to cling to power too long before going to the electorate.

See also: Attlee, Gaitskell, Wilson

Further reading

Callaghan, J., 1987, *Time and Chance*, London: Collins.
Donoghue, B., 1987, *Prime Minister: The Conduct of Policy under Harold Wilson and James Callaghan*, London: Collins.
Jefferys, K. (ed.), 1999, *Leading Labour: From Keir Hardie to Tony Blair*, London: I. B. Tauris.
Morgan, K. O., 1997, 1999, *Callaghan: A Life*, Oxford: Oxford University Press.

HENRY CAMPBELL-BANNERMAN 1836–1908

Henry Campbell Bannerman was the 'Unknown Prime Minister' of the Liberal Party, to coin a phrase applied to Andrew Bonar Law who became Conservative Prime Minister in the 1920s. Bannerman was a politician of conviction and pragmatism who healed many of the divisions within Liberalism at the beginning of the twentieth century. His career was, however, cut short by his untimely death in 1908.

Campbell-Bannerman was born on 7 September 1836, the second son of James (later Lord Provost Sir James) Campbell and Janet Bannerman, and raised in a strict Presbyterian household. He was educated at Glasgow High School the University of Glasgow, from which he failed to graduate, and the University of Cambridge. At the age of twenty-two he joined the family's prosperous retail firm, becoming a partner two years later. In 1860, he married Charlotte, the daughter of Major-General Sir Charles and Lady Charlotte Bruce. In 1868, he changed his name to Campbell-Bannerman on inheriting an uncle's estate in Kent. He was a wealthy man and was later to own an estate in Scotland.

Campbell-Bannerman entered politics in 1868, when he became MP for Stirling District Burghs. He remained MP for this constituency until his death in 1908. Throughout the late nineteenth century he was a prominent and rising political figure within the Liberal Party. He became Financial Secretary of the War Office during Gladstone's administration, between 1871 and 1874, and fulfilled the role again between 1880 and 1882. He was also Parliamentary and Financial Secretary to the Admiralty, 1881–4, and Chief Secretary to Ireland between 1884 and 1885. In 1886 he was, briefly, Secretary of War, and then again between 1892 and 1894. Then, following the retirement of Gladstone and the withdrawal of Lord Rosebery from politics, he rose quickly within the Liberal ranks to become in 1899 the Liberal Leader, a position he held until shortly before his death. In this post he was a great critic of Lord Salisbury and the Conservatives and their conduct of the Boer War.

Campbell-Bannerman's major task as Liberal Leader was to keep the Party together. The Boer War divided its leading figures into three main camps. There were those, such as Lord Rosebery and H. H. Asquith, who were Liberal Imperialists and opposed to the Boers. There was a second group of pro-Boers, including Campbell-Bannerman himself, and a third group which attempted to maintain a balance between the two. Campbell-Bannerman managed to outflank the Liberal Imperialists by appointing Asquith to mount the attack upon the Unionist campaign for tariff reform. In 1905 the leading Liberal Imperialists attempted to replace Campbell-Bannerman, by elevating him to a position in the House of Lords (the Relugas Pact), but at this they failed. Indeed, Campbell-Bannerman strengthened his position by giving the three conspirators (Herbert

H. Asquith, Sir Edward Grey and R. B. Haldane) senior posts whilst he offered support in their ministerial posts.

Campbell-Bannerman formed a Liberal administration in December 1905, which was endorsed in the 1906 general election by a Liberal landslide victory. His appointment as Prime Minister was a landmark in British politics, for he was the first to rise from business rather than land and the first who was not an Anglican. The diversification of British politics in the twentieth century had begun.

Unlike many previous holders of this post, Campbell-Bannerman was more an enabler and moderator than an instigator of reform. Indeed, his approach was very much like that adopted by Clement Attlee in later years, that of a leader who attempts to negotiate a balance and harmony between his various talented ministers. He was careful to ensure that the rival sections of the Party were all represented and on board in his administration. Apart from the Liberal Imperialists, mentioned above, there were Gladstonian Liberals (John Morley, Ripon, Herbert Gladstone, and Campbell-Bannerman himself), a number of Whigs (Elgin and Crewe) and a number of radicals (Lloyd George, John Burns and Winston Churchill). The Party was balanced but there was little in the way of great or controversial legislation in his government; that only came when Asquith took over from him in 1908. Yet he left some marks. Most particularly, he supported self-government for the Boers, as he had done between 1899 and 1902, and he overturned the Trades Dispute Bill that his ministers had prepared in 1906, replacing it with a Labour backbencher's bill that removed the financial penalties imposed upon striking trade unions by the Taff Vale Case of 1900/1.

This latter action was a reflection upon the way in which Campbell-Bannerman wished to embrace the Labour Party, rather than to reject it. Indeed, it was as Leader of the Liberal Party that he endorsed the Lib–Lab Pact of 1903, agreed between Gladstone, Liberal Chief Whip, and Ramsay MacDonald. The agreement was a reciprocal one and allowed both parties thirty seats for which there would be either no Liberal or no Labour opponent. Whilst this may have helped the Liberal Party it was certainly an important breakthrough for the Labour Party (at that time known as the Labour Representation Committee).

With failing health, Campbell-Bannerman resigned as Prime Minister on 3 April 1908, and died on 22 April. He will hardly be remembered for his premiership, but he can claim to have encouraged a co-operative relationship between the Liberal and Labour parties and for having kept the Liberal Party together at a period when it was doubtful whether it would ever achieve office again. Effectively, he did much to heal the divisions within the Liberal Party and to prepare it for office, and in this respect he can be compared with Andrew Bonar Law, who fulfilled a similar role for the Conservative Party a few years after Campbell-Bannerman's death.

See also: Asquith, (Bonar) Law

Further reading

Harris, J. and Hazlehurst, C., 1970, 'Campbell–Bannerman as Prime Minister', *History*, 5.

Rowlands, P., 1968, *The Last Liberal Governments: The Promised Land, 1905–1910*, London: Barrie & Rockliff, Cresset Press.

Russell, A., 1973, *Liberal Landslide: The General Election of 1906*, Newton Abbot: David & Charles.

Wilson, I., 1973, *CB: A Life of Sir Henry Campbell-Bannerman*, London: Constable.

EDWARD (HENRY) CARSON 1854–1935

Edward Carson is most famously known as the leader of the Irish Unionist bloc of the Conservative Party at the time of the First World War and as organizer of the Ulster Volunteers. A strong opponent of Home Rule for Ireland, he finally committed himself by creating a type of Home Rule within Britain for the six Protestant counties that formed Northern Ireland.

Carson was born in Dublin on 9 February 1854 and was educated at Trinity College, Dublin. He trained to be a barrister and was admitted to the Irish Bar in 1877 and the English Bar in 1893, being made a Queen's Counsel in 1889 and knighted in 1900. Carson earned a good reputation as a barrister, being the senior Crown prosecutor in Dublin between 1889 and 1892. He was famously involved in defending the Marquess of Queensberry against the libel suit Oscar Wilde had brought against him in 1895, the outcome of which led to Wilde's imprisonment in Reading Gaol for sodomy. He was just as famously involved in a case defence in the Arthur–Shee case of 1910, clearing a naval cadet accused of theft. This famous case was later the basis of the Terence Rattigan play performed in 1946 and the subsequent film *The Winslow Boy*. His legal successes raised his profile and he was appointed Solicitor-General for Ireland for 1892 and for Great Britain from 1900 to 1905, both of which were political appointments.

Carson's legal career went hand in hand with his political career. He was returned as a Conservative MP for the University of Dublin in

1892 and remained so until 1921, filling the above posts in two Conservative governments. He was strongly opposed to Irish nationalism and the Home Rule policy of the Liberals and identified strongly with the Ulster Unionists, succeeding Walter Long in leading that group in 1910. In 1911 he declined to contest for the Conservative Party leadership, which went to Andrew Bonar Law, instead dedicating himself to opposing Home Rule for Ireland.

When Asquith's government introduced a Home Rule Bill in 1912, Carson decided that since the House of Lords had lost its veto under the Parliament Act of 1911, he would have to go outside the law in opposing the move. He thus raised and trained an 80,000-man armed force of Ulster Unionists (a largely Protestant force) to oppose Home Rule by force if it became law. In a treasonable act, he made arrangements for the Ulster Unionist Council to become the provisional government in Belfast once Home Rule was introduced. He also made arrangements to import guns illegally from Germany.

Remarkably, the Asquith Liberal government took no action against Carson and his supporters and, indeed, offered the compromise that the six mainly Protestant counties of the North of Ireland would be excluded from any Home Rule agreement on Ireland. This offer was rejected, and on the eve of the First World War, the prospect of civil conflict in Ireland arose. However, the threat receded when Carson offered to make the Ulster Volunteers a division of the British Army, an offer that was accepted by the British government. Home Rule was also passed in 1914 but suspended for the duration of the First World War, and Carson was made Attorney-General in Asquith's Coalition Cabinet in May 1915, although he was quick to resign over military policy.

After the Easter Rebellion of Irish nationalists in 1916, Carson entered negotiations with Lloyd George on a new but nevertheless ill-fated scheme to exclude the six northern counties from Home Rule and joined Lloyd George's wartime Coalition Government as First Lord of the Admiralty until July 1917, and then as Minister without Portfolio in the War Cabinet until January 1918. After the First World War Carson accepted that Irish Home Rule was inevitable and agreed that the six counties should be excluded from any agreement and tied to the British government. Indeed, in 1920 he supported the Government of Ireland Act, which set up a separate government for Northern Ireland within the United Kingdom.

Carson retired from politics in 1921 when he became a Lord of Appeal, a post he held until 1929. At the same time he was given a life peerage with the title of Baron Carson of Duncairn. He died on 22 October 1935.

There is no doubting that Carson was a charismatic character and a barrister of the first order. However, he was not the best of administrators in public office and his effectiveness at the head of the Ulster Volunteers is questionable.

See also: Attlee, (Bonar) Law

Further reading

Hyde, H. Montgomery, 1953, *Carson. The Life of Sir Henry Carson*, London: Heinemann.

Marjoribanks, E. and Colvin, I., 1932–6, *The Life of Lord Carson*, 3 vols, London: Victor Gollancz.

Stewart, A. T. Q., 1981, *Edward Carson*, Dublin: Gill & Macmillan.

BARBARA (ANNE) CASTLE (BARONESS CASTLE OF BLACKBURN) 1910–

Barbara Castle is one of the most controversial politicians of her day, representing Blackburn in the House of Commons between 1945 and 1979. At first she was considered a somewhat troublesome Labour Party left-winger and was closely associated with the Bevanites in the 1950s. Later, however, she was drawn into government and filled a variety of prominent posts in the administrations of Harold Wilson, most obviously as the Secretary of State for Social Security between 1974 and 1976 and in introducing the controversial Social Security Act of 1975. She finally left government when James Callaghan became Prime Minister in 1976. After that she played a major part in European politics and became a member of the House of Lords in 1990.

Barbara Castle was born on 6 October 1910, the third of three children, to Frank Betts and Annie Rebecca Ferrand, who were married at Vine Street Chapel, a Quaker Chapel in Coventry in 1905. Frank was an assistant tax surveyor in Sheffield at that time, earning the reasonably good salary of £130 per year but subject to constant movement around the country. By the time Barbara was three years old she was living in the coal-mining area of Pontefract, at Beechhurst House in Love Lane. She attended a school overlooking the Pontefract racecourse for a number of years before her family moved to Toller Lane, Bradford, in 1922, when her father became Inspector of Taxes in the Bradford District. She then went to Bradford Girls' Grammar

School with Marjorie, her elder sister. The strain on the family finances was almost crippling since neither of the girls had access to a scholarship and the family had to pay the fees. Barbara developed a passion for music, attending many of the concerts held at St George's Hall.

It was in Bradford that Barbara became an active socialist. Her mother was already a socialist of the William Morris variety, preferring beauty to ugliness, and was committed to living the life of a socialist. Her father had political leanings to the Left, although his early left-wing writings had to be done under a pseudonym because of his job. Indeed, Frank Betts became editor of the *Bradford Pioneer*, the local socialist journal, going under the initials F. B., and writing numerous articles on Jesus of Nazareth as the socialist working man. Her father invited many young socialists to write for the *Pioneer*, including Vic Feather, a young man who became General Secretary of the Trades Union Congress forty years later when Barbara was Secretary of State for Employment and Productivity. In fact, Feather led opposition to her 1969 White Paper *In Place of Strife*. At the age of sixteen Barbara joined the Independent Labour Party's (ILP) Guild of Youth and campaigned for Norman Angell in the general election of May 1929, when the Bradford ILP fielded four Labour candidates. She then went to St Hugh's College, Oxford in October 1929, participated in the activities of the Labour Club and finished with a Third Class degree.

After Oxford Castle moved back to her family home, now in Hyde, worked in Manchester and then moved to London where she began to build up a name as a Labour activist. Her reputation was boosted in 1943 when she attended the Labour Party Conference, representing the St Pancras Labour Party branch, and spoke against the Party's acceptance of the Beveridge Report of December 1942, stating that it was always 'Jam yesterday, Jam tomorrow, but never Jam today'. As a result she earned a reputation as a heroine of the Labour Left and drew the attention of Aneurin Bevan, Shortly afterwards, on 28 July 1944, she married Ted Castle, a night editor with the *Daily Mirror*. That same month she was selected as one of the two Labour candidates for the Blackburn constituency, still a two-member parliamentary constituency. A year later, as the Second World War drew to a close, Labour won the general election and Castle was returned as MP for Blackburn, along with 22 other women MPs and as part of a massive Labour landslide victory. As a left-winger within the Party she had little prospect of minor office within the Attlee government. Instead she associated herself with Michael Foot, Ian Mikardo and the 'Keep Left' group of left-wing friends who gathered together to offer a policy of planned socialism which would make Britain financially independent from the United States and create a 'Third Force' of European armed forces to help maintain peace between the United States and the Soviet Union. Nevertheless, she acted as the Parliamentary Private Secretary of Sir Stafford Cripps, the Chancellor of the Exchequer, a non-ministerial position which allows a minister to keep in touch with the backbenchers.

In the early 1950s Castle identified closely with Aneurin Bevan, who had left the Labour government in April 1951 over the decision to introduce prescription charges for his beloved National Health Service (NHS). The Bevanites, unlike their forbears the Keep Left movement, were more concerned with immediate issues than with a long-term policy for socialism and consisted of a group of more than 50 MPs who opposed the moderate revisionist views which were emerging around Tony Crosland and Hugh Gaitskell, who wished to end the commitment of the Party to public ownership. Unfortunately, it was not a well-organized group, as Castle reflected in her autobiography *Fighting All the Way* (1993, p. 203). Indeed, whilst Bevan and a group of friends, including Michael Foot, used the left-wing journal *Tribune* to present their ideas, others such as Harold Wilson and Richard Crossman seemed to operate in different circles. Castle was much nearer to Bevan than to the others but she found herself dumbfounded by him when he changed his stand on nuclear disarmament, moving from unilateralism to multilateralism at the 1957 Labour Party Conference at Brighton, where he stated that he did not want a future Labour Foreign Secretary sent 'naked into the Conference chamber'. He was prepared to negotiate away, but not to abandon, nuclear weapons.

Castle also moved more to the centre of the Labour Party at this time. Having been a member of the National Executive Committee in the 1950s she became Party Chairman in 1958–59 and was deeply involved in the general election campaign, appearing on Labour's poster between Bevan and Gaitskell. By 1964, when Labour's chance of government came again, both Bevan and Gaitskell were dead and Harold Wilson was Labour's Leader.

Castle was in the House of Commons for nineteen years before a general election victory in October 1964 made Wilson Prime Minister and brought Castle ministerial office. She joined the Cabinet as Minister of Overseas Development, where her main concern was to boost the economic efficiency of Indian factories, although she was generally concerned about Ian Smith's declaration of independence from British control of Rhodesia. Castle's effectiveness as a minister led her to become Minister of Transport on 21 December 1965, Wilson commenting to her that 'I want a tiger in my tank', in the words of the famous petrol advert (Castle, 1993, p. 364). Her best-remembered achievement was the introduction of the random breathalyser test for drivers, although she did attempt to bring about the integration of the national transport system which Labour had promised in its previous general election manifesto. Her next post, as First Secretary of State and Secretary of State for Employment and Productivity, came on 4 April 1968 and was the most fraught of her career.

In this new post, Castle had first to secure the passage of legislation of the government's increasingly unpopular prices and incomes policy. She introduced the 1968 Prices and Incomes Act which extended the 1966 Prices and Incomes Act, laid down a legislative ceiling of 5.5 per cent pay increases, and stopped incomes and dividends above this level being paid. But her real problems arose over the contentious proposals to regulate the activities of the trade unions in her White Paper *In Place of Strife*.

The Prime Minister had set up a Royal Commission in 1966, under Lord Justice Donovan, to examine ways in which to improve industrial relations in Britain. In 1968 the Donovan Commission, as it was known, concluded that the machinery of collective bargaining should be made more effective by offering more opportunities for conciliation. At the same time the Conservative Party had produced their *Fair Deal at Work* programme advocating a complicated legal system of constraints upon industrial action. Castle needed to act quickly since she felt that the Donovan proposals would not stop wildcat strikes and that the Conservative solution would be opposed by the trade unions. In 1969, Castle produced her policy *In Place of Strife*. She has claimed of it that 'all I asked was the unions should co-operate in avoiding unnecessary strikes' (Castle, 1993, p. 417). Her proposals included the suggestion that unofficial strikes could be suspended for 28 days and that employers would withdraw their action during this 'conciliation pause'. It also included the need for a secret ballot before any strike could be declared and giving an Industrial Relations Commission the power of approving trade union recognition in a dispute, although this could pose problems where there were several unions competing for that official approval. The scheme was approved by the Cabinet on 14 January 1969 and then published. However, the trade unions strongly opposed the plan and she and Wilson were humiliated by the Cabinet's subsequent rejection of legislation due to pressure from the trade unions (TUC opposition was led by Vic Feather, a teenage friend of Castle's). Castle did have one enduring success at the

Department of Employment and Productivity, the passing of the Equal Pay Act of 1970, which was an attempt to improve the rights of working women.

Labour lost the general election of June 1970 and Castle lost her post. However, on Labour's return to office in 1974, Castle became Secretary of State for Health and Social Services. Here her notable success in securing the Child Benefit Act was overshadowed by problems arising from the attempt to phase pay beds (that is, beds paid for by private patients) out of NHS hospitals. This Act, passed in May 1975, replaced the family allowance and the child tax allowance with a child benefit paid directly to mothers by the state for each child, including the first, as from 1977. Castle also introduced the Social Security Act of 1975, which made all insurance contributions earnings related, instead of fixed rate, although specific groups and women were allowed to opt out of paying full insurance contributions.

By 1976, at the age of 66, Castle was contemplating resigning and decided to do so when Harold Wilson decided upon the same course of action in March 1976, withdrawing from office in the James Callaghan Labour government. She eventually retired from the House of Commons in 1979 and stood for the European Parliament – despite her previous long-standing opposition to British membership of the European Economic Community (EEC): in 1975 when she had opposed Labour's continued membership of the EEC, in the referendum she had said that 'If Britain votes to stay in the Common Market, my country will need me more than ever' (Castle, 1993, p. 476). She served two five-year terms, becoming leader of the British Labour Party group for six years and Vice-Chairman of the Socialist group for seven years. She readily admitted that the lack of cut-and-thrust of debate in the European Parliament, where politicians made prepared speeches for the record and then disappeared, usually to a restaurant, was not appealing to her but she was pleased that during her period there the Labour groups kept together despite the divisions within Labour ranks that were occurring in the late 1970s and early 1980s. She also fought in 1979 for the reduction of Labour's contribution to the EEC Budget, in line with her manifesto commitments. In 1980, when she left the European Parliament, she was awarded the Commander's Cross of the Order of Merit of the Federal Republic of Germany and declared herself still to be an anti-marketeer but not anti-European. She reflected upon this in relation to Mrs Thatcher's style, writing that 'I believe the peace of the world depends on nations treating each other's problems with great

sensitivity. It was an art of which Margaret Thatcher was incapable'
(Castle, 1993, p. 538).

Castle was one of the most energetic and widely known politicians
of her day. Indeed, her two volumes of *The Castle Diaries* (1980 and
1984) provide illuminating insights into her work within the Wilson
governments. She also achieved significant reforms in the fields of
social service and welfare provision, which more than washed away the
pallor of defeat over *In Place of Strife*, the document for which she is
often best remembered.

See also: Bevan, Callaghan, Crosland, Gaitskell, Wilson

Further reading

Castle, B., 1980, *The Castle Diaries, 1974–76*, London: Weidenfeld Nicolson.
Castle, B., 1984, *The Castle Diaries, 1964–70*, London: Weidenfeld Nicolson.
Castle, B., 1993, *Fighting all the Way*, London: Macmillan.

JOSEPH CHAMBERLAIN 1836–1914

Joseph Chamberlain was a major political figure of the nineteenth
century, deeply involved in the Home Rule Crisis of 1886 which split
the Liberal Party. However, he can also lay claim to being one of the
major political figures of the early twentieth century, because of his
tariff reform campaign of 1903–6, which split the Conservative and
Unionist Government of Arthur James Balfour. Whilst notable in
dividing both the Liberals and the Conservatives, the two major
political parties of British politics, he was also the father of Austen and
Neville, who became leaders of the Conservative/Unionist Party, the
latter becoming Prime Minister in 1937. Of Joseph, it may be said that
there can be few political figures in British history who were so
important and controversial that the political offices they held were
almost irrelevant.

Joseph Chamberlain was born at Camberwell Grove, London, on 8
July 1836. He was the son of Joseph, who was the fourth generation of
boot and shoemakers, and Caroline (Harben), the daughter of a
provision merchant from London. In 1850 he was sent to University
College School in London, but left there at the age of sixteen to enter
his father's business. At the age of eighteen he went to Birmingham to
protect his father's £10,000 interest in the Birmingham screw-making
firm of Mr Nettlefold, his uncle. Chamberlain worked with that firm
for twenty years and retired from industry at the age of thirty-eight,

with a substantial private fortune of more than £100,000 from the £600,000 the Chamberlain family had sold their interest for in 1875. Throughout this period, Chamberlain was a practising Unitarian, an old dissenting religion which emphasized the need for social salvation to its members and which inspired his part in the development of the so-called 'Civic Gospel' in Birmingham between the 1850s and 1870s. In 1861 he married Harriet Kenrick (1836–63), who brought with her a dowry of almost £5,000. She bore him two children, the second being Austen, whose birth led to complications from which she died in 1863. In 1867 he married Florence Kenrick (1848–75), Harriet's cousin, who, in March 1869, gave birth to Arthur Neville Chamberlain. Florence was a staunch Radical and edited and advised Joseph on some of his Radical articles in the *Fortnightly Review.* Chamberlain was greatly upset when she died in 1875 after giving birth to twins, one boy and one girl. In later years he had minor affairs or flirtations, one with Beatrice Potter, who later became Beatrice Webb, but eventually, in November 1888 he married Mary Endicott (1864–1957). In the late 1860s and early 1870s, however, he was still essentially a businessman of the old Dissent who was interested in social reform.

Yet even before retiring from business in 1874, Chamberlain was building up for himself a formidable political reputation. In the 1850s and 1860s Birmingham was becoming a centre of Liberal reformism, where George Dawson, the Rev. R. W. Dale and Joseph Chamberlain preached the need for the Civic Gospel, which advocated that a good city must provide for its inhabitants what a nation provides for its citizens. The Civic Gospel that emerged was carried on to fruition by Chamberlain in the 1860s and early 1870s. He became a City Councillor in 1869 and was returned for the Birmingham School Board in 1870. He was Chairman of the National Education League in 1869, promoting an enormous campaign to create a state system of elementary education in Britain. When W. E. Forster MP pushed the 1870 Education Act through Parliament, creating a dual system of educational provision by allowing the state to finance both school board (state) schools and voluntary schools Chamberlain was mortified. He wrote to George Dixon (Marsh, 1994, p. 38) that 'It is not National Education at all – it is a trick to strengthen the Church of England ... we must strengthen ourselves in the House of Commons at all risks. I would rather see a Tory ministry in power than a Liberal government truckling to Tory prejudices.'

Chamberlain became the Lord Mayor of Birmingham between 1873 and 1875. He was a reforming leader and his schemes of civic improvement made Birmingham a model city. It bought up the gas and water companies in Birmingham, creating the so-called 'gas and water socialism', building sewage works, and demolishing the slums at the centre of Birmingham and building Corporation Street. In 1875 he and his Liberal councillors adopted the Artisans' Dwelling Act which allowed them to build working houses for the working classes.

Chamberlain also helped to create a remarkable political caucus and, through the efficient campaigning and organization of the Liberal Party, re-created Birmingham as a centre of Liberal political power. In 1876 he was returned to Birmingham as MP in a parliamentary by-election. Shortly afterwards, in 1877 at a meeting in Birmingham, he set up the National Liberal Federation, out of the winding up of the National Education League, thus uniting many Liberal associations throughout the country. W. E. Gladstone was invited to this meeting and Chamberlain, as an inducement, stressed the importance of the 'Eastern Question' and criticized the Turkish authorities for the Bulgarian massacres. Although technically this organization welded Liberalism together behind Gladstone, it was in fact a strong power base for Chamberlain's political ambitions.

Chamberlain's organizational and political ability ensured that he rose quickly in the parliamentary ranks of the Liberal Party. In 1880, when Gladstone became Prime Minister, Chamberlain was appointed President of the Board of Trade, despite Gladstone's dislike of his populist and radical style. Although this was about the lowest ranking of all Cabinet posts, it gained him a foothold at the very top of British politics. During this period, in the early 1880s, Chamberlain was particularly interested in promoting economic policies which would help reduce the economic and political unrest in Ireland and promote British interests in Africa, particularly southern Africa, where he hoped that British influence might be increased in the face of German and French colonial expansion. He was also concerned that Britain's economic position was being challenged by the United States and wished to strengthen British relations with her colonies.

Also during this period Chamberlain made Highbury, his house just outside Birmingham, a centre of radical Liberal opinion to such an extent that it became a serious political challenge to Gladstone's political power base which revolved around Hawarden. Two cabals began to emerge in these two rival power bases. Through parties and meetings at Highbury, Chamberlain built up the connections which supported his radical policies such as manhood suffrage (in 1884), graduated income tax, pre-elementary education, and the disestablishment of state churches. His reforming zeal was evident for all to see and cut across the views held by many members of his own Party as well as the Conservatives. As a result, he published *The Radical Programme* in 1885 and 1886, written by himself and various supporters, offering policies such as the disestablishment of the Church of England which Gladstone felt was unjust. Chamberlain was thus obviously emerging as the rival to Gladstone as Liberal Party Leader. In the difficult political atmosphere of the mid 1880s he favoured the Conservatives being allowed to come to power, but he did become a member of Gladstone's short-lived and turbulent ministry of 1886 as President of the Local Government Board, introducing the famous Chamberlain Circular on 15 March 1886 which encouraged local authorities to offer work to relieve artisans and other workers and thus help them avoid being driven to the Poor Law and 'the stigma of pauperism' (Laybourn, 1995, p. 281).

Later that same year Chamberlain split with the Liberal Party over the issue of Home Rule for Ireland. Gladstone announced his Home Rule for Ireland policy, his 'Hawarden kite' as it was known, as Chamberlain responded with a letter to *The Times* on 8 May 1886 suggesting that Gladstone's Home Rule Bill would be 'a fulcrum for further agitation' and that it 'brought us within measurable distance of civil war in Ireland'. Indeed, Chamberlain believed that Home Rule for Ireland would lead to the break-up of the United Kingdom and, in contrast, argued in favour of each country in the United Kingdom having its own Parliament as part of a federation of the United Kingdom. He also believed, as did many socialists in later years, that Home Rule could stifle the cause of social reform. Thus he resigned and split with Gladstone, severing his links with the Liberal Party where many had considered him a possible successor as Leader.

Chamberlain was followed out of the Liberal Party by many old Liberal Whigs, the Hartington Whigs as they were called, and his Liberal Unionist group. He hoped to form a new centre party in British politics, and built up his power base in Birmingham, but eventually he joined with the Conservative Party. Indeed, when the National Union of Conservative Associations decided to hold its annual conference in Birmingham in 1891 it was Hartington's duty to ensure that the Liberal Unionists produced a political programme acceptable to the Conservative Party.

In the Conservative government of 1895 Chamberlain was made Secretary of State for the Colonies. He was still a supporter of social reform, most notably favouring the introduction of old age pensions, but was able to do little to introduce them. Also, and in spite of his reputation for radicalism, earned in the political debates of the late

1860s, he accepted the Conservative Government's Education Act of 1902 which transferred the powers of the school boards (created by the 1870 Education Act) to local education authorities (LEAs) and allowed for private schools (both elementary and secondary) to receive financial support from the local ratepayers as long as they allowed two of the normal six school governors to be representatives of the LEA. However, his position within the Conservative government soon brought controversy.

Chamberlain wished for political, rather than simply economic reasons, that the whole of southern Africa should be in British hands. As it was, Cecil Rhodes's British South Africa Company was spreading British influence north of the Transvaal, there were white colonies at the Cape and Natal, the black protectorates of Bechuanaland, Swaziland and Zululand, and the Boer Republics of the Transvaal and the Orange Free State. It was clear that Rhodes wished to extend his and British influence by fomenting a rebellion in the Boer republics, and particularly the Transvaal. He encouraged Dr Starr Jameson, in charge of about 500 men on the border between Bechuanaland and Transvaal, to invade the Transvaal on 30 December 1895, on the pretext of coming to the assistance of a rebellion by the *Uitlanders* (Outsiders), the English and non-Boer alien groups within the Transvaal whose interests were being denied by the Boers. Chamberlain was aware of the political dangers this action presented and finally attempted to prevent this ill-fated venture. However, during the following year he saw some of the Jameson raiders and plotters put on trial and sentenced, was drawn into conflict with Rhodes, was linked, through telegrams, to having a prior knowledge of the raid, and was responsible for setting up a parliamentary committee to investigate the events. The parliamentary report, signed by Chamberlain in 1897, implicated Rhodes in the plot to invade the Transvaal but exonerated Chamberlain himself. It is now clear that Chamberlain was distantly involved in the events that led to the raid but knew little about the actual events until they occurred. Whilst Chamberlain's reputation with the Boers, and with Kruger their president, deteriorated, his position in British domestic politics was not harmed.

Within two years, however, Chamberlain's policy of expanding British influence in South Africa had led him to use military threats as a means of pressuring the Boers to accept that the Transvaal, and indeed the Orange Free State, were subordinate states to Britain and not politically independent. When the British Cabinet published its ultimatum to the Boers on 9 October 1899, demanding that all legislation detrimental to aliens be withdrawn and allowing for a redistribution of rights in their favour, the Boer War began. It was popularly known as 'Joe's War', presented to the British public as necessary in order to secure future British greatness in the world, and though it was concluded successfully the war was a Pyrrhic victory taking well over half a million troops to quell 30,000 or so Boer farming families. Support for 'Joe's War' was based partly upon support from Lord Salisbury, the British Prime Minister, but also from the jingoistic nature of the event. At the end of it Chamberlain remained a popular figure in Britain but he was now in a political party whose leadership had moved from Salisbury's hands into those of A. J. Balfour.

By the early twentieth century Chamberlain was convinced that Britain, which was gradually falling behind Germany and the United States as an economic power, should abandon free trade and protect her domestic markets by erecting trade barriers. He believed that the revenue from tariffs would then pay for the social reforms he wished to introduce. He also favoured a preferential tariff for the Colonies as a means of strengthening their union with Britain. In these views, Chamberlain was opposed by some Unionists, the 'Unionist Free-Fooders', and by Balfour, now the Conservative Prime Minister, who attempted to steer a middle course. From September 1903, Balfour's solution was to use the threat of protection to force protectionist countries to negotiate and he outlined his views in his pamphlet *Insular Free Trade*. This did not solve his government's problems for Chamberlain resigned in order to advocate outright protectionism.

The campaign was doomed from the start for any proposal for higher taxes on food courted disaster at the ballot box and the Conservative and Unionist Party lost heavily in the general election of January 1906, even though Chamberlain secured six Birmingham parliamentary seats to the Unionist and protectionist cause. Although the majority of the defeated Conservative Party probably supported Chamberlain, this was his last great cause. Having undermined the Conservative and Unionist Party with division he agreed to the Valentine Compact of 14 February 1906 which, almost verbatim from one of Balfour's speeches, committed the Conservative Party to fiscal reform 'to secure more equal terms of competition for British trade and closer commercial union with the Colonies' (Marsh, 1994, p. 636). In the summer of 1906 Chamberlain's thirty years as one of Birmingham's MPs was widely celebrated throughout the city but this event signified the end of his political career. Shortly afterwards he was incapacitated by a stroke, and although he did not die until 2 July 1914 his political career was finished.

Joseph Chamberlain certainly left his mark on British politics in both the nineteenth and twentieth centuries. He was a social reformer in both Birmingham and government, drawn in by his interest in education, and an immensely talented and ambitious politician. He was also a destroyer of political parties: he helped to divide the Liberal Party in 1886 and the Conservative/Unionist alliance between 1903 and 1906. As he emerged as a politician he became the archetypal Social Imperialist, with a powerful political base (in Birmingham) which could not easily be defied. However, his great talents and abilities were wasted as his commitment to specific political causes – Unionism and Protectionism – meant that he never reached the political heights to which he seemed destined to rise.

See also: Balfour, Chamberlain (Neville), Churchill

Further reading

Amery, J. L., 1951–69, *The Life and Times of Joseph Chamberlain*, vols 4–6, London: Macmillan.

Fraser, P., 1966, *Joseph Chamberlain: Radicalism and Empire 1868–1914*, London: Cassell.

Garvin, J. L., 1933–5, *The Life and Times of Joseph Chamberlain,* vols 1–3, London: Macmillan.

Jay, R., 1981, *Joseph Chamberlain: A Political Study*, Oxford: Clarendon.

Laybourn, K., 1995, *The Evolution of British Social Policy and the Welfare State c.1800–1993*, Keele: Ryburn Publishing, Keele University Press.

Marsh, P. T., 1994, *Joseph Chamberlain: Entrepreneur in Politics*, New Haven and London: Yale University Press.

(ARTHUR) NEVILLE CHAMBERLAIN 1869–1940

Neville Chamberlain was one of the most controversial of Britain's Prime Ministers, being closely associated with the attempt to secure peace in Europe through the 'appeasement' of the European dictators, the climax of which was reached at the Munich Conference in September 1938. He was Prime Minister for three years between 1937 and 1940 but, with the failure of appeasement, was removed in 1940 by a backbench revolt. Subsequently, he was dubbed by Michael Foot, and other writers, as one of 'the Guilty Men' who had led Britain into war because of his failure to confront Hitler. There have, however, been attempts recently to rebut this charge, to revive Chamberlain's reputation and to understand his actions. Indeed, his life has become immensely controversial and subject to the changing mood of historical interpretation.

Arthur Neville Chamberlain was born on 18 March 1869, the eldest child of Joseph Chamberlain and his second wife, Florence Kenrick. Although Joseph never held any of the highest offices of state, he was one of the great political figures of the late nineteenth and early twentieth centuries, who split the Liberal Party by opposing Home Rule and maintaining the need to keep the union with Ireland. He led the Unionist section of the Liberals into an alliance with the Conservative Party and was also famous for his protectionist campaign of the early twentieth century. His first marriage produced his famous son (Joseph) Austen Chamberlain, who was going to follow in his political footsteps. However, Austen never quite rose to the highest of political offices, although he did lead the Conservative Party between 1921 and 1922, and has the distinction, shared with William Hague, of being the only Conservative Leader of the twentieth century never to have become Prime Minister. On the other hand, his half-brother Neville was guided towards a business career, and spent the years 1890 to 1897 on the Andros Islands in the Bahamas, presiding over an unsuccessful family business venture in growing sisal which cut deep into the wealth of his father, Joseph. On his return, and until 1911, it was the family business activities that dominated his life.

Neville's move into politics occurred only gradually. He was returned as City Councillor for Birmingham in 1911 and rose to become Lord Mayor in 1915–16, during the First World War. It was at this stage that he was drawn into the war effort because of his municipal experience. With Lloyd George taking over the premiership from Asquith, Neville Chamberlain was offered the post of Director-General of National Service in December 1916, dealing with the civilian manpower for industry. However, he had no parliamentary seat, was soon at odds with Lloyd George, and was forced to resign in the summer of 1917. This led to a lifelong hostility between Chamberlain and Lloyd George. It was also at this point that the loss of a close family friend convinced him that war was to be avoided in the future, if at all possible.

Chamberlain began his parliamentary career in 1918 when he was returned as MP for Birmingham Ladywood, a seat he held until 1929. From 1929 until 1940 he was then MP for the Edgbaston seat, also in the Birmingham area. Ostensibly, he was a supporter of the Lloyd George Coalition Government but had little feeling for it and only began to rise in politics when Andrew Bonar Law replaced Lloyd George in October 1922 at the head of a Conservative government, a political change which was opposed by Austen and cost him his position as Leader of the Conservative Party. Neville was appointed to junior ministerial posts but eventually joined the Cabinet in March 1923 as Minister of Health. His main achievement in this role was the passing of the Housing Act of 1923 which provided substantial financial incentives for private builders to build houses for sale. For a few weeks, at the end of 1923 and the beginning of 1924, Chamberlain became Chancellor of the Exchequer but he lost his post with the return of Ramsay MacDonald's first Labour government in January 1924. However, when the Conservatives returned to office at the end of 1924, Neville again became Minister of Health, having rejected the post of Chancellor of the Exchequer. In the next four-and-a-half years, Chamberlain embarked upon a massive rationalization programme in which he sought to provide a better financial basis for local government, and prepared the way for the transfer of the Poor Law to local government through the Local Government Act of 1929. This process had been deemed necessary because of the problems of controlling the Board of Guardians of the Poor Laws and Labour-controlled local borough and city councils, as revealed by the lavish expenditure they seemed to be distributing in the events surrounding the government's battle with Poplar Borough Council throughout the 1920s and with Labour-dominated Boards of Guardians during the General Strike of 1926. The second Labour government, which was returned after Labour became the largest party in the May 1929 general election, completed the process with the Poor Laws Act of 1930.

With the defeat of the Conservative Party in the May 1929 general election, Chamberlain occupied himself with politics within the Conservative Party. He chaired the Party's newly-formed Research Department, acted as Chairman of the Party from June 1930 to March 1931, shaped the future economic thinking of the Party and, in March 1931, helped resolve the differences between Lord Beaverbrook, the press baron, and Baldwin. About this time, Chamberlain passed on a memo to Baldwin, from Robert Topping who was the Party's senior official, recommending that Baldwin resign as Party Leader. Indeed, for a time it appeared that Chamberlain might replace Baldwin as Conservative Leader. However, the Party seems to have accepted the adage 'Better the Devil you know than the Neville you don't', and relations between Chamberlain and Baldwin soon returned to normal. Shortly afterwards, in August 1931, Chamberlain was deeply involved in the negotiations which led to the end of MacDonald's second Labour government and the formation of the National Government.

Chamberlain was offered the post of Chancellor of the Exchequer in the National Government after the departure of Philip Snowden and he filled that office between November 1931 and May 1937, when he became Prime Minister. Chamberlain proved to be a pragmatic Chancellor, although he was much criticized for the slowness of the two National Governments to tackle the unemployment problems of the country. Nevertheless, he presided over a slow economic recovery which was a product of the early economic decisions he made. Most obviously he introduced the type of protectionist measures which his father had sought about thirty years before, and pushed ahead with the idea, if not the reality, of an Empire Free Trade area at the Ottawa Conference of 1932. Although not all his economic policies went well they did allow British interests rates to fall to 2 and 3 per cent and thus played a part in stimulating the private housing boom and the boom in the new consumer industries (of cars and electrical goods) in the 1930s. Nevertheless, unemployment blackspots still persisted and he, and the government, faced significant criticism from Lloyd George over the limited financial support being put forward in its Special Areas Act of 1934.

Stanley Baldwin, the Prime Minister, was often ill throughout 1936 and Chamberlain became acting Prime Minister. It was at this stage that he encouraged the slow re-armament of the country and the expansion of the Royal Air Force at a pace that would not damage the fragile British economy. Ultimately, however, his interests were to move in this direction, away from the economy, as he replaced Baldwin as Prime Minister on 28 May 1937. He had become the obvious, and indeed the only, candidate for the post, but he was not a natural leader. Indeed, he had a reputation of being a cold-hearted administrator, a stubborn and persistent politician, a good debater, but a limited orator. Yet his strengths outweighed his weaknesses and he dominated the Cabinet and ran his administration with the support of the inner cabinet of Sir John Simon, Sir Samuel Hoare and Lord Halifax, who had replaced Sir Anthony Eden as Foreign Secretary in February 1938 because of Eden's opposition to precisely the lines taken in Chamberlain's appeasement policies with Hitler and the other European dictators. Indeed, Hitler and Germany were to be Chamberlain's major problem from now onwards.

With the expansionist policy of 'Lebensraum' (the creation of living space in Europe for the German people), Hitler looked to the east to expand in Austria, Czechoslovakia and Poland. Emphasizing the strong German presence in Austria, and following the Austrian President's order not to oppose the Germans, Hitler was able to announce the *Anschluss* on 13 March 1938, when Germany absorbed Austria into the 'Greater Germany'. Chamberlain does not seem to have been too perturbed at this development, but he was concerned about German claims in Czechoslovakia. Britain had promised France that she would protect the borders of Czechoslovakia but Hitler demanded that the large German community, particularly in the Sudeten areas, be allowed to vote on whether or not to join Germany or to remain within Czechoslovakia. He announced a deadline of 1 October 1938 for agreement on this. Chamberlain, after a round a meetings which saw him make three trips to see Hitler in September 1938, eventually conceded to Hitler's demands on 30 September 1938, in the infamous Munich Agreement. A year later, however, in September 1939, Britain declared war on Germany following the German invasion of Poland.

The great concern of British politicians in the 1930s had been how to deal with Hitler's expansionist activities. The British armed forces were weak, and it did not seem likely that the League of Nations would be able to act in concert to restrain Hitler. Indeed, it had blatantly failed to prevent Italy's invasion of Abyssinia in the mid 1930s.

Realistically, there were only three alternative actions that might have maintained peace – to seek collective security through the League of Nations; to form an alliance with powers opposed to the German and fascist states; or to pursue appeasement. The first option was rejected instantly. Indeed, Chamberlain asked the question, in the House of Commons on 7 March 1938: 'What country in Europe today if threatened by a large Power can rely upon the League of Nations for protection?' His answer was 'None'. The second option seemed unlikely, for whilst Britain had an alliance with France, Chamberlain was unwilling to develop an Anglo-Soviet alliance. That left appeasement.

Chamberlain's pursuit of appeasement has, of course, been subject to intense scrutiny. At one time it was suggested, by Michael Foot and the other authors of *The Guilty Men* (1940), that Chamberlain had stumbled into war because he naively believed that Hitler could be appeased. Instead of facing up to Hitler, he gave him everything he asked for and thus, ironically, hastened the onset of war. Keith Feiling attempted a modest defence of Chamberlain from such accusations in *The Life of Neville Chamberlain* (1946). Since then, there have been mixed responses. Martin Gilbert and Richard Gott were critical of his actions in *The Appeasers* (1963) but in a later book, *The Roots of Appeasement* (1966), Gilbert was more considerate of his 'honourable quest' to maintain peace. Indeed, since the late 1960s, the availability of new records has led to the defence of Chamberlain, suggesting that he was far from being naive and cowardly, that appeasement was the only realistic policy available to him, and that the policy was in fact widely supported by the British public. David Dilks has been foremost in defending Chamberlain's reputation in this respect, suggesting that he did the best that was possible given that Britain needed time to build up her defence capability and that he was prepared to give an undertaking to defend Poland.

These revisionist views have been challenged. Ian Colvin, for instance, has suggested that Chamberlain was naive in his personal diplomacy. His problem was that in pursuing appeasement he ignored the other alternatives that might have prevented war. Richard Cockett goes even further and suggests that Chamberlain manipulated the 'free press' in such a way as to give the impression that both the government and the nation were united in support of appeasement, when neither was. R. C. A. Parker has gone yet further in suggesting that Chamberlain ruled out alternatives to appeasement that might have secured peace. Clearly, the debate will continue.

With the outbreak of the Second World War, Chamberlain continued to serve as Prime Minister. However, both the Liberal Party and the Labour Party refused to serve in his wartime ministry, even though Anthony Eden and Winston Churchill, staunch pre-war critics, did serve. At first, Chamberlain adopted the defensive strategy of building up the armed forces and avoiding offensive action but rising public pressure forced his ministry to attempt to block the flow of iron ore from Scandinavia to Germany. When British forces failed to prevent the subsequent invasion of Norway, the Labour Party, the Liberal Party and some sections of the Conservative Party came together to remove Chamberlain as Prime Minister. Following several heated debates in the House of Commons, the government majority fell from 240 to 81 and Chamberlain resigned, on 10 May 1940. He was replaced by Winston Churchill who headed an all-party government. However, Chamberlain continued in government as Lord President of the Council, with a seat on the War Cabinet, and as Leader of the Conservative Party until his declining health forced him to resign. He eventually died of cancer on 9 November 1940.

See also: Baldwin, Churchill, MacDonald

Further reading

Aster, S., 1989, '"Guilty men": the case of Neville Chamberlain', in Boyce, R. and Robertson, E. (eds), *Paths to War*, Basingstoke: Macmillan.

Charmley, J., 1989, *Chamberlain and the Lost Peace*, London: Curtis.

Cockett, R., 1989, *Twilight of Truth: Chamberlain, Appeasement and the Manipulation of the Press*, London: Weidenfeld & Nicolson.

Colvin, I., 1971, *The Chamberlain Cabinet*, London: Gollancz.

Dilks, D., 1984, *Neville Chamberlain. Vol 1: Pioneering and Reform, 1868–1940*, Cambridge: Cambridge University Press.

Dilks, D., 1987, '"We must hope for the best and prepare for the worst." The Prime Minister, the Cabinet and Hitler's Germany 1937–9', *Proceedings of the British Academy*.

Feiling, K., 1946, *The Life of Neville Chamberlain*, London: Macmillan.

Fuchser, L. W., 1982, *Neville Chamberlain and Appeasement*, New York and London: Norton.

Gilbert, M., and Gott, R., 1963, *The Appeasers*, London: Weidenfeld & Nicolson.

Gilbert, M., 1966, *The Roots of Appeasement*, London: Weidenfeld & Nicolson.

Jefferys, K., 1991, 'May 1940: The Downfall of Neville Chamberlain', *Parliamentary History*, 10.

Parker, R. A. C., 1993, *Chamberlain and Appeasement: British Policy and the Coming of the Second World War*, Basingstoke: Macmillan.

SIR WINSTON (LEONARD SPENCER) CHURCHILL 1874–1965

Sir Winston Churchill's parliamentary career was one of the longest in British parliamentary history, extending continuously from 1900 to 1964, with the exception of one break between 1922 and 1924. During all this period he was very much in the public eye. Nonetheless, until 1940 his career was unfulfilled, despite his having headed eight separate government departments between 1908 and 1929, and regardless of the fact that he seemed to have overcome having started life as a Conservative and transferred to the Liberals before returning to the Conservative fold. There was always a suspicion about Churchill's political reliability and he was cast into the political wilderness during the 1930s. Nevertheless, his position and reputation were restored in 1940 when he replaced Neville Chamberlain as Prime Minister. It is as a wartime leader that he is best known, leading Britain to victory in the Second World War in 1945. Although he was Prime Minister again between 1951 and 1955, nothing surpassed his wartime leadership, the crowning glory of his political career.

Winston Leonard Spencer Churchill was born into the aristocracy on 30 November 1874, the son of Lord Randolph Churchill and Jennie Jerome, and the grandson of the seventh Duke of Marlborough. He was educated at Harrow and at Sandhurst, where he was trained for a career in the army. Indeed, he was in the army from 1895 to 1900 and served in India and fought in the Battle of Omdurman in 1898.

He had left the army and was a journalist at the time of the Boer War, during which he was captured and famously escaped. From then onwards, he moved into a political career.

After failing to win a parliamentary by-election in 1899, Churchill was returned as Conservative MP for Oldham in 1900. Upset by Joseph Chamberlain's protectionist campaign within the Conservative Party and within the country, Churchill, a firm believer in free trade, joined the Liberal Party in 1904. He successfully contested the North West Manchester seat in 1906, but then switched to Dundee, which he represented until 1922. As a result of his switch of Party he gained a junior ministerial post in Henry Campbell-Bannerman's Liberal government. However, Campbell-Bannerman's death in April 1908 opened the way for H. H. Asquith to become Prime Minister. Asquith made Churchill President of the Board of Trade and gave him a seat on the Cabinet. In his new role, he worked closely with David Lloyd George, the Chancellor of the Exchequer, in pressing forward with old age pensions (1908), labour exchanges (1909), and other Liberal welfare legislation. He became Home Secretary in February 1910, a post he held until October 1911. He was most controversial in this role, particularly when he sent troops into South Wales, which led to two deaths at Tonypandy, and with his involvement in the 1911 Sydney Street siege, connected with East European revolutionaries. The first of these events earned Churchill the hatred of several generations of miners.

In 1911 Churchill became First Lord of the Admiralty and, from a position of opposing increases in naval expenditure as President of the Board of Trade, he found himself demanding naval expansion, clashing over this issue with Lloyd George. His interference in naval operations caused problems which culminated in his vilification over the failure of the Gallipoli campaign in early 1915. When the first wartime Coalition Government was formed, under Asquith, in May 1915 the Conservative members demanded Churchill's removal from the Admiralty. He spent six months as Chancellor of the Duchy of Lancaster, effectively a minister without a department or portfolio, and then went to the Western Front as a battalion commander.

Lloyd George replaced Asquith as Prime Minister in December 1916, split the Liberal Party, and was forced to seek what little support he could attract from within the Liberal Party. As a result, Churchill was called back to become Minister of Munitions in July 1917, a post he held until January 1919. Between 1919 and 1921, Churchill served as Secretary of War and Air and then as Colonial Secretary from February 1921 until October 1922. Churchill was a close friend of Lloyd George and so, when that Coalition collapsed and Lloyd George was replaced by Bonar Law, Churchill lost office. He also lost his seat at the 1922 general election.

Now faced with a divided and defeated Liberal Party as his platform for political power, Churchill gradually became a 'Constitutionalist', and was adopted by the Conservatives for the safe seat of Epping, which he represented for just over forty years from 1924. When Baldwin became Prime Minister at the end of 1924, Churchill was given the post of Chancellor of the Exchequer, a post he retained until May 1929. As a free trader he was committed to balancing the budgets, much in the way that his Liberal counterpart, Philip Snowden, had done in 1924. He also returned Britain to the Gold Standard, which was synonymous with free trade, in April 1925 – even though the process saw the pound re-flated by 10 per cent in order to raise it to its pre-war parity with the dollar. Churchill was a particularly belligerent opponent of the Trades Union Congress (TUC) during the General Strike of 1926, refusing to accept the TUC demands for the maintenance of the wages of the miners and acting as editor of the *British Gazette*, a paper which Lloyd George described as being a first-class indiscretion 'clothed in the tawdry garb of third-rate journalism'. Once the dispute was called off by the General Council of the TUC, Churchill attempted to bring the coal dispute to a settlement by bringing the coal owners and the coal miners together. However, he could get nowhere and reflected that he had never met a more stubborn and pig-headed set of men than the coal miners, that is until he met the coal owners.

With the Conservative Party defeat at the May 1929 general election and increasing antipathy towards Baldwin, Churchill moved into the political wilderness for the next eleven years. He began to write biographies, returned to his journalistic roots and travelled the world. Indeed, he neglected Parliament and was frequently in conflict with the Conservative Party, first in opposing the bipartisan attitude towards India and, second, in his support for Edward VIII in the Abdication Crisis of 1936. In the case of India he was out of step with British public opinion in denouncing the concessions made to the Indian National Congress and the influence of Mahatma Gandhi, who he describes as 'a seditious Middle Temple lawyer, now posing as a fakir of a type well-known in the East' (Rhodes James, 1974, p. 485).

Churchill was also at odds with the Conservative Party regarding the Spanish Civil War. At first he supported the fascist cause in Spain but then, realizing that a fascist Spain when coupled with a fascist Germany and a fascist Italy would surround France, began to fear that France would be invaded and that Britain would be drawn into war.

As a result he opposed Franco in Spain, demanded re-armament and the development of the Royal Air Force. He was most certainly a minority voice in the Conservative Party until the Munich Agreement of 1938 effectively sacrificed Czechoslovakia to Germany in order to maintain peace. At this stage Churchill forged an alliance with Anthony Eden to oppose appeasement.

On 3 September 1939 Britain declared war on Germany. Churchill was called into Neville Chamberlain's wartime administration as First Lord of the Admiralty. He typified the 'bulldog' spirit to such an extent that when Chamberlain resigned in May 1940 it was clear that he was the only possible replacement. Indeed, the Labour Party insisted upon Churchill as Prime Minister before it would join the wartime Coalition in May 1940. Churchill was to become the great wartime leader, as Prime Minister and Minister of Defence, who took Britain to victory. His reputation for the 'bulldog' tradition was enhanced by his gathering of public support to continue the fight following the fall of France. Even so there were moments in 1941 and 1942 when there were setbacks – military setbacks, when Sir Stafford Cripps was suggested as a possible replacement for Churchill, although left-wing ambitions in this direction were stifled by Stalin.

Churchill's apparently close friendship with Franklin D. Roosevelt led to significant help for Britain even before the United States joined the war. He met with Roosevelt and Stalin at Yalta in order to win the war and prepare the way for a peaceful post-war world.

In 1945, after 'Victory in Europe', but before victory over Japan, Churchill decided to call a general election. As a successful wartime leader, he expected to win even though the Gallup polls had indicated a strong lead for Labour since about 1942. It was thus a shock when the Conservative Party suffered a heavy defeat. Although Churchill was Leader of the Opposition between 1945 and 1951 he had less interest in British politics than in the world stage. As a staunch believer in Empire, he opposed Britain's withdrawal both from the Indian subcontinent and from other far-flung corners of Empire. However, at this stage he is best remembered for his speech, on 15 March 1946, at Fulton, Missouri, in which, referring to Soviet expansion in Eastern Europe, he coined the phrase the 'Iron Curtain'. This speech anticipated the development of the 'Cold War' between the Communist world and the Western World during the post-war years.

Churchill became Prime Minister again in October 1951. During his four years in office he seems to have attempted to reconstruct some of the wartime unity, offering a possible alliance with the Liberals and deciding not to revoke nationalization introduced by the Attlee government, except in the case of the iron and steel industry. Churchill attempted to play the role of great world leader and to bring some type of international agreement that might reduce international tensions. But his efforts were impaired by the fact that he suffered a stroke in July 1953 and from then until his eventual resignation in 1955, he had limited influence. In reality it was Sir Anthony Eden who, from then onwards, ran the day-to-day operation of Churchill's administration, until he took over in 1955. Churchill had received a knighthood in 1953 and the Nobel Prize for Literature the same year. From 1955, he gradually withdrew from politics although he did not retire from the House of Commons until 1964, dying on 24 January 1965. He was given an elaborate national funeral and dubbed 'The Greatest Englishman', a man whom some subsequent prime ministers have sought to emulate.

Had Churchill retired from politics in the 1930s he would have been remembered as a modestly successful politician who had secured some claim to fame through his involvement with Lloyd George in building up the Liberal government's welfare state between 1906 and 1914. Given his talent, that would have been something of a failure. It was the Second World War which rescued his reputation and raised him to the status of one of the most successful British politicians of the twentieth century.

See also: Asquith, Attlee, Baldwin, Lloyd George

Further reading

Addison, P., 1992, *Churchill on the Home Front 1900–1955*, London: Cape.
Blake, R. and Louis, W. R. (eds), 1993, 1996, *Churchill*, Oxford: Oxford University Press and Clarendon.
Cannadine, D. (ed.), 1996, *The Speeches of Winston Churchill*, London: Penguin.
Charmley, J., 1993, *Churchill: The End of Glory*, London: Hodder & Stoughton.
Gilbert, M., vols 1971–88, *Winston S. Churchill*, London: Heinemann.
Rhodes James, R. (ed.), 1980, *Churchill Speaks. Winston S. Churchill in Peace and War. Collected Speeches, 1897–1963*, New York: Chelsea House.
Robbins, K., 1991, *Churchill*, London: Longman.
Stansky, P. (ed.), 1973, *Churchill: A Profile*, London: Macmillan.
Taylor, A. J. P., *et al.*, 1969, *Churchill: Four Faces of the Man*, London: Allen Lane.

WALTER (McLENNAN) CITRINE 1887–1983

Walter Citrine's great claim to fame is that he was General Secretary of the Trades Union Congress (TUC) from 1926 to 1946, having been Assistant and Acting General Secretary prior to that. In this role he acted as a moderator and was one of those within the TUC who believed that there was no possibility of winning the General Strike of 1926 and urged the quickest of settlements. Indeed, moderation was to be his style throughout his industrial and political life.

Citrine was born in 1887 at Liverpool; he was of Italian extraction, although both his father and grandfather had been British seamen. He was a small and physically weak man, with a soft-spoken whiny voice. He began work as a labourer in a flour mill before becoming an electrician. Although raised in a Conservative working-class family atmosphere, he soon gravitated towards the Labour Party, which he joined in 1906. He also joined the Electrical Trades Union (ETU) in 1911 and by 1914 had become its first full-time District Secretary in Liverpool. By 1920 he had become Assistant General Secretary of the ETU and was based in Manchester. Then in 1924 he became Assistant General Secretary of the TUC, to Fred Bramley, who died in 1925. Citrine filled the post of Assistant General Secretary between October 1925 and September 1926, when he was finally appointed General Secretary.

His major activity at this time was to organize the General Strike of 3 to 12 May 1926. Throughout 1925 and the early months of 1926 he had attempted to prepare the way for the Strike by getting all the unions to accept the authority of the TUC when it came to calling for strike action. This was not achieved until a special conference vote on 1 May 1926, which mean that preparations for the General Strike in support of the miners, who had been locked out in an attempt to reduce their wages, were arranged at the last minute. Citrine had was sure that the strike could not be won: 'A general strike ... is a literal impossibility' (Citrine, 'Mining Crisis and National Strike', 4 January 1926, manuscript in the British Library of Political and Economic Science, London). Not surprisingly, he was strongly supportive of the Samuel Memorandum, arranged between Sir Herbert Samuel and the TUC, which aimed to end the dispute and to open up the possibility of negotiations between coal owners and coal miners, subject to the extension of the government's subsidy to coal mining whilst wages and conditions were worked out in the context of its re-organization. Citrine urged the coal miners' leaders to accept this arrangement since it was held to represent 'sufficient assurances ... as to the lines upon which a settlement could be reached to justify terminating the General Strike'. When the miners' leaders refused, it was Citrine who called a meeting with them to discuss the Samuel Memorandum. The miners rejected the proposal for settlement and the TUC contacted 10 Downing Street on the night of 11 May in order to formally call off the dispute the next day. In the end, the General Strike was called off unconditionally and without any guarantees, and the Samuel Memorandum was abandoned.

With the end of the General Strike Citrine was faced with fending off criticism of the TUC levelled against it by the Communist Party of Great Britain and in presenting the TUC as a moderate democratic movement. The first action eventually led to the Black Circulars of 1934, banning both trade unions and trades councils from choosing communists as delegates. The second was to be seen in the way in which Citrine supported the talks between the TUC and the large industrialists of the Federation of British Industry – the Mond-Turner talks – which aimed to unite the two sides on pressuring the government to tackle vital issues concerning industry and unemployment.

Along with Ernest Bevin, the General Secretary of the Transport and General Workers' Union, and the dominant trade unionists of the inter-war years, Citrine represented trade unions on many government-sponsored and public bodies. During the 1930s he served on the National Economic Council, the Consultative Committee of the Treasury and on a Royal Commission that investigated economic and social conditions in the West Indies (1938–9), and continued to serve on a government committee throughout the Second World War. His public role was recognized by the offer of a peerage in 1930 and a knighthood in 1932, both of which he refused, although he eventually accepted a knighthood in 1935. He also eventually accepted a peerage in 1946, upon his retirement as General Secretary of the TUC, and was created first Baron Citrine of Wembley.

In the post-war years of the Attlee Labour governments, Citrine was connected with many public bodies. He was a member of the National Coal Board (1946–7) before becoming Chairman of the British Electricity Authority (1947 to 1957). He was also part-time member on the United Kingdom Atomic Energy Authority (1958–62). Whilst in retirement he wrote his two-volume autobiography.

Although Citrine's fame arises from his industrial activities he was an immensely important person in British twentieth-century political history. His commitment to moderation, particularly at the time of the General Strike, helped to prevent the destruction of the political constitution that would have occurred had an industrial struggle defeated the government of the day. Equally, he was a leading figure of the right wing of the trade union movement whose approach to socialism fitted well with the ambitions and programme of the Attlee Labour government of the post-war years.

See also: Attlee, Bevin

Further reading

Citrine, W., 1964, *Men and Work: An Autobiography*, London: Hutchinson.
Citrine, W., 1967, *Two Careers*, London: Hutchinson.
Laybourn, K., 1993, *The General Strike of 1926*, Manchester: Manchester University Press and New York: St Martin's Press.
Lovell, J. C. and Roberts, B. C., 1968, *A Short History of the TUC*, London: Macmillan.
Martin, R. M.,1980, *TUC: The Growth of a Pressure Group, 1868–1976*, Oxford: Clarendon.

SIR STAFFORD CRIPPS 1889–1952

Sir Stafford Cripps was one of the Labour Party's most controversial political figures. In the 1930s he rose quickly to the position of Deputy Leader of the Labour Party, then was expelled from the Party and, later, when restored to Party membership, became Attlee's Chancellor of the Exchequer, the famous 'Austerity Cripps' of the first post-war Labour government. Throughout his political career he excited criticism because of his arrogance and certitude, evoking comments such as: 'There but for the grace of God goes God' (Winston Churchill). Nevertheless, he was particularly important in leading the Labour Left in the 1930s and acted as British Ambassador to Moscow at the beginning of the Second World War.

Cripps was born on 24 April 1889, the fifth child of Charles Alfred Cripps, later the first Lord Parmoor, who was to act as Lord President of the Council in the first two Labour governments of 1924 and 1929–31. His mother was Theresa Potter, the sister of Beatrice Potter (later Beatrice Webb), the famous socialist writer and activist. Cripps was educated at Winchester and at University College, London, where he intended to become a research chemist. However, he eventually decided to follow both his father and grandfather into a legal career. He married Isobel Swithinbank in July 1911 and became a barrister, shortly afterwards, in 1913.

Cripps's legal career was interrupted by the First World War during which he acted as a Red Cross lorry driver, having been rejected for military service on medical grounds. From 1915 onwards he worked with the Ministry of Munitions explosives department. At the end of the war, Cripps returned to the legal profession and quickly established a successful practice, mainly in patent and compensation cases. As a result, he became in 1926 the youngest King's Counsel at the British Bar. It was through his legal work for the London County Council (LCC) that he came to the attention of Herbert Morrison, who persuaded him to join the Labour Party in 1929, and he was appointed Solicitor-General to Ramsay MacDonald's Labour government in October 1930, being knighted the same year. Cripps was a committed Christian, and prior to entering politics had been active in the World Alliance of Christian Churches between 1923 and 1929.

Cripps entered Parliament as Labour MP for East Bristol at the 1931 general election which saw the return of MacDonald's National Government and the Labour Party reduced to 52 MPs (46 in some listings, according to how they are counted) from more than six times that number in 1929. Cripps's obvious ability in a much-reduced Parliamentary Labour Party allowed him to rise to the top of British Labour politics within months of entering Parliament. From the beginning of his parliamentary career he argued that Labour's gradualist approach to socialism was dead, adopting a more assertive approach and demanding the introduction of measures to ensure the swift movement of a future Labour government towards public ownership. Indicative of this was his decision to help form the Socialist League in 1932 – a body of ex-members of the Independent Labour Party, the Labour Left and the Socialist Society for Information and Propaganda – and through it Cripps sought to mount a Unity Campaign between various socialist groups, including the Independent Labour Party and the Communist Party of Great Britain, to face the rising challenge of fascism in the mid and late 1930s. The forlorn hope was that the Labour Party might eventually adopt socialist unity to fight against fascism. Instead, in 1937 the Labour Party, of which Cripps became Deputy Leader at the time, forced the Socialist League to disband. Cripps therefore channelled his efforts into making a success of the *Tribune*, a left-wing journal formed in January of that year. Labour's hostility to other socialist and non-socialist parties did not, however, curb his ambitions permanently. Indeed, he mounted a Popular Front movement in 1938 and 1939, to bring together all those who opposed fascism. This led him to demand the removal of the government of Neville Chamberlain, to oppose appeasement and to issue the 'Cripps Memorandum' on the need for a Popular Front of all anti-fascists against fascism. This move, which was opposed by the Labour Party, led to Cripps's expulsion from the Labour Party at the beginning of 1939.

With the outbreak of the Second World War, Cripps acted as an unofficial government envoy touring China, India and the Soviet Union, a position promoted by Lord Halifax and the wartime government. Churchill, upon becoming Prime Minister, then made him British ambassador to the Soviet Union in May 1940, a post he held until January 1942. His job was to improve relations with the Soviet Union and to gain its support for Britain in the war effort. This was no easy task, given the existence of a non-aggression pact between Germany and the Soviet Union, but the German invasion of the Soviet Union (Operation Barbarossa) in the summer of 1941 changed matters. The Soviet Union entered the war on the Allied side and Cripps returned to Britain in 1942 to such popular acclaim that there was some speculation that he might replace Churchill as Prime Minister, a move which was opposed by the Soviet Union which played down the hopes of some left-wingers in this direction by indicating its satisfaction with Churchill. Cripps was admitted to the War Cabinet, but Churchill sent him off to India to secure an accommodation with the nationalist leaders and, having returned empty-handed, he was then removed from the Cabinet to the important post of Minister of Aircraft Production.

In 1945, Cripps was formally re-admitted to the Labour Party and appointed President of the Board of Trade in Attlee's first post-war Labour government, in which he was primarily responsible for the rationing programme. He was also involved in another unsuccessful Cabinet mission to India in 1946. At this stage it was clear that he was amongst those pushing for Ernest Bevin to replace Attlee. However, Attlee cleverly headed off this challenge by placing Cripps at the head of the newly created Ministry of Economic Affairs. Indeed, the relations between Cripps and Bevin had never been all that good and the Foreign Office view, presumably reflecting the view of Bevin, was that Cripps was half-way to Moscow in his political leanings and favoured Britain switching her friendship from the United States to the Soviet Union.

The resignation of Hugh Dalton as Chancellor of the Exchequer in November 1947 led to its amalgamation with the Treasury and Cripps's promotion to the post of Chancellor in the wake of the economic crisis of spring of that year, which had seen the end of the convertibility of the pound in connection with the American loan. As Chancellor, Cripps introduced three deflationary Budgets between 1948 and 1950, in which he attempted to control the level of welfare spending, particularly on Aneurin Bevan's National Health Service. In addition, he introduced import controls, a voluntary wage freeze, a limit on dividends, and announced the devaluation of the pound in September 1949. The purpose of his policies was to reduce British imports, to encourage exports and to control inflation. Cripps's efforts to restore credibility to the Labour government led him to be referred to as 'Austerity Cripps'. Nevertheless, he was generally successful in his policies. British exports increased rapidly, unemployment levels fell to around 200,000, with more jobs available than the number of those seeking them, and the new value of the pound ($2.80 to the £1) lasted for eighteen years.

In many respects, Cripps's work as Chancellor reflected his own personal views about how economic planning was essential to economic growth. When he was President of the Board of Trade he had written the economic planning section of the first *Economic Survey*, produced in 1947. His belief was that planning had to be achieved by a mixture of government direction and voluntary co-operation. The *Survey* suggested that a democratic state in normal times could not expect the people to subordinate their desires to the demands of the state and that '[a] democratic government must therefore conduct its economic planning in a manner which preserves the maximum possible freedom of choice to the individual citizens'. He recognized this need in his Budget of April 1948, when he effectively accepted the Keynesian demand management technique of pumping money into the economy at times of depression and reducing it at times of inflation, and of allowing his policies to work upon the free choice of the rest of the nation. He also recognized the value of this co-operation between the state and the individual by stressing the need to continue with a voluntary wage freeze, although the Trades Union Congress found this increasingly difficult to maintain in the late 1940s. The Budget was vital to the steering policy he encouraged as Chancellor and in his Budget speech of 15 April 1950, and he stated that he regarded the Budget as 'the most powerful instrument for influencing economic policy which is available to the government'.

In a confidential letter to Attlee on 26 April 1950, Cripps indicated that he could not continue as Chancellor for much longer. He intended to resign in the summer of 1950 but continued until 19 October of that year, although he was not present at the Treasury for the last few months of his period in office. He resigned from the House of Commons at the same time. He was suffering from ill health and he died eighteen months later, while recuperating in Zurich.

Cripps led a distinguished, if somewhat chequered, political career. In his various roles of leader of the Labour left in the 1930s, opposer of appeasement and proactive British ambassador in Moscow, he won huge recognition and support. Unfortunately, in later years his obvious administrative and political skills were lost as his name came to be associated with austerity and devaluation. What is often forgotten is that he helped to rescue Britain from the economic precipice of 1947, when it looked as though the whole economy was liable to collapse into ruins. Whilst Cripps may not have been an economist, he was a more than adequate Chancellor of the Exchequer.

See also: Attlee, Bevan, Bevin, Churchill, Gaitskell

Further reading:

Bryant, C., 1997, Stafford Cripps. The First Modern Chancellor, London: Hodder & Stoughton.

Cooke, C., 1957, The Life of Richard Stafford Cripps, London: Hodder & Stoughton.

Morgan, K. O.,1984, Labour in Power, 1945–1951, Oxford: Clarendon.

Morgan, K. O., 1987, Labour People: Leaders and Lieutenants, Hardie to Kinnock, Oxford: Oxford University Press.

(CHARLES) ANTHONY (RAVEN) CROSLAND 1918–1977

Tony Crosland was one of the leading British socialist thinkers of the post-Second World War years. He rose to fame as one of the leading 'revisionist' socialist thinkers within the Labour Party in the 1950s, giving his name to the ideology 'Croslandism', and he held a number of ministerial posts in the Labour governments of the 1960s and 1970s, most prominently, albeit briefly, that of Foreign Secretary.

Crosland was born on 28 August 1918 in Sussex and was educated at Trinity College, Oxford, where he read Classics before switching to Economics. His academic life was interrupted by the Second World War, during which he became an officer in the Royal Welsh Fusiliers and served in North Africa. He returned to Oxford after the war, becoming Chairman of the Democratic Socialist Club, president of the Oxford Union and also a member of the National Executive of the Fabian Society. He then became a tutor and lecturer in economics at Oxford in 1947. However, he abandoned his academic career in 1950 and became MP for South Gloucestershire. He lost that seat in 1955 but established his prominence within the Labour Party by publishing his main work, The Future of Socialism, in 1956. Regarded as a major piece of Labour revisionism, this work built upon his article in the New Fabian Essays, published in 1952, in which he attempted to balance a theoretical analysis of socialism with its practical application.

He stressed that Labour's socialism should not be simply about nationalization and the provision of welfare benefits but should be about tackling the gross inequalities of wealth (not income) which persisted, the reform of the educational system and the creation of a less confrontational system of industrial relations. *The Future of Socialism* developed these ideas further by stressing that socialist aims were essentially ethical and moral, and sprang from the need to stress such ideals as liberty, fellowship, social welfare and equality. It argued that to establish these principles, particularly equality, required the redistribution of resources and wealth in society through social expenditure and progressive taxation. This could be achieved with ease because society had mastered production and could sustain economic growth. Thus it followed that public ownership of the means of production – Labour's famous Clause Four – was no longer essential to the development of socialist policy. It was also deemed essential that there should be educational reform to create the new egalitarian type of society, and this meant the sweeping away of the 11-plus exam and the selective and discriminatory nature of secondary provision that it created.

Crosland's views were taken up by Hugh Gaitskell, who argued that educational reform and taxation were more likely than public ownership to achieve ethical socialism. For this reason Gaitskell attempted, unsuccessfully, to get the Labour Party Conference of 1959 to remove Clause Four, which he felt was the basis of Labour's unpopularity in the 1959 general election. However, trade union opposition ensured that the Labour Party leadership did not get its way.

In 1959 Crosland was returned to Parliament as the MP for Grimsby. At this time he supported Gaitskell on the removal of Clause Four, and also on the need to ensure that the Labour Party abandoned its policy of unilateral nuclear disarmament. However, the momentum of revisionism faded in 1963, when Gaitskell died and was replaced by Harold Wilson, a pragmatic and more compromising Labour Leader. As a result, Crosland was given the middling government posts rather than the higher posts he might have expected under Gaitskell.

Crosland was Wilson's Minister to the Department of Economic Affairs in 1964 before becoming Secretary of State for Science and Education between 1965 and 1967. In the latter role he was largely responsible for Circular 10/65 which requested all local authorities consider plans for the re-organization of education along comprehensive lines. This created controversy as it became clear that he meant to replace the selective direct and assisted grammar schools with all-embracing comprehensive schools. Crosland was President of the Board of Trade between 1967 and 1969, and Secretary of State for

Local Government and Regional Planning between 1969 and 1970. In June 1970 the Labour Party was defeated in a general election and Crosland was in opposition until 1974. However, it is clear that during that period, and particularly between 1972 and 1974, he was pushing forward arguments within the Party in favour of a future Labour government seeking Britain's permanent entry into the European Economic Community, although he compromised on this issue from time to time in the face of considerable anti-European sentiment within the Labour Party.

In Wilson's 1974 Labour government, Crosland was appointed Secretary of State for the Environment. Again, this was a post of middling importance but it gave him a seat on the Cabinet. When Wilson resigned, Crosland entered the Party leadership contest but came last of six candidates, polling a mere seventeen votes in the first ballot, in an election which eventually saw James Callaghan installed as Labour Leader. Despite the contest, Callaghan promoted Crosland to Foreign Secretary, a post he held from April 1976 until his death on 19 February 1977, and during which his main concern was dealing with Ian Smith's declaration of independence for Rhodesia.

It was during the last year of his life that he began to re-think the revisionist ideas he had first put forward in the 1950s. The deepening economic crisis in 1976 had forced Denis Healey, the Chancellor of the Exchequer, to seek a loan from the International Monetary Fund. This was obtained but only at the cost of massive cuts in expenditure. At this juncture, James Callaghan, the Prime Minister, spoke of the fact that the party was over and that vast inputs of investment and expenditure in the economy could not be expected in order to ensure that there was continued full employment. The Keynesian expansionist policies that Labour had adopted since 1945 were now unaffordable. The redistribution of income and wealth promised to the trade unions by the Labour government in 1974, in return for the 'Social Contract' to control wage demands, would not be achieved. The Crosland idea was also dead: economic growth could not ensure high social expenditure and the redistribution of income and wealth because it could not be sustained.

Crosland was a successful politician and an effective Cabinet Minister but, above all, he is best remembered for being a great socialist thinker. His book *The Future of Socialism* is still regarded as one of the most influential socialist tracts of twentieth-century Britain, even if its demands for the redistribution of wealth do not form a major plank in Tony Blair's 'New Labour' strategy. Crosland's lasting legacy is his commitment to Britain as a parade of equals and not the 'parade of dwarfs and giants' that the *Guardian* (28 July 1997) felt characterized the Thatcher and Major administrations.

See also: Attlee, Bevan, Callaghan, Gaitskell, Wilson

Further reading

Brivati, B., 1996, *Hugh Gaitskell. A Biography*, London: Richard Cohen.
Crosland, C. A. R., 1956, *The Future of Socialism*, London: Cape.
Crosland, C. A. R., 1962, *The Conservative Enemy*, London: Cape.
Crosland, C. A. R., 1974, *Socialism Now*, ed. Dick Leonard, London: Cape.
Crosland, S., 1982, *Tony Crosland*, London: Cape.
Jefferys, K., 1999, *Anthony Crosland: A New Biography*, London: Richard Cohen.

(EDWARD) HUGH (JOHN NEALE) DALTON 1887–1962

Hugh Dalton became one of the most prominent Labour figures during the 1930s, following the disastrous general election of 1931 which saw the Parliamentary Labour Party reduced to about one-sixth of its former size. Later, he became a member of Winston Churchill's wartime Coalition Government and subsequently was the first Chancellor of the Exchequer in Attlee's post-war Labour government. Ben Pimlott, in his introduction to *The Political Diary of Hugh Dalton* (1986, p. 465) described Dalton as 'the most economically literate of all modern Chancellors apart from his protégé Hugh Gaitskell'.

Dalton was born at Neath in Glamorgan, Wales, on 26 August 1887, the son of the Rev. Canon J. N. Dalton, an Anglican cleric and sometime tutor to the sons of Queen Victoria. Dalton was educated at Eton and then at King's College, Cambridge, where he studied economics under John Maynard Keynes. It was here, in 1907, that his socialism began when he joined the Fabian Society, which was committed to the slow extension of public control over industry. After completing his degree he began a law degree but soon moved on to hold a Hutchinson Research studentship at the London School of Economics between 1911 and 1913. In 1914 he married Ruth Fox and also qualified as a barrister.

During the First World War, Dalton joined the Army Service Corps before moving to the Royal Artillery Corps. Towards the end of the war he fought in Italy. At the end of the war he took up a lecturing post at the London School of Economics, teaching economics. At this stage an academic career looked to be beckoning and he was appointed the Sir Ernest Cassell Reader in Commerce at the University of London (1920–5) and Reader in Economics at the

University of London (1925–36). However, he managed to combine his academic career with rising political activity in the Labour Party and in Parliament.

In the early 1920s he was active in developing the policies of the Labour Party, and in October 1924 was returned as MP for the Peckham Division of Camberwell. Later, in 1929, he switched to and won the Durham seat of Bishop Auckland which he held until 1931 and again from 1935 to 1959. Dalton rose rapidly in the Labour ranks, becoming a member of the National Executive Committee (NEC) of the Party in 1925. His prominence earned him a key position in the second Labour government of 1929 to 1931, when he became Under-Secretary to Arthur Henderson at the Foreign Office.

With the collapse of the second Labour government and the disastrous 1931 general election, Dalton found himself both out of government and out of Parliament. During this period, between 1931 and 1935, he built up his power base within the Labour Party and became deeply involved in developing the role of planning within the Labour Party, along with Herbert Morrison. Indeed, Dalton was the powerhouse behind Labour's new moderate, but planned, socialist policies. Essentially Fabian, and gradualist, in outlook he argued that 'Labour needed better policies and better people'. At first he joined the New Fabian Research Bureau and, after a trip to the Soviet Union, became convinced of the need for planning. He then pressed forward his ideas for planning the redistribution of wealth and income in Britain, in order to tackle the horrendous problem of unemployment, to the various committees of the NEC and maintained, in his Labour Party document *Socialism and the Condition of the People* (1933), that the only means was a well-planned rush. His ideas were elaborated further in *For Socialism and Peace* (1934), which committed the Labour Party to a programme of nationalization, and in various other documents. The ideas that emerged were finally put into shape, under his direction, in a short manifesto called *Labour's Immediate Future*, adopted at the Labour Party Conference in 1937. It committed Labour to a programme of nationalization, narrow and limited though it was, in a more specific manner than had ever occurred before. Effectively, it provided the nationalization blueprint for the post-war Labour governments of Attlee, although public ownership was to be introduced in only a few industries.

Dalton was also instrumental, along with Ernest Bevin, in turning Labour away from the pacifist policies of George Lansbury, Labour Leader between 1932 and 1935, and into a Party prepared to support re-armament and to stand up to the European fascist dictators. This was evident in *International Policy and Defence*, adopted by the Party in 1937.

In the 1935 general election, Dalton was returned as Labour MP for Bishop Auckland. From then onwards he was able to exert his influence within the Parliamentary Labour Party as well as within the Labour Party itself. Friendly with Herbert Morrison, whom he supported in the 1935 leadership contest against Attlee, he was a close friend of Hugh Gaitskell and many of the other up-and-coming young members of the Party.

Dalton's prominence ensured that greater honours were predicted when the Labour Party joined Winston Churchill's wartime Coalition Government in May 1940. Dalton was in fact Minister of Economic Warfare between 1940 and 1942, being responsible for the economic blockade of Germany, then President of the Board of Trade between 1942 and 1945, dealing with issues such as rationing and reconstruction. In this respect, he was responsible for the Distribution of Industry Act (1945), which was designed to re-locate industry in the depressed areas.

With Attlee's post-war Labour victory of 1945, Dalton was appointed Chancellor of the Exchequer. As such he was faced with the immensely difficult and important task of reconstructing the post-war British economy. In this role, he encouraged cheap money, and presided over the nationalization of various industries and services, including the Bank of England. He was certainly committed to socialist planning but the economy was weak and depended upon the post-war American loan of $3,750,000,000 negotiated by John Maynard Keynes for its survival. It faced a serious economic crisis in 1947 when a condition of the loan, that of making sterling convertible/payable in gold and bullion, ensured that Britain's gold and bullion reserves, and thus the loan, were quickly dissipated. As a consequence, Dalton was forced to suspend convertibility in August 1947.

Dalton was, by any standards, an effective Chancellor given the economic problems that he faced. He tried to make Britain more self-sufficient and provided £20 million over five years for the Forestry Commission. In his first Budget speech of 9 April 1946, he announced the formation of development areas for Scotland, Wales, the North East and the North West. Dalton also arranged the formal mechanism for the extension of public ownership and the development of a modern welfare state, even though the National Health Service and the National Insurance arrangements did not come in place until July 1948. He was particularly associated with the nationalization of the

Bank of England and was committed to promoting a policy of cheap money. In this emerging 1946 Budget the object was 'to strengthen still further, and without delay, our budgetary defences against inflation'. He kept food subsidies at £329 million per annum and his intention was to build up a Budget surplus. In other words it was to be a deflationary Budget, something which ran counter to his general predisposition to spend. At this stage it looked as though he was already becoming disillusioned with his role and that Attlee was preparing to remove him. However, this did not occur for nearly eighteen months, and then for other reasons.

Dalton was forced to resign in November 1947 for revealing the contents of the Budget to a journalist shortly before presenting it to the House of Commons. He did return to the Cabinet later, in 1948, as Chancellor of the Duchy of Lancaster (responsible for European Affairs) and as Minister of Town and Country Planning between 1950 and 1951.

After Labour's defeat in the 1951 general election, Dalton gradually withdrew from his previous dominant position within the Labour Party. He lost his seat in the 1952 NEC elections and withdrew from the Parliamentary Committee of the Labour Party. By the mid 1950s he was acting the role of elder statesman in the Party and attempted to shape and influence Hugh Gaitskell and Anthony Crosland. He was created a Life Peer in 1960 and died in February 1962.

Dalton's life was a remarkable mixture of academic achievement and political guile. It is also one of sharp contrasts. Most obviously, having shaped Labour's commitment to nationalization he drifted away from that in his later life and instead encouraged the socialist ideas of Hugh Gaitskell, his protégé, and Anthony Crosland. Nevertheless, he will be remembered as a politician of immense intellectual ability and as a Chancellor of the Exchequer whose socialist credentials were as good as any, even if limited by the economic problems of post-war reconstruction in the mid and late 1940s.

See also: Attlee, Bevan, Bevin, Churchill

Further reading

Dalton, H., 1953, *Call Back Yesterday. Memoirs, 1887–1931*, London: Frederick Muller.

Dalton, H., 1957, *The Fateful Years. Memoirs, 1931–1945*, London: Frederick Muller.

Dalton, H., 1962, *High Tide and After. Memoirs, 1945–1960*, London: Frederick Muller.

Pimlott, B., 1985, *Hugh Dalton*, London: Cape.

Pimlott, B. (ed.), 1986, *The Political Diary of Hugh Dalton, 1918–1940, 1945–60*,

London. Cape in association with the London School of Economics and Political Science.

Pimlott, B. (ed.), 1986, *The Second World War Diary of Hugh Dalton, 1940–45*, London. Cape in association with the London School of Economics and Political Science.

SIR (ROBERT) ANTHONY EDEN (FIRST EARL OF AVON) 1897–1977

Anthony Eden is invariably remembered for his involvement with the Suez Canal Crisis in 1956 when Britain and France, with the aid of Israel, invaded Egypt in response to the decision of Colonel Nasser to nationalize the Suez Canal Company. The ignominious withdrawal of British and French forces, in the face of American pressure, led to Eden's resignation on grounds of ill health. Yet the Suez Crisis was an unfortunate end for a politician who emerged as diplomat of some distinction during the inter-war years.

Eden was born on 12 June 1897 at Windlestone Hall near Durham, the third son of Sir William Eden and Sybil Gray, although there is some suggestion that his real father might have been the politician George Wyndham. He had an unhappy childhood and did not enjoy his time at Eton. Nevertheless, he distinguished himself in the First World War, winning the Military Cross and becoming the youngest brigade major in the British army. After the war he went to Christ Church, Oxford where he obtained a first-class honours degree in Oriental Languages. In 1923 he married Beatrice Beckett.

Eden's political career began in 1923 when he became Conservative MP for Warwick and Leamington, a seat he held until his retirement from the House of Commons in 1957. He performed a number of junior roles in Stanley Baldwin's Conservative government of 1924 to 1929. He was Parliamentary Private Secretary to the Parliamentary Under-Secretary at the Home Office between 1924 and 1926, and fulfilled the same role at the Foreign Office in 1926 before rising to become Parliamentary Private Secretary to the Foreign Secretary (Sir Austen Chamberlain) between 1926 and 1929. He rose further in the National Government of the 1930s, becoming Parliamentary Under-Secretary at the Foreign Office between 1931 and 1933, Lord Privy Seal between 1933 and 1935 and Minister without Portfolio for League of Nation Affairs in 1935. By 1935, then, he had gained wide political experience and was focusing upon foreign affairs.

Eden's formidable political reputation was based upon his role as Foreign Secretary, a position which he held on three occasions throughout his career. He was first appointed to the post in 1935 but resigned in 1938. That led to him being associated with Winston Churchill in his opposition to the 'appeasement' policies of Neville Chamberlain that seemed to be drawing Britain into war. Whether Eden deserved the image of an anti-appeaser seems open to question but it is clear that he was not always opposed to fascism, as shown by his reluctance to oppose the re-militarization of the Rhineland in 1936. Even his resignation can be seen as a fit of pique at Chamberlain's interference in Anglo-Italian relations. Whatever the situation, his reward for being seen as an anti-appeaser was that he became Churchill's Foreign Secretary from December 1940 until the end of the Second World War in 1945. This involved him in extensive diplomatic work.

It has been suggested that Eden enjoyed a close working relationship with Churchill during the war years, almost that of father and son. However, recent evidence suggests that they were often bitter rivals. Attempting to see the Soviet point of view on major issues, Eden often clashed with Churchill and was on the point of resignation on a number of occasions. This difference was revealed after the war when Eden privately indicated his strong disapproval of Churchill's attack upon communism in his 'Iron Curtain' speech at Fulton, Missouri, in 1946.

With the return of Attlee as Labour Prime Minister in 1945, Eden was out of office from 1945 to 1951. During these years Eden aspired to become Conservative Leader but found his way blocked by Churchill who refused to stand down despite defeats in both the 1945 and 1950 general elections.

Nevertheless, the return of Churchill's Conservative government in 1951 saw Eden assume, once again, the post of Foreign Secretary. As in wartime, Eden often found himself in conflict with Churchill over foreign policy, but he was responsible for three major developments. First, he helped to organize the Geneva Conference of 1954, which ended the conflict between the French and communists in Indo-China. Second, he negotiated the 1954 agreement with Egypt which arranged for the withdrawal of British troops from the Suez Canal Zone in 1956. Third, he was influential in forcing France to accept that West Germany could re-arm under the auspices of the North Atlantic Treaty Organization (NATO).

Eden succeeded the ailing Churchill as Conservative Leader on 6 April 1955 and led the Conservative Party to a general election victory the following month. As Prime Minister, he gained world attention by arranging a three-power (the United States, Britain and the USSR) summit at Geneva in July 1955 to help improve international relations. There was some Western optimism (Britain and the United States) that the Soviet leadership was different after the death of Stalin in 1953. In fact, Eden's efforts to mediate between the United States and the USSR proved of limited value, but he invited Nikolai Buganin and Nikita Khrushchev to make a state visit to Britain in 1956. Unfortunately, the Soviet invasion of Hungary in October/November 1956 put an end to efforts to improve East–West relations and revived concern about the predatory ambitions of the USSR.

In other areas, Eden's premiership faced increasing problems. There was a deep financial crisis developing in 1955. R. A. Butler, Churchill's Chancellor of the Exchequer, had introduced an expansionist Budget immediately before the May general election but was forced, by expansionary pressures, to introduce an emergency deflationary Budget in October 1955. Eden then replaced Butler with Harold Macmillan in December 1955. Macmillan attempted to impose further deflationary measures in 1956 although the feeling is that these were broadly neutral in terms of the economy as a whole.

The final months of Eden's premiership were dominated by the Suez Crisis, an event which has tended to blight assessments of his political achievements. It arose partly out of Eden's belief, influenced by Churchill, that Britain could continue to be a major player in international politics alongside the United States and the Soviet Union, and that Britain was not necessarily dependent upon the United States. In 1944, as wartime Foreign Secretary, Eden had been determined to preserve Britain's involvement in the Middle East irrespective of American interests. This situation continued throughout his period as Foreign Secretary during the 1950s. John Foster Dulles, the American Secretary of State, was equally adamant that the United States would not be seen to be involved in any act of imperialist aggression. These two approaches clashed during the Suez Crisis.

The Suez Canal had been controlled by a company based in Paris. However, at the end of 1955 Gamal Abdel Nasser led Egypt into an arms deal with Czechoslovakia, a communist-dominated country, and mounted an aggressive campaign against British interests in the Middle East. Then, on 26 July 1956, he nationalized the Suez Canal Company, aiming to use canal revenues to finance the Aswan Dam project, which both the British and the Americans had refused to finance. Nasser's action annoyed the French and Eden also felt that Britain's access to the oil supplies of the Middle East was seriously threatened. Action had to be taken.

It is clear that the Egypt Committee of the British Cabinet was discussing the need to restore the Suez Canal to international control by the end of July 1956 and that its concern was also to topple Nasser from power in Egypt. It is also evident that the United States made its opposition to military intervention in Egypt perfectly clear. Regardless, Eden was drawn into a plan whereby Israel would invade Egypt and British and French forces would intervene by invading and occupying the Canal Zone. The Israelis invaded Egypt on 29 October 1956 and, following an Anglo-French ultimatum the following day asking both sides to withdraw their troops from the Canal Zone, the Anglo-French invasion began on 31 October 1956 and culminated when it then landed a task force at Port Said on 5 November 1956. The United Nations demanded a cease-fire throughout the whole affair, the Soviet Union supported Egypt and the United States refused to give support to sterling which had come under speculative pressure throughout the whole Suez episode. Faced with strong opposition to their actions, Britain and France agreed to a cease-fire and the humiliating withdrawal of their forces on 6 November 1956.

Why Eden became involved in the Suez fiasco has been a matter of some debate. Whilst David Carlton suggests this arose in an attempt to distract the British from their domestic problems, Robert Rhodes James suggests that Eden acted in order to counter the Soviet Union's growing influence in the Middle East. There is also some doubt about how much the Cabinet knew about the plan to involve Israel in the invasion of Egypt. Richard Lamb suggests that Eden misled the Cabinet whilst David Carlton feels that no minister could claim that he had been deceived.

Eden had suffered ill-health throughout his life. More recently, his health had been weakened in 1953 when a bile-duct operation had gone wrong. He also appears to have faced renewed ill health throughout 1956 and, therefore, he decided to resign on 9 January 1957. Yet ill health was merely the pretext for his resignation and the Suez Crisis was the determining factor. His political reputation had suffered as a result and it is clear that he had misled the House of Commons on 20 December by denying collusion with Israel. This latter action was bound to be exposed in the fullness of time.

Eden left the House of Commons in 1957 and was ennobled in 1961 as the first Earl of Avon. He died on 14 January 1977. His obituary writers recognized that he was the last British Prime Minister to believe that Britain was still one of the great powers. Suez exposed that belief as an illusion.

See also: Baldwin, Chamberlain, Churchill, Macmillan

Further reading

Carlton, D., 1981, *Anthony Eden: A Biography*, London: Allen Lane.
Dutton, D., 1996, *Anthony Eden: A Life and Reputation*, London: Arnold.
Lamb, R., 1987, *The Failure of the Eden Government*, London: Sidgwick & Jackson.
Rhodes James, R., 1986, *Anthony Eden*, London: Weidenfeld & Nicolson.
Rothwell, V. H., 1991, *Anthony Eden: A Political Biography 1931–1957*, Manchester: Manchester University Press.

MICHAEL (MACKINTOSH) FOOT 1913–

Michael Foot has had many distinguished careers, most obviously as a journalist, author, campaigner and left-wing Labour MP. However, he is often remembered for his one major failure, that of Labour Leader between 1980 and 1983 which culminated in Labour's disastrous general election campaign based upon a left-wing manifesto which Gerald Kaufmann referred to as 'the longest suicide note in history'. It was a harsh experience for an otherwise brilliant writer and generally effective politician.

Foot was born in Devon in 1913 into a family of seven children, and was raised as a Liberal, his father, Isaac, being a staunch Liberal. Three of his brothers – John, Hugh and Dingle – maintained this tradition although both Hugh and Dingle did later serve in a Labour government. Michael was educated at a Quaker School and at Oxford University before working in a shipping firm in Liverpool. Influenced by the poverty he saw around him he joined the Labour Party and became a lifelong socialist. He was friends with Labour's left-wing politicians, such as Aneurin Bevan, and began to write for *Tribune*, the Labour left-wing weekly established in 1937. Also, with others, in 1940 he wrote *The Guilty Men*, condemning the appeasement policies of Stanley Baldwin and Neville Chamberlain that had led to the Second World War. In 1945 he became MP for Plymouth Devonport. At this stage of his career (1946) he became editor of the *Tribune* and was briefly associated with Ian Mikardo and other left-wing MPs in the formation of the Keep Left group, being one of the co-authors (with Ian Mikardo and Richard Crossman) of the *Keep Left* pamphlet, written in 1947. At that stage Foot believed in the need to extend public ownership more widely throughout British industry, but also in the need to create a 'Third Force', based upon an Anglo-French pact and associated with a regional European

Security System which would act independently of the United States and the USSR in an attempt to bring the two superpowers closer together and maintain the peace. However, Foot detached himself from the Keep Left group over the formation of the North Atlantic Treaty Organization (NATO), which he decided to support in the face of Russian expansionism in Eastern Europe in an impressively written article in the *Tribune*, 20 May 1949, which suggested that the Americans had received nothing in return for the Marshall Plan whilst the Soviet Union was prepared to swallow up democratic socialist nations in Eastern Europe and impose communist dictatorship. Mikardo left the editorial board of *Tribune* as a result of this article although he continued to write for the journal, justifying the actions of the Soviet Union by maintaining that she needed to be confident of the safety of her borders.

Foot continued to be a scion of radicalism within the Labour Party throughout the early 1950s and associated closely with Bevan and the Bevanites from 1951 onwards, although he was dismayed by Bevan's about-turn at the 1957 Labour Party Conference, at which Bevan proclaimed in favour of supporting the construction of a British hydrogen bomb. At this point Foot missed the opportunity to lead the Labour Left, having lost some of his influence because of the loss of his seat at the 1955 general election. In 1960 Foot was returned as MP for Ebbw Vale, in a parliamentary by-election caused by the death of his hero Bevan, on whom he was to later write a two volume biography, *Aneurin Bevan* (1962 and 1973). Once again in Parliament, he continued in a radical vein, pursing nuclear disarmament. It was a long time before he began again to rise up the political ladder. In 1964 he remained firmly on Labour's backbenches when Harold Wilson formed the first Labour government for thirteen years, and was one of the most prominent members of the newly formed *Tribune* Group of MPs which challenged the Wilson governments over the support it gave to United States policy on Vietnam. But in 1970 he became a member of Labour's Shadow Cabinet and in 1971 unsuccessfully contested for the position of Deputy Leader of the Labour Party. He was still the most prominent voice of the Left and became the Shadow Leader of the House of Commons in 1972, attempting to bring together the two wings of the Labour Party. In 1974 he became Secretary of State for Employment in the new Labour government led by Harold Wilson, although the Conservatives considered him too soft in dealing with the powerful trade union movement for he greatly extended the collective and individual rights of employees at work. Indeed, he was seen as the representative of the trade unions in the

Cabinet, and at a time when the Labour government was operating a social contract with the unions was advocating that pay should be governed by a norm of £9 per week increase, equivalent to about 15 per cent of the national average wage.

Harold Wilson resigned as Labour's Prime Minister in March 1976 and in Labour's leadership succession contest Foot was only defeated when he became the final challenger to James Callaghan; he did however become Labour's Deputy Leader. Throughout the next three years he acted as Leader of the House, steering legislation through the Commons. During these years Callaghan, with the Right, and Foot, with the Left, kept the Labour Party united in government. Even Labour's defeat in 1979 did not create disunity and warring within the Party. However, Callaghan resigned as Labour Leader in November 1980 and Foot was elected in his place in the subsequent leadership contest, Denis Healey becoming Deputy Leader.

Foot's leadership was disastrous for Labour. He was hapless in staunching the rise of the anti-parliamentary left-wing Militant Tendency within the Labour Party and, damagingly, was involved in the attempt to prevent Peter Tatchell, the Australian radical, from standing as Labour candidate for Bermondsey in the general election of 1983. Indeed, Foot was unable to control the increasingly left-wing dominated National Executive Committee of the Party which in 1982 took over responsibility for drawing up the Labour Manifesto, a responsibility normally assumed by Labour's Shadow Cabinet, many members of whom felt that they had been forced into accepting a too strongly left-wing programme.

This left-wing drift within Labour led to members of the Labour Right, such as David Owen, Shirley Williams, Bill Rodgers and Roy Jenkins, producing their Limehouse Declaration and forming the Social Democratic Party (SDP) in 1981.

The SDP's subsequent alliance with the Liberals proved to be an effective, if temporary, challenge to the Labour Party, which was further buffeted by a bruising contest between Tony Benn and Denis Healey for the post of Deputy Leader. Healey won by the narrow margin of 50.4 per cent to 49.6 per cent of the vote, and only after Neil Kinnock and some leading left-wing MPs had switched their votes at the last minute.

Although there was a small switch to the Labour Right, it was the Labour Left who drew up the manifesto for the 1983 general election. Unfortunately, *The New Hope for Britain* manifesto was not seen to be politically attractive by the electorate, despite its commitment to reduce unemployment, increase social benefits, reverse Conservative trade union legislation and to return to the public sector all those industries privatized by the Thatcher administration. There were other factors at play – most obviously the feeling that Labour had not been patriotic enough in the Falklands War – which also told against Labour. As a result, the Labour Party performed badly and, with 27.6 per cent of the votes, was a mere 1.6 per cent ahead of the Liberal–SDP Alliance vote. Labour had reached its political nadir. The switch to the Left had not worked and Michael Foot promptly resigned and was replaced by Neil Kinnock.

Foot remained in the House of Commons until 1992, representing Ebbw Vale between 1960 and 1983 and Blaenau Gwent from 1983 until 1992. He was particularly prominent in the House of Commons, commenting in humorous fashion on the Westland affair of 1985/6, which saw Michael Heseltine, the Defence Secretary, resign from Margaret Thatcher's Conservative government on the issue of the style in which government was conducted.

Michael Foot has always been a great debater, journalist and writer but, as Labour Leader, he lacked the administrative skill and inclination to keep the Labour Party united, attempting to use platform oratory rather than the power and communication lines within the Labour Party to effect his will. It took many years for Labour to recover from the failure of Foot to win the 1983 general election. In the final analysis, he was a formidable parliamentarian but a poor Leader.

See also: Attlee, Bevan, Callaghan, Gaitskell, Wilson

Further reading

Foot, M., 1980, *Debts of Honour*, London: Poynter.
Hoggart, S. and Leigh, D., 1981, *Michael Foot; A Portrait*, London: Hodder & Stoughton.
Shaw, E, 1999, 'Michael Foot 1980–1983', in Jeffreys, K. (ed) Leading Labour: From Kier Hardie to Tony Blair, London: I. B. Tauris.
Jones, M., 1994, *Michael Foot*, London: Gollancz.
Morgan, K. O., 1987, *Labour People: Leaders and Lieutenants, Hardie to Kinnock*, Oxford: Oxford University Press.

HUGH (TODD NAYLOR) GAITSKELL 1906–1963

Hugh Gaitskell led the Labour Party from December 1955 until his death in January 1963. During that period he developed a brand of socialism which became known as 'Gaitskellism', and which was identified with a retreat from public ownership and the creation of a society in which all would have greater equality of opportunity. It was a vision which did not win over the trade-union based Party bosses of Labour at that time, although some, if not all, of his objectives have come to fruition in Blairite Britain. Essentially, Gaitskell was more interested in promoting equality and removing inequality, and the means by which this was achieved was unimportant.

Gaitskell was born on 9 April 1906 into a wealthy family which had a background in the Indian Civil Service. He was educated at Winchester and New College, Oxford, where he came under the influence of G. D. H. Cole, the famous socialist theorist. It was at this time, in the mid 1920s, that Gaitskell became a socialist. After Oxford he was briefly employed as an adult education tutor in the Nottinghamshire coal field but then became an economics lecturer at University College, London, holding the post from 1928 until 1939. It was during this period that he became associated with a small group of Oxford-educated London-based socialist intellectuals, and with Douglas Jay and Evan Durbin. The group was convinced of the need to plan economic development and was attracted to the ideas of economic management – including both expansionism and contractionism – of John Maynard Keynes. Their views were presented through the New Fabian Research Bureau and through it in the Labour Party policy document *Labour's Immediate Programme* (1937).

As a German-speaking economist, Gaitskell spent the Second World War as a civil servant. He worked at the Ministry of Economic Warfare and then at the Board of Trade under Hugh Dalton, who in the 1930s had been the chief architect of Labour's nationalization policies and long-term planning strategy presented in *Labour's Immediate Programme*.

Gaitskell's parliamentary career began in 1945 when he was returned as MP for Leeds South. In Attlee's first post-war Labour government he was appointed Parliamentary Secretary and then became Minister of Fuel and Power. In this latter role he was responsible for nationalizing the gas industry. As an economist he played a major role in pressuring the government to devalue the pound during the economic crisis of 1949, to the benefit of British exports. Up until that point, Attlee and the Labour government had been hesitant to grasp the idea of devaluation and were considering the orthodox methods of cutting expenditure that had destroyed the second Ramsay MacDonald government in August 1931. By now it was becoming increasingly obvious that Gaitskell was an important economic voice within the government and, after the return of the Attlee government in the 1950 general election by a six-seat majority, he was appointed Chancellor of the Exchequer, in the place of Sir Stafford Cripps and on the recommendation of Hugh Dalton. In this post he was faced with the problems of the rising cost of re-armament, provoked by both the Korean War and his strong support for the Anglo-American alliance. He was also thrown into conflict with Aneurin Bevan (formerly the Minister of Health and Housing though by then Minister of Labour) over the issue of imposing prescription charges on the National Health Service – the 'teeth and spectacles' episode – although it was the subsequent Conservative government which eventually introduced them. Gaitskell had been a member of the Ministerial Committee set up after the 1950 Budget to monitor the cost of the health service, and this was the basis of the antipathy they held towards each other.

Gaitskell's threat to impose prescription charges towards the end of 1950 and the beginning of 1951 led Bevan to the point of resignation. The final straw was Gaitskell's 1951 Budget which set a ceiling of £400 million for National Health Service expenditure (not the £422 million requested by the Ministry of Health) and announced the intention of imposing prescription charges on dental and optical services. This led to the resignation of Aneurin Bevan, Harold Wilson and John Freeman in April 1951 which, in turn, led to deep divisions within the Labour Party as the Labour Left organized itself into the 'Bevanites'. Later that year the Labour government was forced into a general election, because of the fragility of its majority, and was defeated by Winston Churchill and the Conservative Party.

In December 1955 Gaitskell replaced Clement Attlee as Leader of the Labour Party. This came as a result of Gaitskell's persistent campaigning throughout the early 1950s which involved him holding gatherings of his friends at regular intervals in his home at Frognal Gardens in London. The appointment, however, proved immensely controversial and divisive.

At first Gaitskell consolidated the Labour Party over British involvement in the Suez Crisis, when British troops were parachuted into Egypt in order to secure the Suez Canal. He opposed this action by Eden's Conservative government, arguing that it could not be supported without the Atlantic Alliance and the United Nations. Neither was forthcoming and it soon became clear that it was the United States who forced Britain to withdraw her troops from Nasser's Egypt. Michael Foot later recalled that 'Gaitskell's relentless, passionate marshalling of the whole legal and moral case against the government's expedition to Suez' and Bevan's reflective and sardonic commentary upon it 'was one of the most brilliant displays of opposition in parliamentary history'.

As a right-wing revisionist, Gaitskell advocated the creation of equality through high social expenditure financed out of economic growth very much along the lines outlined by Anthony Crosland in his book *The Future of Socialism* (1956). 'Gaitskellism' saw no purpose in the extension of public ownership but found it difficult to budge the Party on this issue. However, the defeat of Labour in the 1959 general election persuaded Gaitskell that Labour was almost unelectable without some changes in its policies. This resulted in his attempt to amend Clause Four, the public ownership clause, of the Labour Party's Constitution in 1959 and 1960. Indeed, within a few days of Labour's defeat Gaitskell was meeting with Party friends to discuss the need to replace Clause Four with a new statement of the Party's aims. His views were put to a special post-mortem conference where they were defeated, so entrenched was the mythology of Clause Four in the Labour Party. They were rejected, once again, in 1960. His efforts had been blocked by trade unionism and particularly by the Transport and General Workers' Union.

When Gaitskell spoke at the Labour Party Conference in 1960 he was also fighting on another matter – the defence policy of the Labour Party. An advocate of multilateral nuclear disarmament he fought on an issue on which he was almost certain to be, and was, defeated. Before the Scarborough Conference he had made a number of speeches on the multilateralist case, and they provided the backcloth for his famous 'fight and fight again' speech once the Conference had rejected his recommendation. However, at the Blackpool Conference in 1961 it was Gaitskell's pressure that helped to reverse the unilateral resolution. Gaitskell also upset many of his supporters at the 1962 Labour Party Conference at Brighton by opposing Britain's entry into the Common Market (now known as the European Union) at a time when the Party appeared to be moving in that direction. He argued that the debate in the Press had not been of a high standard and, on the prospects of a Federal Europe, stated that:

> We must be clear about this: it does mean, if this is the idea, the end of Britain as an independent European state. I make no apology for repeating it. It means the end of a thousand years of history. You may say, 'Let it end', but my goodness, it is a decision that needs a little care and thought. And it does mean the end of the Commonwealth. How can we seriously suppose that if the mother country, the centre of the

Commonwealth, is a province of Europe (which is what Federation means) it could continue to exist as the mother country
of a series of independent nations? It is sheer nonsense.
(Labour Party Annual Conference Report, 1962, p. 30)

He concluded by presenting the image of a Britain operating with the
Commonwealth, in the European Free Trade Association, protecting her
agriculture and operating an independent foreign policy in a wider and
looser association with Europe. Having mesmerized his audience, and
received an overwhelming ovation, Gaitskell won the day: the Labour
Party appeared united behind him and preparing for political power.

At the height of his powers Gaitskell died, in London on 18 January
1963, 108 days after his anti-Common Market speech. He is
remembered for his assertive and confrontational style of leadership,
which was not always in tune with the more working-class sentiments
of the then Labour Party. His objective of revising the Labour Party,
and particularly its commitment to Clause Four, failed because of trade
union opposition although he won the day on the need for multilateral
nuclear disarmament and with his opposition to the Common Market.
His modernizing approach to the Party was, however, carried forward
by later leaders such as Neil Kinnock, John Smith and even, to some
extent, by Tony Blair.

See also: Attlee, Bevan, Blair, Churchill, Cripps, Dalton, Wilson

Further reading

Brivati, B., 1996, *Hugh Gaitskell: A Biography*, London: Richard Cohen.
Jefferys, K., (ed.) 1999, *Leading Labour: From Keir Hardie to Tony Blair*, London:
I. B. Tauris.
McDermott, G., 1982, *Leader Lost: A Biography of Hugh Gaitskell*, London: Leslie
Frewin.
Morgan, K. O., 1984, *Labour in Power, 1945–1951*, Oxford: Clarendon.
Williams, P. M., 1979 *Hugh Gaitskell : A Political Biography*, London: Cape.

EDWARD GREY (VISCOUNT GREY
OF FALLODEN) 1862–1933

Sir Edward Grey was the Liberal politician who was Foreign Secretary
at the outbreak of the First World War. To many socialists, such as the
Independent Labour Party MP Fred Jowett, it was his 'secret

discussions' with France in the pre-war years that forced Britain to become involved in the war.

Grey was the son of a landed army officer and a descendant of Lord Grey, the Whig Prime Minister of the early 1830s. He was educated at Winchester and Balliol College, Oxford. Expelled from Oxford in 1884, he moved into public life by becoming private secretary to Evelyn Baring, later Lord Cromer, and then to the Liberal Chancellor of the Exchequer, H. C. E. Childers.

Grey's political career began in 1885 when he won Berwick-upon-Tweed, a seat he retained until raised to the peerage as Viscount Grey of Falloden in 1916. He was an impressive politician who remained within the Liberal Party during and after the split over the issue of Irish Home Rule in the mid 1880s. Grey rose to become a junior Minister at the Foreign Office in the Liberal governments of W. E. Gladstone and Lord Rosebery, between 1892 and 1895. Indeed, in 1895 he declared his opposition to the French advance in the Sudan, the eventual outcome of which was the Fashoda Incident between the French and British in 1898.

With the fall of the Liberal government in 1895, Grey followed Rosebery into the Liberal Imperialist section of the Liberal Party. As a result of this, he found himself supporting the Conservative government's actions during the Boer War (1899–1902), Lord Lansdowne's treaty with Japan in 1902, and the Entente Cordiale with France in 1904. Indeed, Grey believed in the need for treaties to maintain the balance of power in Europe and acknowledged that Britain needed the military strength to observe her treaties. He also supported strongly Britain's re-armament in the face of European military rivalry.

At this time, the Liberal Party was deeply divided, with Radicals such as David Lloyd George opposing imperialist ambitions and foreign entanglements, the National Liberals accepting the need to protect British interests, and the Liberal Imperialists being concerned to protect Britain's current and future imperial interests. Consequently, when the Conservative government resigned in December 1905, Grey joined with H. H. Asquith and R. B. Haldane, both Liberal Imperialists, in attempting to replace the radical Sir Henry Campbell-Bannerman as Liberal Leader and thus as Prime Minister. Despite this intrigue, Grey was appointed as Foreign Secretary, a post he occupied from December 1905 until December 1916.

As Foreign Secretary, Grey was determined to maintain the balance of power in Europe in order to neutralize Germany's growing military strength in Europe and her imperialist strengths in Africa and Asia.

Central to the containment of Germany was Britain's alliance with France, which Grey sought to preserve regardless of the military and diplomatic difficulties. In order to maintain the alliance, Grey acted as an arbiter in the first Moroccan crisis between France and Germany, in 1907, but maintained Britain's alliance with France. Indeed, without the knowledge of most of his Cabinet colleagues, Grey developed an Anglo-French military strategy. Fearful also that Russia, defeated in the Russo-Japanese war of 1904–5, would ally with Germany he cemented the anti-German alliance of Britain, France and Russia with the Anglo-Russian Convention of 1907.

The strategic interests of Britain were far more important to Grey than the Liberal Radical interest in peace, even though in domestic matters he supported the Radical issues of women's suffrage, Irish Home Rule and land reform. Equally, the maintenance of peace in Europe was vital to him. Britain was still under no formal obligation to her French and Russian allies but the second Moroccan crisis of 1911, between France and Germany, eventually led to a declaration from David Lloyd George that Britain might be obligated to fight alongside France. The crisis revealed, however, that there had been secret discussions between Britain and France. Asquith's Cabinet was split over this revelation but the illusions of some Liberals that Britain could remain in splendid isolation were soon pricked. Grey continued to struggle to maintain the balance of power within Europe, containing the Balkan Wars with German help in 1912–13, but the assassination of the Austrian Archduke Franz Ferdinand at Sarajevo in June 1914 tested Grey's balancing act beyond its limits.

Grey was unable to persuade Austria-Hungary and Germany to pull back from war with Serbia, Russia and France, and thus a European war, involving Britain, became inevitable. On the eve of the First World War, Grey spoke, with great effect, in the House of Commons on the balance of power that he had attempted to maintain in Europe – but he admitted the inevitability of Britain being drawn into the conflict. Although many, such as Fred Jowett MP, took this speech as evidence of how Britain had been brought into the conflict by secret discussions, treaties and understandings, it is clear that Grey had sought to avoid the conflict that was now upon Europe. Yet once Britain was in the Great War, Grey worked to draw Italy into the Allied Alliance in 1915 and attempted to maintain good relations with the United States.

When, in December 1916, David Lloyd George replaced Asquith as Prime Minister, Grey lost his post as Foreign Secretary. From that moment onwards, Grey withdrew from the centre stage of politics. He devoted the rest of his life to a variety of public duties. Although still active in the Liberal Party he was mainly associated with the post-war League of Nations' Union and was Chancellor of Oxford University from 1928 until his death in 1933.

See also: Asquith, Churchill, Lloyd George

Further reading

Grey of Falloden, Viscount, 1925, *Twenty-Five Years, 1892–1916*, 2 vols, London: Hodder & Stoughton.
Hinsley, F. H. (ed.), 1977, *British Foreign Policy Under Sir Edward Grey*, Cambridge: Cambridge University Press.
Robbins, K., 1971, *Sir Edward Grey: A Biography of Lord Grey of Falloden*, London: Cassell.

(JAMES) KEIR HARDIE 1856–1915

James Keir Hardie's life and career are closely associated with the formation of the Independent Labour Party (ILP) (1893) and the Labour Representation Committee (LRC) (1900), which became the Labour Party in 1906. Indeed, he was the first Member of Parliament to represent the new Independent Labour movement in the House of Commons and acted as the chairman of the Labour parliamentary group from about 1903 onwards, although the position was not formalized until 1906. Along with James Ramsay MacDonald, J. Bruce Glasier and Philip Snowden, he was one of the four leading members of the Labour Party in its pre-First World War years.

Hardie was born at Legbrannock, Lanarkshire in Scotland, on 15 August 1856, the illegitimate son of a Scottish farm servant. He was raised in poverty and forced to work in the coal mines of the Lanarkshire coalfield from the age of ten. However, he became involved in organizing the Lanarkshire coal mining trade unions and was victimized for his activities, being driven to live in Cumnock in Ayrshire in the early 1880s where he began to develop a journalistic career and fervently supported the Liberal Party.

By the mid 1880s, however, his political views were beginning to change. He was greatly affected by hearing Henry George, the American radical advocate of land reform, speak on the need for land nationalization and was already contemplating moving towards socialism when, in 1886–7, he attempted and failed to form a Scottish miners' trade union. In January 1887 he established a newspaper, *The Miner*, and began to discuss socialism with members of William Morris's Socialist League and Henry Mayers Hyndman's SDF. It was as an Independent Labour candidate, of socialist leanings, that he contested the Mid-Lanark parliamentary by-election in April 1888. Whether or not he had broken with official Liberalism seems debatable, but he made a reasonable electoral challenge, receiving 617 votes, or 8.2 per cent of the total vote in a three-cornered contest. Although he still carried many of the Liberal progressive beliefs of his youth he now moved swiftly to form a new political party for the working classes. Indeed, Hardie formed the Scottish Labour Party, uniting radicals, land reformers and trade unionists in August 1888. It was an alliance that combined Liberal progressive ideas with the demand for political independence for the working classes and was typical of Hardie's broad-based Radical and Independent Labour approach that dominated the rest of his life.

Hardie shot to fame as the founding father of Independent Labour politics when he was returned to Parliament as Independent Labour MP for West Ham in July 1892 having been selected to represent the South West Ham Radical Association. It was a dramatic success and one that propelled him forward as the first Independent Labour MP in Parliament. From his parliamentary platform he attacked the Liberal government on labour questions, became known as the 'Member for the Unemployed', and was remembered for his first attendance in Parliament in a cloth cap (actually a deerstalker). His maiden speech in the House of Commons in February 1893 saw him attack the protectionist and emigration solutions to unemployment at that time in vogue, then without suggesting specific reforms arguing that 'the Labour party aims at uprooting causes which produce those untoward results.... To raise the level of existence of every one there is one enduring means available – the action of the State'. This speech in fact reflects upon an essential feature of Hardie's political life – his relative ignorance of detailed economic solutions to unemployment and his claimed lack of understanding of Marxist economics.

It was not surprising that Hardie was asked to chair the meeting in January 1893 which saw the formation of the ILP in Bradford, at the Labour Institute in Peckover Street, and later at St George's Hall. On this first occasion Hardie once again revealed his commitment to a flexibility of approach in dealing with electoral matters, opposing the attempt by Conference to impose a constitution. He also opposed the Manchester Fourth Clause, which would have committed ILP members and supporters to abstaining from voting if there were no appropriate ILP candidate standing in an election, and stressing the need for 'each locality ... [to] be left to apply the Independence principle in its own way' (*Workman's Times*, 8 October 1892). Instead,

Hardie wished for fundamental principles, such as a commitment to socialism, to be agreed. Given his prominence within the Independent Labour movement it is not surprising that he also acted a Chairman (President 1894–6) of the ILP from 1893 to 1900, although he had at first refused the offer. Hardie's position was further strengthened by the creation of the *Labour Leader*, successor to *The Miner*, which became a weekly publication from March 1894. He owned and edited the paper until 1904, providing him with a journalistic and propagandizing base.

There was great hope, as the 1895 general election occurred, that since 'the Liberal party is shedding its members at both ends' the ILP would pick up more parliamentary seats. That did not occur. Hardie lost his seat at West Ham South but contested the Bradford East seat in the parliamentary by-election of 1896. Why he stood for Bradford had been open to conjecture. Kenneth O. Morgan suggested that the reasons for the candidature remain unclear: 'a mystery, unless it was the general assumption that any section of the town which had witnessed the birth of the ILP must be worth fighting for' (1975, p. 91). Yet Fenner Brockway suggested that Hardie expected to win (Brockway, 1944, chap. 1). However, it is possible that he wished merely to demonstrate that the ILP was still alive in its birthplace. Indeed, shortly before the election he stated: 'This was the first time since the general election that the ILP had had the chance in a three-cornered contest to prove what strength was left in it' (*Bradford Observer*, 4 November 1894).

For a time it looked as though this seat, which had been won by the Conservatives in 1895, would fall to Hardie since there was no Liberal candidate but then Alfred Illingworth, the local Liberal bigwig, brought in Alfred Billson as Liberal candidate. Thus the progressive vote was divided and the Conservative candidate was returned. Nevertheless, Hardie failed to be nonplussed by these events, predicting that socialism would come in 1953 and reflecting upon the number of votes he had received:

> He did not regret the defeat, nor even feel downhearted or discouraged (cheers). Eight years had passed since he had fought his first Parliamentary contest. He then got 617 votes and now had got 1953 votes. He had fought the contest not expecting to win but because there was a cause to fight for.
> (*Bradford Labour Echo*, 11 November 1896)

The following day Hardie held a post-election inquest which

criticized those trade unionists who had not voted for him and which pointed the way ahead:

> They [the ILP] must see to it before the next election they made these sections of the electorate understand that although [the Independent Labour Party] were Socialists they also supported the principles maintained by those sections as far as they could, and that their place was within the party of Independent Labour.
>
> (*Bradford Labour Echo*, 19 November 1896)

The future of the ILP was now open to question. Should it join with other socialist groups in forming a Party of Socialist Unity or should it seek a broader alliance of socialists and trade unionists? Hardie decided upon the latter course, thwarting efforts to get the ILP and the Socialist Democratic Federation (SDF) to combine. The 'Informal Conferences' between the two organizations held in 1897 led to a joint referendum, in 1897, which produced a five-to-one majority in favour of fusion. However, Hardie pointed out that less than a third of the ILP's paying members had voted and he therefore delayed a decision until the annual ILP conference in 1898. In the meantime he mounted opposition against the idea of fusion through the pages of the *Labour Leader* (4 September 1897) and the *ILP News*, maintaining that 'Rigidity is fatal to growth as I think our SDF friends are finding out'. Ultimately, Hardie's campaign proved successful and, in a second referendum, 2,397 ILP members voted in favour of federation and only 1,695 for fusion. The SDF would not contemplate federation and Hardie pushed on with his idea of an alliance between socialists and trade unionists. The matter was pushed forward at the Trades Union Congress (TUC) in 1899 and consummated on 27 February 1900 with the formation of the LRC.

Shortly afterwards, in September 1900, Hardie was returned to Parliament once again as one of the two MPs for the Merthyr Tydfil constituency. This was partly because of the split within the local Liberal Party, which traditionally had won both seats, and despite Hardie's open opposition to the Boer War. It was truly a remarkable success. From that point onwards, Hardie represented the constituency until his death in 1915, maintaining a robust commitment to political independence but willing to do electoral deals with the Liberals, a constant, if somewhat contradictory, feature of his political career.

Once in Parliament, Hardie appealed, through the pages of the *Labour Leader*, to John Morley, the pro-Boer Liberal figure, and to John

Burns, the Lib-Lab and ex-Liberal Minister, to lead the Labour group in the House of Commons. In the case of Burns this was because 'his ability, experience and position in the Labour movement mark him out as the political head of the movement' (Maclean, 1975, p. 89). Hardie wished to unite the Labour movement and in his personal appeal he wrote that 'The time, John, is one for drawing together, for consolidating, for strengthening all the forces which made for the emancipation of Labour'. Burns did not respond and nothing was done to form a Labour group in the House of Commons until after the parliamentary by-election successes of 1902 and 1903. Then, on his own initiative, Hardie persuaded the LRC to agree to the formation of 'a distinct Labour group with their own Whip', in other words to the formation of the Parliamentary Labour Party (PLP). Until this point Labour members were effectively followers without leaders and, at this stage there was no guarantee that the LRC would be successful, although the affiliated membership had risen from 350,000 in 1901 to 450,000 in 1902 and 850,000, or 56 per cent of TUC membership, in 1903. Hardie seems to have been kept informed about the possible pact with the Liberals which MacDonald was brokering throughout 1903, although he always remained elusive on the question of alliances.

No sooner had Hardie become Chairman of the PLP than he fell ill with appendicitis, had an operation and was forced to recuperate. He was out of circulation from January to June 1904, at which point he resumed his position – though only for two months before he went off to the International Socialist Congress in Amsterdam. Upon his return Hardie was particularly active in condemning the Aliens Bill of 1905, which sought to control the entry of aliens resulting from the pogroms in Eastern Europe, and was particularly concerned about the Unemployed Workmen Act of August 1905, which he felt did not give sufficient powers and financial help to local authorities in dealing with the unemployed.

During the 1905/6 general election, Hardie rather neglected his own constituency and found his victory to be rather narrower than he expected. Nevertheless, the successes of the LRC/Labour Party meant that the PLP was now a more viable group than before and needed a prominent Chairman prepared to undertake the enormously increased administrative burden that success entailed. Hardie's leadership was necessary given that '[o]f the thirty Members at the General Election twenty-six [were] without experience of Parliamentary procedure' (*Labour Party Annual Conference Report, 1907*, p. 37). Unfortunately Hardie had the name, the experience and the prestige for administration, but not the aptitude for leadership. In a letter dated 11 February 1906, J. Bruce Glasier tried to put him off contesting the post, writing that: 'You should not accept nomination for the chairmanship unless it unexpectedly happens that the feeling in favour for you doing so is *unanimous and enthusiastic – and hardly so even if it were so* [...]'. He added that

> It is much more important – much more important indeed to our side of the movement that you should be *free to lead the Socialist policy*, than that you should be stuck in the official chairmanship where you would be bound for unity and decorum's sake to adopt a personal attitude acceptable to the moderates. You must not be tied down in any way whatever that would destroy your Socialist initiatives. I feel that this is vital to us.... If Henderson, Shackleton, or even Barnes accepts the position, you will nevertheless be the fighting front.

Glasier was clearly acting as a conduit for the frustrations of other leading figures in the Labour Party. However, regardless of his advice, Hardie did contest the election, defeating Shackleton by 15 votes to 14, a victory which the *Labour Leader*, no longer in Hardie's hands, confirmed by stressing that Hardie was the only man for the job and that he had a unique political record which even Ramsay MacDonald and Philip Snowden could not rival.

Hardie was officially Chairman of the PLP in 1906 and 1907. At first, with the newly expanded Labour Party in buoyant mood, Hardie seemed to be successful, securing the reversal of the Taff Vale Judgement through the Trade Disputes Bill, which he and Shackleton promoted, thus securing immunity from prosecution for financial losses incurred during a strike. He was also placed upon two select committees of the House of Commons – one on the procedures of the House and the other on income tax. On the latter he gave full support for Sir Charles Dilke's report favouring a graduated income tax. Yet, it soon became clear that there were limits to Labour's power and criticism of Hardie's less-than-diligent attention to the needs of the PLP began to develop.

In the summer of 1906 MacDonald made the point that 'I voted for Hardie as chairman with much reluctance as I could not persuade myself that he could fill the place'. On another occasion he added that 'we never know where to find him. The result is that we are coming to the objectionable habit of coming to decisions without him.' Philip Snowden made much the same point about the unbusinesslike attitude and unreliability of Hardie. Indeed, he was able to assure T. D. Benson of the 'intense dissatisfaction amongst the ILP members. I doubt he would get two votes if the leadership were voted upon today.' Such comments regarding Hardie's waywardness might be considered the rumour-mongering of two frustrated potential leaders of the PLP were it not for the fact that Glasier himself, who was a close friend of Hardie, recorded that after Labour's poor performance in the Cockermouth parliamentary by-election of August 1906 he met Hardie and found 'that he does not realize how strong the move is against him'.

Apart from his reluctance to act as a Party man Hardie developed his own individual political interests with a passion which often cut across those of the Labour Party. Most obviously he found himself at odds with the Party over the women's suffrage question. As a close friend of the Pankhursts, Hardie had agitated with them for the right of free speech at Boggart Hole Clough in 1896. He was particularly close to Sylvia and associated himself with the activities of the Women's Social and Political Union (WSPU). Founded in 1903 the organization supported the idea of women being given voting rights on the same basis as men – 'the limited franchise', rather than complete enfranchisement which still seemed a distant prospect. Almost obsessional about the issue, and the imprisonment of suffragettes in 1906 and 1907, Hardie raised the 'limited franchise' issue at the Labour Party Conference in 1907. The Conference, held at Belfast, voted against the limited move by 605,000 votes to 268,000, suggesting that it was a retrograde step. Conference was not impressed by the fact that the WSPU had advised voters to elect the Unionist rather than the Labour candidate at the Cockermouth parliamentary by-election. This rejection provoked Hardie, in his winding-up speech, to threaten that 'he would have to seriously consider whether he could remain a Member of the Parliamentary Party'. Arthur Henderson saved the day by finding a formula allowing individual members of the PLP to vote as they wished on the 'limited franchise'. A similar fit of petulance occurred at the ILP Conference at Easter 1907 when Hardie annoyed those attending by supporting the limited franchise and demanding that a telegram of support be sent to WSPU women who had recently been imprisoned. MacDonald, Glasier and the Conference objected to this action.

There were other points of conflict as well, most obviously that concerning the power of the Conference to instruct the PLP on its parliamentary programme. The 1907 Labour Party Conference committed the National Executive and the PLP to joint discussions on this issue. From the beginning Hardie was opposed to this, and saw the resolution rejecting the 'limited suffrage' franchise for women passed at this Conference as an attempt to impose Conference decisions upon the PLP. In this respect, of course, Hardie expressed the view, endorsed by all Chairmen and Leaders of the Labour Party ever since, that Conference cannot dictate the policies of the PLP. This view was endorsed in a compromise resolution, passed by 642,000 votes to 252,000, that Conference resolutions were 'opinions only' and that the timing of them would be left to the PLP. It was a point which Hardie reiterated three years later when he argued that '[i]n the House of Commons, the members of the Party have to decide their own policy without interference from the Executive or any outside authority'.

Evidently, the responsibilities of balanced and constant leadership did not seem to fit well with Hardie's propagandist instincts. It was thus a relief to many that, after a serious illness in the spring of 1907, Hardie decided upon a world tour. It was left to David Shackleton, Vice-Chairman of the PLP, to explain to Hardie the PLP's initial opposition to this tour and, ultimately, to stand in during his absence. Whilst Hardie was away, the PLP elected Arthur Henderson as the new Chairman in 1908.

Between 1908 and 1914 Hardie acted as the elder statesman of the Labour Party. He continued to criticize what he saw as the reluctance of the Labour Party to sponsor the women's suffrage cause but on most issues fell into line with the Party's policies, although often in his own idiosyncratic way.

Indeed, Hardie was quite defensive of the PLP on some matters. His personal animosity towards Ben Tillett, the famous trade union leader, positively encouraged him to criticize Tillett's pamphlet *Is the Parliamentary Labour Party a Failure* (1908) which claimed that 'The lion has no teeth or claws, and is losing his growl too; the temperance section being softly feline in their purring to Ministers and their patronage'.

Loyalty to Labour also led Hardie to admonish Victor Grayson, who had been elected as MP for Colne Valley in 1907. Grayson made two personal demonstrations in the House of Commons in October 1908. He was ejected because of his refusal to be bound by the rules of the House on the first occasion and, on the second, because he stated that 'This House is a House of murderers'. Hardie felt that Grayson's actions were pre-meditated and that the man had been high-handed in failing to work with the PLP. This feud between Hardie and Grayson extended further when Hyndman, Leader of the SDF, and Grayson refused to speak on the same platform as Hardie at Holborn Town Hall in November 1908. The issue surfaced again at the ILP Conference at Edinburgh in 1909. The National Administrative Council (NAC) of the ILP sought to censure Grayson but the Conference decided to refer the main passage of criticism back for reconsideration. This one revolt of the Conference was on a substantively trivial point, but to the NAC leadership it was a symbolic challenge to their authority. As a result Hardie, MacDonald, Glasier and Snowden all resigned from the NAC, Hardie explaining that he disliked Grayson's criticism of the 'Old Gang' as 'limpets clinging to the rock of office'. The Conference quickly changed its mind and passed the original report, which condemned Grayson, by 249 votes to 110 and asked the 'Big Four' to withdraw their resignations. They refused and remained outside the NAC, despite a countrywide campaign to get them to rejoin. This release from the NAC of the ILP, as with Hardie's withdrawal from the Chairmanship of the PLP, gave him the space to operate as the free agent he wished to be.

These were heady political times, with the People's Budget being fought in the House of Commons and the House of Lords, and Hardie quite strongly supported the suggestion of 6d in the £ supertax on incomes above £5,000 per annum. The resistance of the Lords led Hardie to complain that the House of Lords was the 'cut of the tail of the mad dog'.

In Hardie the Labour Party also had a figure of international importance. In his world tour in 1907–8 he caused controversy by being ambiguous on the White Australia policy but was denounced strongly because of his condemnation of British rule in India. His brief visit to South Africa brought riots when he condemned racial discrimination as well as the practice of white-only trade unions.

Yet above all Hardie was concerned with rising militarism in Europe, and he focused his hopes upon the Second International, of which he had been a founding member in 1889, averting war in Europe. It failed to do so and collapsed at the outbreak of the Second World War.

Shortly after war broke out Hardie faced, on 6 August 1914, a bruising encounter with his constituents in the Aberdare valley in which the meeting was cut short by patriotic disorder, the singing of *Rule, Britannia* and shouting of 'Turn the German out'. As a political force he was now spent, and little over a year later, on 26 September 1915, he died of pneumonia in a Glasgow nursing home. Not one word of regret was expressed in the House of Commons, in which he had served for eighteen years. *The Times* of 27 September 1915 gave him a grudging obituary in which it suggested that

> He never caught the ear of the assembly [the Commons] and was an ineffective leader of the independent group which owed its existence in great measure to his unflagging energy. He ... did not at any time gain the complete confidence of the working class. The Labour Party disappointed his hopes. He was out of tune with the more modest views of the trade unionist majority for a considerable time, and his views ceased to have any influence in the councils of the party with the coming of the war.... The bitter passions which he aroused in his life were in great measure forgotten before his death.

Only the Labour movement was more generous, with the *Labour Party Annual Conference Report*, January 1916, declaring that 'he pioneered the coming of the Labour Party as we know it, and fully earned the honour of being the first Chairman of the Parliamentary Labour Party when it entered the House of Commons in 1906'.

See also: MacDonald, Snowden

Further reading

Benn, C., 1992, *Keir Hardie*, London: Hutchinson.
Brockway, F., 1944, *Socialism over Sixty Years*, London: Allen & Unwin.
Hughes, E. (ed.), 1928, *Keir Hardie: Speeches and Writings (from 1888–1915)*, Forward Printing and Publishing Co.
Maclean, I., 1975, *Keir Hardie*, London: Allen Lane.
Morgan, K. O., 1975, *Keir Hardie: Radical and Socialist*, London: Weidenfeld & Nicolson.

EDWARD (RICHARD GEORGE) HEATH 1916–

Edward Heath was Prime Minister of the controversial and unsuccessful Conservative government of 1970–4. Amidst his government's industrial problems his major achievement was to secure Britain's entry to the European Economic Community (EEC), with the signing of the Treaty of Accession in 1972, followed by entry in 1973. Ever since, Heath has been a determined supporter of the EEC in the face of much Conservative Euro-scepticism and the hostility of

Margaret Thatcher to such policies. Removed as Conservative Party Leader in 1975 and replaced by Margaret Thatcher, Heath was a determined opponent of the strident and confrontational style of leadership adopted by Thatcher after her victory in the general election of 1979. Indeed, his support for the EEC often worked in tandem with his opposition to Thatcherism.

Heath was born at Broadstairs on 9 July 1916, the first child of William Heath and Edith Pantony. His father was a carpenter, who later ran a small building firm, and his mother had been in domestic service before she married. Heath won a scholarship to Chatham House School, Ramsgate, a fee-paying grammar school, and then went to Balliol College, Oxford, where he read Politics, Philosophy and Economics. Whilst at Oxford he was both President of the Oxford Union and President of the Oxford University Conservative Association. Revealing an early independence of thought, he worked for an anti-Munich Agreement candidate in the 1938 Oxford parliamentary by-election, opposing a settlement that allowed the German-dominated district of Czechoslovakia to join Germany. During the Second World War he was a colonel in the Royal Artillery. He then entered the Civil Service before becoming MP for Bexley in the 1950 general election, holding the seat until 1974 when he became MP for Sidcup (1974–83) and then Old Bexley and Sidcup (1983–).

Heath rose steadily within the Conservative Party and governments of the 1950s and early 1960s, becoming Chief Whip in 1955, Minister of Labour in 1959 and Lord Privy Seal in 1960, through which office he was responsible for the unsuccessful negotiations in 1960 and 1961 to arrange for Britain's entry into the EEC. In 1963 he became Minister of Trade, Industry and Regional Development in Sir Alec Douglas Home's Conservative Government. It was whilst in this office that he partially abolished Resale Price Maintenance, which he felt fixed prices high at the expense of the customers. This action, which was unpopular with businessmen, marked him out as a reforming and modernizing Conservative.

After the Douglas Home government was defeated in the 1964 general election, Heath was made Shadow Chancellor of the Exchequer and then won the Conservative leadership contest in 1965, defeating Enoch Powell and Reginald Maudling in the process. Heath's success was probably because he was seen to be the modern type of Conservative politician who might provide a successful alternative to Harold Wilson's reforming zeal. Nevertheless, he was defeated in the 1966 general election and, accepting that the

Conservatives would be in opposition for a number of years, decided that he would set up a large number of policy review groups to prepare the programme for a future Conservative government.

Heath's moment came during a general election in June 1970 at which he committed the Conservative Party to a policy of modernization aimed at tackling the relative economic decline of the British economy. His approach was largely designed to release private initiative and enterprise by reducing direct taxation, cutting back on government expenditure, reforming industrial relations, and reforming central and local government administration. It was also linked with the need to negotiate entry into the EEC, which Heath felt would guarantee both Britain's political security and economic competitiveness in its post-Imperialist days. Armed with these policies, and faced with a Wilson government which was expressing difficulties with the trade union movement, Heath's Conservative Party was returned with a small majority of thirty.

Heath's premiership was not the most successful in recent British history, although it foreshadowed Margaret Thatcher's willingness to challenge the existing political conventions in Britain by attempting to reduce the government's commitment to the welfare state. He developed a reputation for being abrupt, lacking tact and leading from the front. Yet he could show surprising political skill, as he did on the question of Europe. Allowing a free vote of MPs on the issue of applying for entry to the EEC in 1972, Heath found that thirty-nine Conservative MPs voted against entry but that sixty-nine Labour MPs ignored the Labour Party whip and voted in favour. Securing victory, Heath sought, and eventually obtained, Britain's entry to the EEC on 1 January 1973.

The Heath government's handling of the immigration issue proved no less controversial. The Conservative manifesto of 1970 had accepted that there would be no further large-scale immigration and the Immigration Act of 1971 was introduced to ensure that immigration restrictions were tightened. However, Britain's acceptance of 60,000 Ugandan Asians who held British passports and were threatened with expulsion from Uganda by President Idi Amin, created serious criticism from Enoch Powell, the Conservative MP and well-known opponent of immigration, and some disquiet within the Conservative Party.

The dominating theme of Heath's government was efficiency, and it introduced many initiatives to reduce public expenditure, including creating new larger departments such as the Department of Trade and Industry and the Department of the Environment. His government's financial prudence was, however, offset by rising inflation, wage demands and the failure of high-profile companies such as Rolls Royce, which had to be nationalized, and Upper Clyde Shipbuilders, which had to be subsidized. The government had also removed the Prices and Incomes Board and the Industrial Reorganization Corporation and was determined to fight excessive public-sector wage claims without control. At first it made attempts to negotiate a voluntary prices and incomes policy but, when this failed, Heath moved to make the scheme compulsory, an action which was censured by some Conservative MPs, such as Enoch Powell who felt that 'it is fatal for any government or Party to seek to govern in direct opposition to the principles on which they were established to govern'. Stages 1 and 2 of the scheme worked well enough but Stage 3 created more problems as the miners decided to ignore the wage guidelines.

Of course, this tension concerning wages reflected in part the conflict that had been accumulating since the introduction of the Industrial Relations Act of 1971. The Act sought to tighten the Labour Law, to create 60-day cooling-off periods and to introduce secret pre-strike ballots. However, the trade unions refused to register for it, employers refused to operate under its conditions, and it resulted in a number of serious industrial confrontations. The Act thus created more problems than it solved.

It was against this background of that the miners refused to comply with wage limits. The coal miners' strike of 1972 created serious difficulties for Heath's government but the major confrontation was the 1973–4 strike, following the quadrupling of Middle East oil prices, which saw the government introduce the three-day week to save fuel and prompted Heath to call a general election on 28 February 1974, when his government was defeated.

Heath remained Conservative Leader until 1975, when he was replaced by Margaret Thatcher. From then onwards, and particularly after Thatcher became Prime Minister in 1979, he has been very much an isolated political figure in the Party, committed to Europe in a Party which has been expressing grave doubts about the EEC. He has also fulfilled the function of senior statesman, and in 1992 became 'Father of the House' of Commons (that is, longest-serving member). He retired from the Commons just before the general election of June 2001, which saw the Conservative Party suffer a heavy defeat.

Edward Heath will hardly figure in anyone's pantheon of great prime ministers of the twentieth century, and he was unfortunate to assume office at a time of rapidly changing economic and political circumstances. His great achievement was that he negotiated Britain's entry into the EEC. His great failure was his inability to deal effectively with industrial relations.

See also: Home, Powell, Thatcher, Wilson

Further reading

Blake, R., 1985, *The Conservative Party from Peel to Thatcher*, London: Fontana.
Campbell, J., 1993, *Edward Heath: A Biography*, London: Cape.
Holmes, M., 1982, *Political Pressure and Economic Policy: British Government, 1970–1974*, London: Butterworth Scientific.

ARTHUR HENDERSON 1863–1935

Often referred to as 'Uncle Arthur', Arthur Henderson was a major figure of the trade-union wing of the Labour Party, Labour Party Secretary between 1911 and 1934 and, with Sidney Webb and Ramsay MacDonald, played a major role in formulating the 1918 Labour Party Constitution. He was for most of his political career a moderate trade unionist and Labour loyalist. He dominated the Labour Party's organization for most of the first third of the twentieth century, shaping its policies and practice. He also filled the role of Foreign Secretary in the second Labour government of 1929 to 1931. Indeed, it was his commitment to the Labour Party that led him to split with Ramsay MacDonald in the financial crisis of 1931 and saw him act briefly as Labour Leader at the end of 1931 and in early 1932.

Henderson was born illegitimately and in poverty, in Glasgow, probably on either the 13 or 20 September 1863, to Agnes Henderson, a domestic servant, and to a labourer and sometime cotton spinner. At eight or nine years of age his father died and his mother moved to Newcastle-upon-Tyne where, in 1874, she married Robert Heath, a policeman. Arthur left school when he was about ten to work in a photographers' shop and, at the age of twelve, became apprenticed to an iron moulder. Indeed, he qualified as an iron founder in 1883, becoming active in his union, and later became district organizer for Northumberland, Durham, and Lancashire. By 1892 his life as a manual worker was at an end, and for the next eleven years he focused upon trade union activity. For Henderson, trade union activity also pushed him on to the national stage. He was thus a strong and prominent trade unionist, eventually becoming President of the Friendly Society of Iron Founders from 1911. He made his name as a moderate trade unionist during a major local strike in 1894 and from his earliest days he was committed to industrial conciliation. Eventually, in 1903 he topped a poll to be his union's first parliamentary candidate.

Henderson was deeply religious, a fact that also placed him in the spotlight. Raised in a chapel-going family, after attending a Salvation Army street meeting when he was sixteen, he became a 'born-again Christian'. Indeed, he met his wife, Eleanor Watson, at the Wesleyan Methodist Mission chapel on Elswick Road, Newcastle. Through his religious commitments he emerged as an important non-conformist politician in his local community and then quickly transferred his talents to the national stage. At first he took an active role in his chapel's affairs. Later, he was prominent in national Wesleyan bodies, such as the Wesleyan Methodist Union for Social Service and the Brotherhood Movement (of which he became President). Before he was elected to Parliament, he was also an active lecturer on temperance.

Henderson began his political career as a Gladstonian Liberal, committed to free trade, Home Rule for Ireland, peace and economic retrenchment. At first he served as a radical Liberal councillor in Newcastle from 1892 and he was close to becoming one of the two Liberal candidates for the city in the 1895 general election. However, he accepted the post of Liberal agent in Newcastle and then in nearby Barnard Castle constituency. He then joined the Labour Party and became both a district and county councillor for Darlington, serving as the town's first Labour mayor in 1903.

Henderson's move from the Liberal to the Labour Party followed the decision of his union to join the Labour Representation Committee (LRC). The union had been represented at the inaugural conference of the LRC on 27 February 1900 and was politically committed to this body, which was to become the Labour Party in 1906. Henderson remained a politically moderate member of the Labour Party throughout his life, vehemently opposed to Marxist ideas. His victory in the 1903 by-election in Barnard Castle made him the fifth Independent Labour MP in the House of Commons but given that this was achieved with the support of many Liberal voters and that he was still wedded to Liberal ideas, it is clear that he remained a suspect character in the eyes of the more socialist members of the Independent Labour Party (ILP). Nevertheless, he rose quickly within the LRC, becoming its Treasurer in 1904, preparing a handbook for election agents with Ramsay MacDonald, and acting as its Chairman between 1905 and 1906.

The 1906 general election increased the number to Labour MPs to twenty-nine and, shortly afterwards, to thirty. Henderson was Chief Whip for the Parliamentary Labour Party (PLP) between 1906 and 1908. He was also Chairman of the Parliamentary Labour Party from 1908 to 1910, successor to James Keir Hardie, although Hardie has only actively filled this role until 1907 and Henderson had already been acting on his behalf. Henderson was Chairman of the PLP again from 1914 to 1917, succeeding Ramsay MacDonald who resigned after the outbreak of the First World War. Like most other trade union Labour MPs, Henderson supported Britain's war effort, largely to prevent a major split within the Party. Indeed, still trying to attract MacDonald back to the leadership of the Labour Party, Henderson informed him on 19 October 1914 that 'I am apprehensive that we are dividing ourselves off into small groups . . . . I have done what I could to follow the line which would leave the party at the end of the War as strong, if not stronger than we were before hostilities broke out' (Wrigley, 1990, p. 53). Henderson thus entered the Cabinet in Asquith's Coalition Government, serving first as President of the Board of Education (1915–16) and then as Paymaster-General (1916). This was an historic event for he became the first ever Labour Cabinet Minister. In Lloyd George's Coalition Government he was one of the War Cabinet of five (1916–17) until he resigned when he and the Prime Minister differed over his desire to support Kerensky's Menshevik government in Russia.

Out of office, Henderson returned to organizing the Labour Party and was one of those Labour leaders who were responsible for drawing up the Labour Party Constitution of 1918, which gave more power to the dominating trade unions, and to improving the Party's electoral organization in an attempt to meet electoral demands which resulted from the electorate being increased from seven to twenty-one million in 1918. He was a key figure in revising Labour's policies, helping to provide it with a socialist constitution through the incorporation of Clause 4 (or 3d), which committed the Labour Party to a policy of public ownership of industry and services.

At the end of the war, however, he lost his seat in Parliament, having moved his candidature from Barnard Castle to East Ham South, where he was beaten. He returned to the House of Commons in 1919, having won a by-election for Widnes. He then stood, and was returned, for Newcastle East in 1923, and won the Burnley constituency at the 1924 and 1929 general elections, before being defeated in 1931. Henderson was then returned to the House of Commons in 1933 as MP for Clay Cross, holding the seat until his death in 1935. His chequered parliamentary career reflects both the volatile nature of Labour politics at this time and the fact that he spent much of the time reorganizing the Labour Party both nationally and in the regions, rather than tending to his own constituency.

In 1924 the Labour Party took office for the first time, with Henderson, who was Labour Party secretary at that time, as Home Secretary. In this role he did little other than attempt to introduce a Factory Bill to rectify employee grievances. The measure was dropped when Labour lost office at the end of 1924. Nevertheless, Henderson was a member of the British delegation to the London Conference on the Dawes Plan, which organized the reparation payments to be made by Germany, and was subsequently to be found fulfilling a similar role to the League of Nations, where he supported the Geneva Protocol which advocated a structure to bring about the peaceful resolution of disputes.

Ramsay MacDonald was Foreign Secretary in his own government of 1924 but Henderson was able to secure that post after Labour's victory in the 1929 general election. In this role, Henderson was in his element. He won Foreign Office admiration for his willingness to make decisions and the quietly firm manner in which he ran his department. He carried out Labour's foreign policy, strongly supporting the League of Nations and making great efforts to secure international peace. He also made substantial attempts to end the isolation of both Germany and the Soviet Union. In particular, he attempted to resolve French and German differences over reparations at The Hague Conference of 1929 and in Geneva sponsored the idea of a Disarmament Conference. He also made efforts to improve Britain's standing with both Iraq and Egypt.

In August 1931, when a financial crisis brought down the second Labour government, Henderson opposed MacDonald's efforts to impose cuts on unemployment benefits. Initially, Henderson seemed to favour cuts but, after he realized the depth of trade union opposition within the Labour Party, he decided to oppose such a measure in Cabinet and sought to maintain Party unity in the midst of adversity.

After MacDonald formed the National Government in August 1931, Henderson succeeded him as Leader of the Labour Party. However, like most Labour politicians, he lost his seat in the 1931 general election. He then resigned as Leader in 1932, in favour of George Lansbury, to become Chairman of the World Disarmament Conference in Geneva (1932–4), which gained the principle if not the substance of arms reductions. He received the Nobel Peace prize in autumn 1934, a year after receiving the Wateler Peace Prize. He died in London a year later, on 20 October 1935.

Henderson may not have ranked among the great charismatic leaders of the Labour Party, such as Keir Hardie and Ramsay MacDonald, but the Labour Party owed much of its organizational development to his skills. Committed to maintaining Party unity, Henderson fused the trade unions and the Labour Party together in a bond that was essential to the success of both. By the 1920s he was one of Labour's great leaders and had also projected himself onto the international stage where he became a determined advocate of disarmament and supporter of the League of Nations. In the end, he shaped greatly Labour Party policies both at home and abroad.

See also: Hardie, Lloyd George, MacDonald, Snowden

Further reading

Carlton, D., 1970, *MacDonald versus Henderson*, London: Macmillan.
Hamilton, M. A., 1938, *Arthur Henderson, A Biography*, London and Toronto: Heinemann.
Jefferys, K. (ed.), 1999, *Leading Labour: From Keir Hardie to Tony Blair*, London: I. B. Tauris.
Jenkins, E. A., 1933, *From Foundry to Foreign Office. The Romantic Life-Story of the Rt Hon Arthur Henderson MP. Edwin A. Jenkins*, London: Grayson & Grayson.
Leventhal, F. M., 1989, *Arthur Henderson*, Manchester: Manchester University Press.
Marquand, D., 1977, *Ramsay MacDonald*, London: Cape.
Wrigley, C., 1990, *Arthur Henderson*, Cardiff: GPC Books.

SIR SAMUEL (JOHN GURNEY) HOARE (SECOND BARON AND VISCOUNT TEMPLEWOOD) 1880–1959

A Conservative politician of considerable importance, Sir Samuel Hoare is almost infamous for his role in the controversial Hoare–Laval Pact (1935) and his strong commitment to appeasement before the Second World War. As a result of the latter stance, he gained the reputation of being one of 'the Guilty Men' who failed to check Hitler and paved the way for the foreign policy that resulted in the Second World War.

Samuel Hoare was born on 24 February 1880, the elder son of (Sir) Samuel Hoare, later first Baronet, MP for Norwich (1886–1906), and his wife, Katherine Louisa Hart. He was educated at Harrow and then at New College, Oxford. On leaving Oxford it looked as though he might carve out a career in banking, for he was a member of an old

Norfolk banking family, and also that he might become a landed gentleman, for he married Lady Maud Lygo, fifth daughter of the sixth Earl of Beauchamp in 1909. However, after unsuccessfully contesting the Ipswich constituency in the 1906 general election, he was returned for the Chelsea constituency in 1910, a seat he represented for the Conservative Party until 1944.

During the First World War, Hoare served as a general staff officer with the rank of lieutenant-colonel in his military missions to Russia in 1916–17 and Italy, 1917–18. After the war he was a prominent figure in Conservative politics and in the Conservative governments. He was one of the Conservative MPs who acted to remove David Lloyd George from the premiership of the Coalition Government in October 1922. Hoare also held numerous ministerial offices between the wars: Secretary of State for Air (1922–4, 1924–9, 1940); Secretary of State for India (1931–5); Foreign Secretary (1935); First Lord of the Admiralty (1936–7); Home Secretary (1937–9); and Lord Privy Seal (1939–40). After the fall of Neville Chamberlain, in May 1940, Hoare became ambassador to Spain (1940–4), before being raised to the peerage as Viscount Templewood in 1944.

In the 1920s Hoare did much to make the public more aware of air issues, and his arrival by air at Gothenburg in 1923 to attend the first International Aero Exhibition was a first for ministerial travel. On Boxing Day 1926 he and his wife set off in an Imperial Airways de Havilland aeroplane on the first civil air flight to India, arriving in Delhi on 8 January 1927. It was India that occupied his attention in the early 1930s for, as Secretary of State for India, he was responsible for the drafting of the Government of India Act in 1935. During the Round Table Conferences on India, he attempted to come to an accord with Mahatma Gandhi, and he was a prominent witness when a Select Committee of both Houses of Parliament sat to discuss the outcome of these conferences in 1934 and 1935. Although the resulting Government of India Bill was strongly opposed by Winston Churchill, and a small group of dissident Conservatives, it was passed in 1935.

It was at this point, when Stanley Baldwin replaced Ramsay MacDonald as Prime Minister of the National Government, that Hoare was made Foreign Secretary. It was not an easy post to accept, for Britain had reduced her expenditure on military forces at a time when Germany, Italy and Japan were ignoring the League of Nations and re-arming at a rapid rate. Britain's commitment to collective security through the League of Nations in effect meant nothing unless Britain and France were prepared to act together, especially since the United States was adopting something of an isolationist policy. Hoare's foreign policy was, therefore, one of gaining time for Britain to build up her military strength. As a result he negotiated the 1935 Anglo-German Naval Treaty that permanently fixed German naval strength at 35 per cent of the level of British naval forces, although it allowed Germany parity with submarines. Since this occurred only two months after Germany announced an expansion of its army and the re-activation of its air force, this treaty seemed to be an endorsement of existing patterns of German re-armament.

Hoare's next problem was to deal with the Abyssinian crisis of 1935. The threatened Italian invasion of Abyssinia over its disputed borders with Italian Somaliland created a problem for the League of Nations, which should have acted collectively in opposing the move. However, the French had made it clear that they would not consider military action against Italy over Abyssinia. On 11 September 1935 Hoare attempted to rally the League, by emphasizing the need for collective security: 'If the burden is to be borne, it must be borne collectively. If the risks for peace are to be run, they must be run by all.' He also re-affirmed Britain's support for 'the collective maintenance of the Covenant'. Unfortunately, there was little support from the other member states of the League of Nations, and a committee of five was set up by the League to settle the crisis. Mussolini rejected its compromise, invaded Abyssinia in October 1935 and the League of Nations imposed limited sanctions against Italy. On behalf of the League, Britain and France negotiated together, to produce the Hoare–Laval Pact. By this, Abyssinia would maintain access to the sea and Abyssinian sovereignty over its surviving territories would be guaranteed but Italy would have most of the Tigre district, which its troops already occupied, and would have the right to economically develop a large zone of land in the south and south-west of the country. Unfortunately, this plan was leaked to the press, with the result that many Conservative MPs protested that it was a reversal of Hoare's 11 September speech, and Baldwin and the Cabinet decided against accepting a plan they had at first approved, because of the rising popular opposition throughout the country. Hoare decided to resign rather than withdraw the plan, largely because he felt that any other course of action could have led Britain into a war with Italy, without the support of France. In the event, Mussolini's Italian fascist state did what it wanted in Abyssinia, the League of Nations was discredited and, to many historians, the Second World War was probably brought forward by the weakness of opposition to fascism.

Hoare was brought back into Baldwin's National Government in June 1936 when he was made First Lord of the Admiralty, and in May

1937 he became Home Secretary in Neville Chamberlain's government. His main work in this role was connected with introducing the Criminal Justice Bill in 1938 and 1939, which introduced two new types of prison sentences – corrective training and preventive detention – abolished flogging and provided alternative punishments for juvenile offenders. In addition, as one of Chamberlain's closest colleagues he was invited to join an inner group of four Ministers in September 1938 during the events that led to the Munich Agreement. Indeed, Hoare was a great defender of the Munich Agreement since he felt that there was no alternative without French support and with the Labour Party and public opinion at home opposed to military activity. Hoare continued at the outbreak of the Second World War as one of Chamberlain's key Ministers, although he did become Lord Privy Seal and resigned as Home Secretary. He became a member of the War Cabinet and, in April 1940, again was appointed Secretary of State for Air. Nevertheless, he resigned the following month when Chamberlain was replaced by Winston Churchill. The same month, he was appointed British Ambassador to Spain, a post he filled until December 1944, his main task being to secure the release from Spanish prisons of about 30,000 Allied prisoners of war and refugees.

Hoare became Viscount Templewood about six months before he retired as British Ambassador. Yet he rarely spoke in the House of Lords and effectively retired to his Norfolk estate, building Templewood, a small classical villa. He was however Chairman of the Council of Magistrates (1947–52) and was President of the Howard League for Penal Reform (1947–59). He received many degrees and honours and held the position of Chancellor of the University of Reading from 1937 until his death. He died in London on 7 May 1959, and is still remembered for his commitment to appeasement rather than his diplomatic skills.

See also: Baldwin, Chamberlain, (Bonar) Law, MacDonald

Further reading

Cross, J. A., 1977, *Sir Samuel Hoare: A Political Biography*, London: Cape.

SIR ALEC (ALEXANDER FREDERICK) DOUGLAS HOME 1903–1995

Sir Alec Douglas Home, the fourteenth Earl of Home, became Prime Minister in 1963 by virtue of the fact that the Peerage Act, which only became law on 3 July 1963, permitted him to renounce his title and contest a seat for the House of Commons. Home's premiership was a brief transition period between the resignation of Harold Macmillan and the emergence of Edward Heath as Leader of the Conservative Party, and represented the last throw of the old 'grouse-moor image' of the Conservative Party against the new more radical and modern type of Conservative leader who was to emerge.

The Earls of Home (pronounced Hume) owned substantial estates based upon their mansion at Hirsel, near Coldstream in Scotland. Alec Douglas Home was born on 2 July 1903, the eldest son of the thirteenth Earl of Home and Lady Lilian Lambton. He was educated at Ludgrove before entering Eton (at the same time as George Orwell) and then at Christ Church, Oxford. He graduated with a third-class degree in History but distinguished himself at cricket, touring South Africa and Argentina. He had become Lord Dunglass in 1918. For two years from 1927 he spent his time managing the family estates, shooting and fishing. Then he contested and won the South Lanark seat in 1931, representing it from 1931 to 1945, and again from 1950 to 1951, when his father's death raised him to the House of Lords as the fourteenth Earl of Home. In 1936 he married Elizabeth Alington, the daughter of the headmaster of Eton, later Dean of Durham.

By the late 1930s, Home had begun to attract political attention. From 1937 to 1940, he was Parliamentary Private Secretary to Neville Chamberlain, the Prime Minister, and accompanied him to the famous Munich meeting with Hitler in 1939, which led to Hitler securing parts of Czechoslovakia. Rather like Chamberlain, Home viewed the Soviet Union as a bigger danger than Nazi Germany and refused to contemplate the possibility of a much-mooted Anglo-Soviet Pact. When the war broke out Home continued as Parliamentary Private Secretary to Chamberlain. However, he contracted tuberculosis of the spine in 1940, which meant that he was not involved in the wartime administration of Britain for the rest of the Second World War. He became something of an evangelical Christian whilst in his immobilized state, and criticized the Yalta treaties between the Soviet Union, the United States and Britain which created spheres of influence for the Soviets.

Home (still Lord Dunglass) lost his parliamentary seat in the 1945 general election, when the Labour Party won a landslide victory, but regained it in 1950. He intended to retire to his landed estates but was given the post of Minister of State at the Scottish Office, by Winston Churchill in 1951, in order that the government would have a Minister resident in Scotland capable of defusing the demands for

Scottish Home Rule. Home held this post until 1955, when he became Secretary of Commonwealth Relations. He was, incidentally, Lord President of the Council in 1957 and 1959 to 1960, Deputy Leader of the Lords between 1956 and 1957, and Leader of the Lords from 1957 to 1960. Then Harold Macmillan, the Prime Minister, appointed him Foreign Secretary in 1961. In this role he organized Britain's ill-fated attempt to join the European Economic Community (the Common Market) in 1961, but did little else.

Nevertheless, when Macmillan fell ill in 1963 the Conservative Party and government divided into two camps: the centrist MPs supported R. A. Butler and the constituencies supported Lord Hailsham (Quintin Hogg). Liking neither alternative, Macmillan pressed forward Home's claim and he became both Leader of the Conservative Party and Prime Minister. This process necessitated that he renounce his title and be returned as MP for Kinross and West Perthshire, a seat he held from 1963 to 1974. At first Home's administration was popular, for it heralded the expansion of the universities following the Robbins Report, but when Edward Heath, President of the Board of Trade, removed Resale Price Maintenance, and upset many small businesses, its fortunes went into decline. At this point, in 1964, the balance of payments in Britain was spiralling towards an £800 million deficit which Reginald Maudling, the Chancellor of the Exchequer, seemed unable to check. Home's statement that he worked out economic problems with a box of matches ignited a feeling that the Conservative government lacked economic expertise. As a result of the rising economic crisis, Home lost the October 1964 general election by seven seats, and he then stepped down as Conservative Leader in 1965, making way for the election of Edward Heath as the new Conservative Leader.

Nevertheless, Home remained active in politics. He was Heath's foreign affairs spokesman and in 1968 became the Chair of the Committee on the Constitution for Scotland, which recommended an Assembly for Scotland. This, however, was not implemented by the Heath government which came to power in June 1970. Home was then appointed Foreign Secretary, a position he held until February 1974. His main work concerned the unsuccessful attempt to secure a settlement of the Rhodesia situation which aimed to bring Southern Rhodesia back into the Commonwealth. He also expelled 108 Soviet spies in 1973.

Home retired from the House of Commons in 1974 and was raised to the House of Lords once again, this time with the life peerage of Lord Home of Hirsel. His political activity was limited, although he did work to oppose the Labour Party's devolution campaign for Scotland in February 1979, suggesting that the Conservatives might offer 'something better', although nothing ever emerged. He died on 15 October 1995 and is barely remembered as the interim Prime Minister that he was.

See also: Chamberlain (Neville), Churchill, Eden, Macmillan

Further reading

Dickie, J., 1964 *The Uncommon Commoner: A Study of Sir Alec Douglas Home*, London: Pall Mall Press.
Home, Lord, 1976, *The Way the Wind Blows. An Autobiography*, London: Collins.
Margach, J., 1981, *The Anatomy of Power. An Enquiry into the Personality of Leadership*, London: W. H. Allen.
Young, K., 1970, *Sir Alec Douglas-Home*, London: Dent.

SIR KEITH (SINJOHN) JOSEPH 1918–1994

Keith Joseph is best remembered for being one of the great intellectual figures of the Thatcher governments of the 1980s, although his agonies in decision-making meant that he was a rather ineffectual administrator. Yet it is as an architect of Thatcherism, indeed as Thatcher's guru and defender of entrepreneurial capitalism, that he must be judged for here was a politician prepared to challenge the conventional wisdom of the day.

Keith Joseph was the son of Sir Samuel Joseph, a self-made Jewish millionaire who was partly responsible for building up Bovis, the construction firm, and who became Lord Mayor of London. Keith Joseph was born on 17 January 1918 and was educated at Harrow and then at Magdalen College, Oxford. He served in the Second World War, then returned to a Fellowship at All Souls College, Oxford, before training to become a barrister, although he never practised law.

Always a Conservative, Joseph began his parliamentary career in 1956 after having been returned as Conservative MP for the safe seat of Leeds North East at a by-election in February of that year, becoming one of only two Jewish Conservatives in the House of Commons at that time. He held this seat for thirty-one years, until his retirement during the general election of 1987. His political career was slow to develop but during the 1960s and early 1970s he gained a reputation for being a defender of entrepreneurial capitalism which he felt would guarantee British economic prosperity and thus the welfare of all people in British society, including quality of life for the economically disadvantaged. In his early years he earned a reputation as a political eccentric, regretting, rather than opposing, the Anglo-French invasion of the Suez Canal Zone in 1956 and opposing the use of capital punishment, an unusual position for a Conservative to adopt.

Joseph's first government appointment was as Parliamentary Secretary at the Housing, Local Government and Welsh Affairs office from 22 October 1959 until 9 October 1961. He then became Minister of State at the Board of Trade, and then, on 13 July 1962, was appointed Minister of Housing, Local Government and Welsh Affairs. This period in office came to an end when Harold Wilson's Labour government was returned to office in October 1964.

Although considered to be a political high flyer, Joseph did not gain much political advancement when Edward Heath became Conservative Prime Minister in June 1970. Despite Joseph's interest in economic matters, Heath kept him out of economic roles and appointed him Secretary of State for Social Services. In this position he increased enormously the budget of his department but, after the return of a Labour government, repented of his role. Indeed, he suggested that in 1974, at the age of 56, he had only just become a Conservative. Along with Enoch Powell, he disliked the fact that Heath had resorted to statutory controls and an incomes policy, much in the way that the Wilson Labour governments of the 1960s had.

At this stage, Joseph claimed to be greatly influenced by the ideas of Friedrich von Hayek and Milton Friedman, both of whom opposed collective action and favoured the free market economy. He now supported the views of the free market Institute of Economic Affairs. He also became one of those former Cabinet Ministers of the Heath government who wished to challenge Heath's leadership of the Conservative Party but who were reluctant to do so.

Edward du Cann, Chairman of the powerful 1922 back-bench committee of the Conservative Party began discussions in his City of London office with other critics of Heath. Since du Cann's office was in Milk Street, they became known as the 'Milk Street Mafia'. They favoured Joseph as Heath's replacement because he offered a new economic strategy. Indeed, in the brief period between the two elections in 1974, Joseph had formed the Centre of Policy Studies to chart a new way forward for Conservatism. It was during this period and at Preston in September 1974 that Joseph made a striking speech rejecting Keynesian economics. He maintained that inflation was caused by governments and that tackling inflation was far more important than maintaining full employment. His views appealed to many within the Conservative Party who, after the election defeat of

February 1974, were disillusioned with the existing policies of the Conservative Party.

Thus Sir Keith became the obvious right-wing challenger to Edward Heath for the Conservative leadership. However, as a result of some ill-judged speeches his credentials for that role were undermined. In a speech at Birmingham in October 1974 he repeated his criticism of Keynesian economics but complained about 'the high and rising proportion of children being born to mothers least fitted to bring children into the world' (Howe, 1995, p. 8). This was considered to be a flirtation with eugenics as a solution to poverty and inequality and many of his supporters deserted him. While intellectually better equipped than Thatcher he gave way to her, realizing that he was unsuited to being Leader of the Conservative Party. Instead he threw his political weight behind the person who was to become Conservative Leader in 1975.

In developing the classic Thatcherism of later years Joseph spoke in favour of big cuts in taxes and public spending, the reduction of the power of the trade unions, firm control over the money supply to defeat inflation, and the encouragement of the free market.

When she became Conservative Leader in 1975 Margaret Thatcher gave Joseph responsibility in the Shadow Cabinet for developing Conservative policy. In this role he declared the need to abandon the post-war policy of full employment, which had been inherited from the various wartime publications of William Beveridge. He argued that such policies were not sustainable for they involved the government spending large amounts of money and borrowing from the market, forcing interest rates up and thus denying British industry easy access to relatively cheap money. The welfare state and the maintenance of full employment were thus seen as the reasons for the relative economic decline of Britain – 'the British Disease'. Ironically, within months the Labour government was forced to impose public expenditure cuts as part of its obligations under the International Monetary Fund loan it had negotiated, and James Callaghan, the new Prime Minister, was led to admit that full employment could not be maintained; the economic and political climate was moving in the direction of Thatcherism.

In the Thatcher government of 1979 Sir Keith was made Secretary of State for Industry. In this office he found himself in direct contravention of his own declared aims, providing, in a climate of rapidly rising unemployment, large subsidies for British Leyland (the car-manufacturing firm), British Steel and Rolls-Royce. Naturally, he was greatly criticized for the fact that unemployment more than doubled in his first two years of office. As a result he was more than happy to move to the post of Minister of State for Education and Science on 14 September 1981, as part of Thatcher's mid-term Cabinet shuffle. In this post he upset school teachers by suggesting that they did not need significant pay increases because their wages would be determined by supply and demand, and this led to bad relations, strikes, and long-running pay disputes. He also prepared the way for the education reforms which Kenneth Baker, a later Minister of State for Education, introduced in the Education Act of 1988. These included moves towards creating a national curriculum in education, ending the Burnham pay negotiations for teachers and moving towards the formation of a Pay Review Body, which effectively cut off the negotiation rights of teachers' unions, and suggesting the need to widen choice and undermine the domination of comprehensive education.

Joseph left the House of Commons at the general election of 1987 and was raised to the House of Lords, being made a life peer. He died on 10 December 1994.

Sir Keith Joseph was not a great success as an administrator, was a modest Secretary of State for Social Services, and a poor Secretary of State for both Industry and Education. Indeed, it was suggested in the mid 1980s that there was nothing he was incapable of destroying. Since he was open-minded and almost publicly anguished over his decisions, his critics saw him as indecisive. Indeed it was said of him that he was 'a lion in opposition and a lamb in government'. Nevertheless, Joseph had a creative talent and was a mentor to both Thatcher and Thatcherism, and upset the post-war consensus to such an extent that even in 2001 one is aware, through the actions of the Blair Labour government, that there has been a sea-change in British political opinion which Joseph in part influenced.

See also: Callaghan, Heath, Thatcher, Wilson

Further reading

Evans, B., 1999, *Thatcherism and British Politics 1975–1999*, Stroud: Sutton.
Joseph, K., 1972, *The Cycle of Deprivation*, London: Psychotherapy Centre.
Howe, G. ,1994, *Conflict of Loyalty*, London: Macmillan.

JOHN MAYNARD KEYNES 1883–1946

John Maynard Keynes is most famous for his book *The General Theory of Employment, Interest and Money*, written in 1936, which suggested that the self-regulating Gold Standard system of the nineteenth and early twentieth centuries was ineffective and that governments needed to regulate the economy to avoid unemployment. In periods of slump money needed to pumped into the economy to create demand, and in periods of boom money needed to be taken out of the economy. The mechanism for this was the multiplier effect, whereby putting money into the hands of those who would spend would generate many times the level of investment in terms of demand. Taking money from those who spend would produce the opposite effect. This was demand management, or 'Keynesianism'.

Keynes's ideas were important because of his growing reputation in both intellectual and government circles. His ideas were already becoming widely known before the General Theory appeared in 1936, his criticism of Winston Churchill for returning to the Gold Standard in 1925 being almost legendary. Yet even more important was his influence upon government. He was attached to the Treasury during the First World War and was given responsibility for arranging the reconstruction of international arrangements during the Second World War, organizing the discussions at Bretton Woods in 1944 that led to the formation of the International Monetary Fund. In effect, Keynes straddled the world of academia and public service throughout his life.

Keynes was born in 1883 into a wealthy middle-class intellectual family. He was educated at King's College, Cambridge, and gained a first-class degree in mathematics. Whilst at Cambridge he was President of both the Liberal Club and the Cambridge Union, the student debating society. He was also member of a society known as 'The Apostles', which included Lytton Strachey and Duncan Grant.

Keynes was greatly influenced by Alfred Marshall, the famous economist. As a result he studied probability. He began work as a civil servant in the India Office in 1906 but returned to Cambridge as an economics lecturer two years later. As a result of Marshall's influence, Keynes became editor of the Economic Journal in 1911 as a young university academic. He was soon to combine both of these economic and administrative aspects when he became a member of the Royal Commission on Indian Finance and Currency in 1913.

The First World War drew Keynes into public service once again. He was attached to the Treasury and given the major responsibility for the external finance of the war. He was an expert adviser who knew how the system worked. However, acting as Treasury representative at the Versailles Peace Conference, he became frustrated at the way in which heavy reparations were demanded of Germany by the Allies. He resigned in June 1919 and revealed his frustrations in *The Economic Consequences of the Peace* (1919), in which he argued that a poor Germany was expected to pay a level of reparations to richer nations that could only be achieved by Germany's economic domination of Europe. Such a policy made no economic sense and had political implications.

Having resigned his government post, Keynes adopted a double life. On the one hand, he retained his Fellowship at King's College, Cambridge, which involved part-time academic work; on the other he lived in Bloomsbury where many of his friends of 'The Apostles' group became part of the influential Bloomsbury Group. From his London home he cultivated connections with the cultural, business and political communities of London. In 1925 he married the ballerina Lydia Lopokova and, in part through her, cultivated an interest in the arts as a founder member of the Arts Council of Great Britain. During this period also he speculated on the stock market, and allegedly was worth about half a million pounds in 1936. From the mid 1920s to the mid 1930s he was also Director of the London School of Economics.

Throughout this period, Keynes was regularly called upon to advise the government on economic matters. No issue in this respect was more important than the decision of Winston Churchill, Chancellor of the Exchequer, to return to the Gold Standard in 1925. In 1918 the Cunliffe Committee had advised upon a set of deflationary policies to improve the finances of the government and to strengthen the pound from about $2.85 to the pound to the pre-war parity of $4.86 to the pound. It also laid down a time-scale of seven years. Thus in April 1925, Churchill returned Britain to the Gold Standard, and raised the value of the pound from $4.40 (as it was then) to $4.86 in the process, since it was believed that the pre-war parity had to be reached. What annoyed Keynes is that he had been drawn into Churchill's round of breakfast discussions and that his opposition to returning to the Gold Standard had been ignored. In his short pamphlet *The Economic Consequences of Mr Churchill* Keynes asked why Churchill had done 'such a silly thing', suggesting that he had been 'deafened by the clamorous voices of conventional finance' and because of his 'lack of instinctive judgement'. Rightly, as it happened, Keynes predicted that the government would not be able to reduce the costs of production by the 10 per cent needed as a result of the upward revaluation of the pound and that exports would be lost. He thus suggested that there was a need to look at the immediate consequences of economic actions, reviving thoughts of his famous dictum that: 'In the long run we are all dead'.

Keynes was a deeply political figure. He had been a Liberal from his student days and in 1922 he became chairman of the *Nation*, which was absorbed later by the *New Statesman*. This brought him into close cooperation with David Lloyd George; he certainly influenced the thinking exhibited by Lloyd George in his 'Liberal Yellow Books', which advocated that the 'idle balances' being held by banks should be used by governments to stimulate the economy out of depression. In the late 1920s Keynes was firmly behind such efforts to undermine Treasury dogma of balanced budgets, and the like, and in 1929 he wrote, with H. D. Henderson, the famous pamphlet *Can Lloyd George Do It?* In this, it was argued that a massive programme of public works, including road building, should be used to stimulate the economy using those idle balances of £300 million or so already identified by the Yellow Books.

The failure of Lloyd George's Liberal Party to win direct power as a result of the 1929 general election did not, however, diminish Keynes's political and economic significance. Indeed, he became a member of both the (Macmillan) Committee on Finance and Industry and the Economic Advisory Council, of which he became Chairman. In these capacities he offered a varied collection of solutions to the rising unemployment of the years between 1929 and 1931. His book *A Treatise on Money* (1930) reiterated his earlier belief in cheap money. As the financial and unemployment crises worsened he even contemplated, albeit briefly, the need for tariff protection. Such action would, he argued, allow interest rates to fall and provide the cheap money that might be used to stimulate demand.

With the formation of the National Government in August 1931, Keynes abandoned politics and focused more upon his economic theory. Supported by young Cambridge economists, including R. F. Kahn and J. E. Meade, Keynes began to argue that far from relying upon cheap money to invest, the very act of investment would create demand, employment, income and saving. Through a multiplier effect initial investment and expenditure would tackle the problem of unemployment and also allow savings *en route*. Above all, his theory challenged the notion that wage cuts and deflation were the way forward in reducing production costs and government borrowing, thus releasing money into the finance market, forcing interest rates down and encouraging investment. These ideas became the basis of his *General Theory*, published in 1936.

Keynes's ideas attracted some interest within the British trade union movement and amongst some progressive thinkers but they did not attract widespread attention until the Second World War. This was in part by due to his being invited back to the Treasury in 1940, where he acted as a top-level adviser for the rest of his life. His main attention was focused upon planning for the post-war international economy and replacing the old Gold Standard and projectionist attitudes of the inter-war years. In this respect he played a major part in the Bretton Woods Conference in 1944 which helped to set up the International Monetary Fund and the World Bank. These organizations were created to obtain resources from member nations and to transfer these resources around the international community, as the need arose, to ensure that world trade expanded in the post-war years. Gone was Keynes's commitment to some form of protectionism, which had emerged in the 1930s because of the exigent need of the economy.

At the end of the Second World War, Keynes was also involved in negotiations with the United States following the abrupt end to their lend-lease agreement with Britain. As a result of his efforts he secured a large dollar loan from the United States. It was not an ideal arrangement but it saw Britain through the transition period from war to peace.

Keynes was not a healthy man in his last few years. He had a heart attack in 1937 and, weakened by his excessive workload, died suddenly during Easter 1946. At that time his reputation was being established, and during the next three decades expansion of the British and world economies owed much to his interventionist policies, which worked as a weapon, albeit an imperfect one, in keeping unemployment low. Keynesianism's importance in economic thinking was not attacked until the orthodox economic views of the 1920s and 1930s reappeared in the form of Margaret Thatcher's monetarism in the late 1970s. In recent years Keynes's reputation and ideas have become less dominant than they once were, but they remain a testament to the enormous reputation of Keynes in the twentieth century. Indeed, his economic ideas were a major factor shaping the political and economic decisions made in the mid twentieth century.

See also: Churchill, Lloyd George, Mosley

Further reading

Clarke, P., 1988, *The Keynesian Revolution in the Making 1924–1936*, Oxford: Clarendon.

Hession, C. H, 1984, *John Maynard Keynes*. New York: Macmillan and London: Collier Macmillan.

Moggridge, D. E., 1992, *Maynard Keynes: An Economist's Biography*, London: Routledge.

Skidelsky, R., 1983, *John Maynard Keynes. Vol 1: Hopes Betrayed, 1883–1920*, London: Macmillan.

Skidelsky, R., 1992, *John Maynard Keynes. Vol. 2: The Economist as Saviour, 1920–1937*, London: Macmillan.

NEIL KINNOCK 1943–

Neil Kinnock is famous for acting as Leader of the Labour Party from 1983 to 1992, assuming leadership at a time when its fortunes were at their lowest ebb since the 1930s. Eschewing his past as a left-wing parliamentary rebel in the 1970s he introduced root-and-branch reform in the Labour Party which swept away old shibboleths, such as a commitment to unilateral disarmament, and reformed the Labour Party as a social democratic party. Indeed, he also attempted play down the commitment to public ownership within the Party, to remove Militant Tendency from the Party, and to reduce the power of the trade union movement within the Party. Yet, although he rescued Labour from political oblivion, was appointed because of his 'sensible Left' image, and was a good Party manager, Kinnock was always seen as a political lightweight. Indeed, he was never acknowledged to be a leader capable of returning Labour to power. Eventually he resigned as Labour Leader after the poor general election result of 1992, when Labour won just 35.2 per cent of the vote, and 271 seats, 1.7 per cent lower than in the disastrous 1979 general election.

Kinnock was born in 1943 into a mining family living in Tredegar, South Wales, and can lay claim to having one of the purest of working-class pedigrees. He was educated at University College, Cardiff, where he obtained a poor degree as a result of his deep and distracting involvement in political activities. It was here that he met his wife, Glenys Parry, who had the same strong left-wing views. Leaving university he then became a Workers' Education Association lecturer for a short period of time but was then selected as a prospective parliamentary candidate for the safe seat of Bedwellty.

Kinnock's political career developed within the Labour Party. He became MP for Bedwellty in 1970 and held that seat until 1994 when he became a European Commissioner. In his early days he was a politically rebellious member of the Left of the Party, although never a member of the 'hard Left'. He was left-wing and refused the offer of minor government posts in the Harold Wilson/James Callaghan Labour government of 1974–9. He was elected to the Labour Party's National Executive Committee (NEC) in 1978 and became its education spokesman in 1979.

Kinnock rose quickly within the ranks, due in part to the patronage of Michael Foot, Labour Leader from 1980, although he gradually moved to the middle of Labour politics in the process. Following the general election of 1983, Kinnock succeeded Foot as Labour's Leader. Young and charismatic, and untainted by any association with the Labour government of 1974–9, Kinnock was elected Labour Leader in October 1983, winning 71.3 per cent of the votes cast. Indeed, he then formed a 'dream ticket' with the Labour Right's Roy Hattersley, who became Deputy Leader. This Left–Right balance represented the uniting of the Party.

Kinnock was faced with reshaping a Party which had now lost two successive general elections, which was still divided between the Left and the Right, was faced with a troublesome 'Militant Tendency' group which was infiltrating the Party, and which was losing its traditional working-class base of support. Faced with this situation Kinnock sought to reorganize the Party. However, his immediate problem was the year-long Miners' Strike of 1984–5 which distracted attention from the Labour Party and delayed any reforms.

To deal with these challenges, Kinnock attempted to distance himself, and the Labour Party, from the conflict. He criticized the embarrassing tactics of Arthur Scargill in not calling for a national strike ballot before calling strike action. In June 1984 he further criticized the violence of both the police and the pickets and in October 1984 attacked the confrontational tactics of the National Union of Mineworkers (NUM). This was despite the fact that Scargill received a standing ovation when he spoke to the Labour Party Conference of October 1985, which produced the tellingly hostile news photograph of Kinnock looking over the shoulder of Scargill as he was making his speech. In January 1985, Kinnock further criticized Arthur Scargill for acting like a First World War general, in a clear reference to the comment that the situation was one of 'heroes led by donkeys'. In March 1985 Kinnock further refused to commit any future Labour government to giving amnesty to any miner convicted of serious crime, a commitment requested by the NUM. The final straw came at the Labour Party Conference in October 1985 with Kinnock's attack upon Scargill's conduct of the strike.

Both the non-compliance protests by the mines and the Miners' Strike eventually disintegrated. But they left the Labour Party identified with the extreme Labour Left, something which Kinnock had tried to avoid through his criticism of Scargill's tactics. Kinnock clearly wished to distance himself from the type of trade union and industrial action which had brought Labour into political disfavour in the 'winter of discontent' of 1979 and which had undermined Labour's fortunes in the early 1980s. The Strike had not provided him with much of an opportunity for this but his attempt to remove the Militant Tendency faction proved a more effective means of creating the image of Labour as a party of political moderation.

At the 1985 Labour Party Conference, Kinnock was extremely critical of Derek Hatton, leader of the Militant Tendency faction that ran Liverpool City Council. He was particularly appalled at the action of the Militant Tendency leaders in Liverpool in issuing redundancy notices to all employees in order to place pressure on the Thatcher government to remove its capping of council expenditure. This had annoyed the trade unions and Kinnock, at the 1985 Conference, stated that

> I'll tell you what happens with impossible promises. You start with far-fetched revolutions. You are then pickled into a rigid dogma, a code, and you go through the years sticking to that, outdated, misplaced, irrelevant to the real needs, and you end in the grotesque chaos of a Labour council hiring taxis to scuttle round a city handing out redundancy notices to its own workers. (Applause). ... You can't play politics with people's jobs ... (Applause and some boos).

One front-bench Labour MP was heard to state that 'with one speech [Kinnock] he lanced the boil'.

Indeed, the NEC began an investigation into the Liverpool Labour Party which, in March 1986, was surcharged by the High Court, along with Lambeth Council, for not setting a council rate on time as directed by the Thatcher government. The Party NEC later, at the 1986 Conference, recommended that the Liverpool District Party be expelled.

By his actions, Kinnock was beginning to unite the Labour Right with the soft Left of the Party, represented by David Blunkett, Michael Meacher and the *Tribune* Group within the NEC. He also alienated and isolated the hard Left, the Trotskyists, the Campaign for Labour Party Democracy and related bodies. Yet to present Labour as a party of moderation also required changes in its policy commitments – particularly on the three major policy areas of nationalization, industrial relations and unilateral nuclear disarmament.

Kinnock began to move the Party away from its commitment to nationalization in 1985, when he declared that the re-nationalization of industries privatized by the Conservative government would not be a priority for a future Labour government. The Deputy Leader, Roy Hattersley, re-emphasized this point when his proposals for a variety of forms of social ownership, rather than nationalization, were accepted at the Party Conference in 1985. The unifying symbol of Labour's socialism of 1918 was now being challenged, for pragmatic reasons, by Kinnock and Hattersley. Yet Kinnock, in order to keep the soft Left on board with his political agenda, accepted that there would be a compromise arrangement whereby British Gas and British Telecom, both recently privatized organizations, would be returned to public control with compensation.

Kinnock also wanted Labour to be distanced further from the industrial action that had blighted its fortunes in 1979. He wished to retain much of the new framework of the Conservative government's industrial legislation but eventually compromised on repealing the existing framework whilst insisting that ballots would be held on strikes and that trade union executives would have to have their position constantly re-affirmed.

On the issue of unilateralism, however, Kinnock faced his sternest opposition. This issue had become almost the mark of being a socialist, and the policy had been re-affirmed at the 1984 Party Conference. However, by 1986 Kinnock was receiving evidence that unilateralism was a vote loser. Unable to influence the Party on this issue, by December 1986 Kinnock was suggesting that a non-nuclear policy would be a step towards developing the North Atlantic Treaty Organization's (NATO's) strategy and would release savings for social spending. There was little evidence that this cut any ice with the British public.

The first four years of Kinnock's leadership were thus eventful ones in which he tried to allay the fears of the British public that the Labour Party was irresponsible and too politically extreme. This strategy had been focused in particular against industrial action and the Militant Tendency faction of the Party. Nevertheless, Labour remained committed to unilateral disarmament and re-affirmed its belief in a non-nuclear defence policy at the 1985 Labour Party Conference. It also voted at the 1986 Conference for the removal of American nuclear bases from Britain. Even further, on March 1987, Kinnock was forced to commit a future Labour government to the instant withdrawal of the Polaris submarines from patrol.

Given these policies it was inevitable that the Labour Party would be subject to press criticism. Indeed, the press began a campaign against Labour which exposed to ridicule all its policies, including those connected with gay and Green issues, during the Greenwich parliamentary by-election of March 1987 when a hard-Left candidate was defeated by an SDP candidate. Labour's popularity declined and the campaign culminated in a leaked letter (March 1987) from Patricia Hewitt, Kinnock's press secretary, who stated that: 'It's obvious from our polling, as well as from the doorstep that ... the "loony" Labour left is taking its toll; the gays and lesbian issue is costing us dear amongst the pensioners, the fear of extremism and higher tax/rates is particularly prominent in the GLC area ... '. The omens were not good for the forthcoming general election.

As Labour geared up to the 1987 general election it began to focus upon the need to reverse the tax cuts of the Conservatives, which favoured the better-off sections of society, and to stimulate investment through a British Investment Bank. Such moves were outlined in its policy document *New Industrial Strength for Britain* (1987). In the election itself in June 1987, Labour conducted a most impressive political campaign with its manifesto *Britain Will Win*. Yet the Labour Party was, once again, defeated, winning only 30.8 per cent of the vote and 229 seats, although this was an improvement on the 1983 results.

Labour's campaign appears to have been derailed by two issues: defence and taxation. On defence, Labour was misrepresented as being committed to pacifism, with one advert depicting 'Labour's policy on arms' as a soldier with his hands in the air. On taxation, the Conservative Treasury Ministers costed Labour's election pledges at £35 billion, which would impose an enormous tax burden upon the British people.

Labour's election defeat speeded up the process of reform that led to the politics of New Labour and 'Blairism', even if Kinnock and Hattersley never contemplated going as far as Blair later did in rejecting the role of the state in maintaining full employment. Nevertheless, Neil Kinnock began a course of action between 1987 and 1992 which was designed to remove the image of Labour both as an extremist and as a divided party. The starting point, in many respects, was the Labour Party Conference of September 1987, which overwhelmingly endorsed Kinnock's decision to review the entire range of Labour's policies. The inevitable meaning of this was that more moderate policies would emerge. Indeed, the Policy Review was designed to create a more moderate social democratic party.

Four Policy Review reports were published between 1988 and 1991. The first, *Social Justice and Economic Efficiency* was a vague statement of aims and carried little impact. The second, *Meet the*

Challenge and Make the Change was submitted to, and accepted, by the 1989 Labour Party Conference. The third, *Looking to the Future* suggested a rightward move, as did the fourth, *Opportunity Britain*, which was presented to the 1991 Labour Party Conference. These four reports formed the basis for the Labour Party's 1992 Manifesto *It's Time to Get Britain Working Again*.

These reports, collectively, abandoned many of Labour's established shibboleths. Labour's commitment to public ownership was played down, particularly in *Meet the Challenge and Make the Change*, in which it was suggested that private industry would have an important part to play in Britain's future society. Labour's commitment to intervene in the workings of the City of London, forwarded by Bryan Gould who convened the economic group of the Policy Review, was also watered down when he was replaced as industry spokesman by Gordon Brown. There was going to be no future commitment by Labour to further nationalization, although there remained the problem of the privatization measures which the Thatcher and Major governments had introduced. *Looking to the Future* did suggest that Labour would take back ownership of the water companies but even this was reduced to the issue of control by the time of the 1992 Manifesto.

In effect, by 1992 Labour had abandoned the idea of state interventionism, and public ownership, and had also abandoned the idea of pumping money into and out of the economy in the classic Keynesian desire to respond to economic slumps and booms. It had linked itself instead to the need for fixed and high exchange rates as a means of regulating the economy, even with the deflationary pressures and consequences that had resulted in the Thatcher era. Labour's commitment to full employment was thus ended. Its commitment to social welfare provision was thus also played down. The general election of 1987, and additional research at that time, suggested that the British public were not prepared to accept high taxation. Therefore Labour's attempt to influence the supply of goods and services would have to be abandoned if it were to win wide political support. The Labour Party accepted this situation, which effectively meant limited commitment to increased family allowances and pensions at the 1992 general election. Public expenditure was to be stringently controlled as John Smith, Labour's Shadow Chancellor, was quoted in the *Guardian* of 2 October 1989: 'we can't spend what we haven't earned. We intend to earn it before we can spend it. That will be the guiding light of the next Labour government's economic policy'. Even the minimalist social-security welfare state that Britain had adopted was going to be restrained.

The Policy Review also tackled the thorny issues of trade unions and defence. On trade unionism, Labour had already indicated that some, perhaps much, of the Thatcher legislation would be retained and Tony Blair, who in October 1989 took over from Michael Meacher as front-bench spokesman on Employment and convenor of the industrial relations Policy Review, ensured that much of the legislation, including the banning of closed shops, would be retained whilst allowing picketing and secondary picketing under specifically legally-defined circumstances. The 1992 Labour Manifesto *It's Time to Get Britain Working Again* thus stated that 'there will be no return to the trade union legislation of the 1970s.... There will be no mass or flying pickets' (p. 11).

On defence, Kinnock ensured that the Policy Review Group was dominated by multilateralists and its report was compiled by Gerald Kaufmann, the Shadow Foreign Secretary. The Review suggested that Labour should drop its unilateral stance and Kinnock endorsed this, suggesting that he would resign if the new line were not supported at the Party Conference. The Conference of 1990 endorsed his position, stressing that Britain would reduce her nuclear capacity through multilateral agreements. The 1992 Manifesto confirmed this position, stating that as long as nuclear weapons still existed 'Labour will retain Britain's nuclear capability' (p. 26).

Between 1987 and 1992, then, the Labour Party had removed every major symbol of its former left-wing policies. Unilateralism was abandoned, trade unions would have to endure most of the Thatcherite controls, there was no longer going to be an extension of public ownership, and privatized industries would only be controlled, rather than re-nationalized. Even the welfare state could not expect to be expanded but was dependent upon the success of the British economy and the operation of market forces. Not surprisingly, there was strong reaction within the Party as these policies emerged.

Faced with the prospect of a right turn within Labour, Tony Benn challenged Kinnock for the leadership of the Party in October 1988. In an ill-matched contest, Kinnock won 88.63 per cent of the vote and Hattersley was also returned as Deputy Leader, with 66.82 per cent of the vote against John Prescott and Eric Heffer. Kinnock, and the Labour Party, were not going to be driven from a move rightward towards social democracy. Thereafter, the protest of the Labour Left was limited and Labour's moderation knew no bounds. In March 1990, during the campaign against the poll tax which led to anti-poll tax riots throughout Britain, Kinnock attacked the 'toy town revolutionaries' involved in such tactics. The more radical, and unsuccessful, days of the Foot leadership were felt to have passed.

Kinnock now took increasing control of the Party by centralizing its campaign management and communicating more effectively with the press. He also moved to ensure that MPs were no longer subject to the whims of an activist left-wing minority in their constituencies when facing re-selection by their constituencies. He had attempted to change the rules for the re-selection of MPs in 1984 and 1987, but was unsuccessful. As a result he compromised in 1987, winning from the 1987 Party Conference the decision that trade unions would exercise up to 40 per cent of the vote, depending upon the degree of union representation at the General Committee level, and that the rest of the vote would be based upon an individual ballot of the rank-and-file members. The influence of the Labour Left on the selection and re-selection of parliamentary candidates, and thus MPs, was therefore diminished. Eventually in 1990, because of the unwieldy nature of the system, the electoral college system for electing the Party Leaders was also abandoned at the Party Conference, although it was not replaced until 1993.

Kinnock also managed to get accepted the principle of 'one member, one vote' (OMOV). The NEC of the Labour Party suggested that the principle be used in the voting in the Leadership and Deputy Leadership contests in 1988 and recommended the principle in its own elections for its own constituency sections from 1989. What is clear is that Kinnock was able to push forward with his reforms to such an extent that the Labour Left became marginalized. Indeed, with the changes came an increasingly right-wing-dominated NEC which now supported Kinnock in a way in which its previously left-wing tendencies had not allowed it to operate between the late 1970s and the mid 1980s. The NEC of the Labour Party was operating once again in line with the Party Leadership and the Parliamentary Labour Party. Unified on organization, and unified on a more moderate policy, Labour now had a prospect of political success.

There were growing signs that Labour's strategy of moderation was working. Labour continued to do well in the municipal elections and, in May 1989, won 45 seats in the elections for the European Parliament, in contrast to the 31 seats won by the Conservatives. This was Thatcher's first major political reversal at the national level, and all the more surprising since Labour was still committed to its 1983 promise to withdraw from the European Economic Community (EEC). This was also at a time when Kinnock welcomed the EEC commitment to a social charter of rights for workers which had just been drafted by the French socialist Jacques Delors.

Nevertheless, Labour still lagged in the polls and, in September 1991, on the eve of the Labour Party Conference, there was much rumour among the Press that Kinnock was under pressure to resign in order to improve Labour's electoral prospects. Kinnock denied he was under any such pressures and instead prepared for the general election of 1992.

Since Labour had improved its position in the 1987 general election there was great optimism that the Party would end its political wilderness years at the 1992 general election. In March/April 1992 it issued its general election manifesto, *It's Time to Get Britain Working Again*, which promised an extra £1,000 million for the National Health Service (NHS), £600 million for education, increases in retirement pensions and child benefits, a minimum wage of £3.40 an hour, a 50 per cent higher rate of income tax, the abolition of the National Insurance ceiling, which would have greatly increased the National Insurance contributions of high earners, and the replacement of the House of Lords with an elected second chamber. Unfortunately for Labour it became embroiled in a debate about the costing of its reforms and the suggestion that it would have to raise taxes beyond its declared intent resulting in a 'tax bombshell'.

Nevertheless, the Labour Party was clearly in high spirits for the 1992 general election for it had removed its unpopular policies of nationalization and unilateral disarmament. The Liberal–SDP Alliance of 1987 had been engulfed by a rampant Green Party, which pushed it down to fourth in the opinion polls on the eve of the election. The time looked ripe for Labour's political revival. Yet the Party lost. It has been suggested that this defeat had little to do with Labour's Policy Review, for most electors recognized that 'Labour was now more moderate'. It has also been suggested that Kinnock's leadership was the reason for the defeat. According to one report: 'Mr Major did not win the election. Mr Kinnock lost it.' Another suggested that: 'Voters just did not believe Mr Kinnock was fit to run Britain', whilst yet another argued that the task of winning the election was just 'too much for a man who had to spend time inventing a new identity for himself'. Nonetheless, recent research indicates that there is little evidence to maintain that the quality, or perceived quality, of leadership has much to do with electoral success, for whilst the Labour Leadership can make some minor impact upon elections its influence is seldom decisive.

It is not easy to establish precisely why Labour lost. Perhaps it was to do with a diminished trade union and traditional working-class base for Labour, some minor uncertainty about Kinnock's leadership, or some concern about the extent to which Labour had become more moderate. Yet there were, possibly, other factors. Generally, the newspapers campaigned against Labour and exposed its shortcomings and mistakes. In particular, they made great play of the problems with the Labour Party's Shadow Budget, as already indicated, and campaigns such as the 'War of Jennifer's Ear', which focused upon the different treatment of two girls with the same problem under the NHS and private medicine, and the overconfident, and highly triumphalist, rally that was held at Sheffield Arena on 1 April 1992.

Yet media events, such as Jennifer's Ear and the Sheffield Arena rally, were topped by the *Sun*'s open advice, on 9 April, for the electors to vote for the Conservatives asking, 'in the event of a Labour victory will the last person to leave the UK please switch off the light'. Rupert Murdoch, owner of the paper most widely read by the working class, had declared strongly against Labour and certainly influenced the undecided voters. Indeed, the *Sun* claimed, on 10 April 1992, that it was '[t]he Sun wot won it'. It is uncertain whether this was the case but what is clear is that the Labour Party lost again, winning only 271 seats.

Although Kinnock's new policies were often criticized from within Labour, he had begun the process of rehabilitating the Party as a convincing alternative Party of government. Indeed, with the reaction against the poll tax debilitating Thatcher's Conservative government, Labour rose dramatically in the polls. Had there been a general election in 1990 Labour would probably have won. Unfortunately this was not to be, for John Major replaced Margaret Thatcher, was buoyed up by the war against Saddam Hussein, and went on to win the general election of 9 April 1992.

Kinnock did a remarkable job in restoring the fortunes of the Labour Party, now back from the political oblivion of 1983. However, he was greatly vilified in the press and in April 1992, after Labour's fourth defeat at the general elections, Kinnock decided to retire as Leader. Nevertheless, he had been an important transitional leader who was too closely identified with the old regime of pre-1990 Labour to have taken forward the new Labour Party he had effectively created. Subsequently, he retired from Parliament and has been involved with the European Commission.

See also: Blair, Foot, Keynes

Further reading

Drower, G., 1984, *Neil Kinnock: The Path to Leadership*, London: Weidenfeld & Nicolson.
Harris, R., 1984, *The Making of Neil Kinnock*, London: Faber.

Hughes, C. and Wintour, P., 1990, *Labour Rebuilt: The New Model Party*, London: Fourth Estate.
Jefferys, K. (ed.), 1999, *Leading Labour: From Keir Hardie to Tony Blair*, London: I. B. Tauris
Jones, E., 1994, *Neil Kinnock*, London: Hale.
Leapman, M., 1987, *Kinnock*, London: Unwin Hyman.
Morgan, K. O., 1987, *Labour People: Leaders and Lieutenants, Hardie to Kinnock*, Oxford: Oxford University Press.

GEORGE LANSBURY 1859–1940

George Lansbury was Leader of the Labour Party between 1932 and 1935, a prominent supporter of the women's suffrage movement, and a lifelong pacifist. He is closely associated with the belief that Britain must stand for the moral principle of opposing war but found his views to be anachronistic in the 1930s when European fascism and Hitler posed a threat to both European and world peace.

Lansbury was born on 22 February 1859. He was educated at an elementary school and left when he was very young, working in various jobs before becoming a railway worker at the age of fourteen. He married Bessie (Elizabeth Jane Brine) in 1883 and then emigrated to Queensland, Australia, in 1884 but returned the following year. He then began work in his father-in-law's timber mill. He became active in Liberal politics at that time, set up an Emigration Information Department in 1886 and quickly became a prominent public and political figure in the East End of London, acting as Liberal agent for the Bow parliamentary constituency.

In 1892 Lansbury joined the quasi-Marxist Social Democratic Federation (SDF), but had previously become a Christian Socialist in 1890. He became active in local municipal politics, becoming a member of the Poplar Board of Guardians in 1892 and a councillor for the recently created Poplar Borough of London in 1893; he subsequently became Mayor of Poplar in 1919. As a result of his expertise on the working of the Poor Laws, and the fact that he became a member of the Central (Unemployed) Body for London he was appointed a member of the Royal Commission on the Poor Laws, which sat between 1905 and 1909. When it finally reported he wrote and signed, along with Beatrice Webb, the Minority Report, which advocated the creation of government departments to deal with the aged, children, the unemployed, and other groups who fell under the Poor Laws. In the end, both the Majority Report, which advocated creating local Public Assistance Committees based upon local authorities to deal with the

154

poor, and the Minority Report were rejected as Asquith's pre-war Liberal governments offered social reforms to reduce the burden upon the Poor Laws. From 1909 until 1912 Lansbury was also a socialist member of the London County Council.

Lansbury's socialist and municipal activities nurtured his parliamentary ambitions. He unsuccessfully contested the Walworth parliamentary constituency for the SDF in 1895, and was defeated as the Socialist candidate for Bow in 1900. He was then defeated as Independent Labour Party (ILP) candidate for Middlesbrough in 1906, and again in January 1910. However, Lansbury eventually entered Parliament in December 1910, as Labour member for the Bow and Bromley constituency. Yet, as a keen supporter of the women's suffrage movement he decided to resign from his seat in 1912 and forced a by-election, focused upon women's suffrage, in which he was defeated. Now out of Parliament he was imprisoned for suffragette activity in 1912, but went on a hunger strike and was released.

Lansbury then turned his attentions to editing the *Daily Herald*, which he had helped form as a single-sheet strike bulletin for London printers in April 1912, which emerged to rival the official Labour paper the *Daily Citizen*. He became principal editor in October 1913, remaining so until 1922, and made it the most important and lively paper for the British Left. Indeed, he used this paper as a platform for his criticism of Britain's involvement in the First World War. After this he returned to the House of Commons as MP for Bow and Bromley, holding the seat until his death in 1940. During this phase of his political career, he refused the post of Minister of Transport in Ramsay MacDonald's first Labour government, since it did not carry with it a post in the Cabinet. However, he accepted the post of First Commissioner of Works, which did carry a Cabinet seat, in MacDonald's second Labour government of 1929–31. Indeed, it was solely because he was the only Labour Cabinet Minister to survive Labour's electoral defeat in 1931 that he eventually became Labour Leader. At first the post was held by Arthur Henderson, from 1931 to 1932, with Lansbury leading the Labour Party in the Commons. But with Henderson's resignation in October 1932, Lansbury succeeded to the post of Leader. He resigned from this post in 1935, making way for Clement Attlee, but then devoted all his time and energy to promoting the peace movement, meeting Adolf Hitler, Benito Mussolini, Franklin D. Roosevelt and Leon Blum, the French premier, in a determined but vain attempt to avoid the impending war. He died on 7 May 1940, at a point when the Labour Party was considering joining the wartime Coalition Government under the leadership of Winston Churchill.

Lansbury was a remarkable man and his career, already outlined, covered many aspects of the struggles of the early Labour movement. He played many vital roles in Labour's emergence as a vehicle for working-class ambitions. He is particularly well known for his association with the Poplar Board of Guardians, where he campaigned for the better treatment of both indoor and outdoor paupers. He was active in forming the Laindon and Hollesley Bay farm colonies to which the Poplar poor might be sent to labour. In 1921, he led passive resistance to the introduction of 'precepts' (local taxes) to the London County Council. Lansbury argued that these precepts were a heavy burden to an area with high poverty and called for an arrangement whereby the rates of all London boroughs would be equalized in such a way that the rich boroughs would effectively subsidize the high level of unemployment in the poor ones. This was illegal and the Lloyd George Coalition Government imprisoned some of the Poplar councillors and Lansbury, in September 1921, for contempt in not paying the precept but using it to support the unemployed on generous allowances. In the end, however, the councillors remained firm and were eventually released by the Lloyd George government on 12 October. From then onwards 'Poplarism' became common currency, denoting a council that was unwilling to be restrained in its financial spending on, and commitment to, the poor.

Normally, however, Lansbury was not so successful. In 1912, as already indicated, he lost his seat when he resigned to force a parliamentary by-election at Bow and Bromley over the question of women's suffrage. He rather hoped that the Labour Party would fall into line with his ideas and withdraw support from the Liberal government until the women's franchise was granted. In fact, despite gaining some support for his ideas from James Keir Hardie, the Labour Party did not agree to his policy and he resigned, not to return until after the First World War.

Becoming Leader of the Labour Party in 1932 did not bring him great success. After the defeat of the Labour Party in the 1931 general election he led a party in the House of Commons which could muster only forty-six MPs and six other unendorsed MPs. He hoped to shape it into a party of peace, advocating that it organize an international conference of the 'have' and 'have not' nations. His idea was that nations such as Britain would divest themselves of colonies and reduce their armed forces to the level allowed to Germany under the arrangements of the Treaty of Versailles, agreed at the end of the First World War. Indeed, on 8 April 1932 *The Times* quotes him as stating of the Disarmament Conference that he did not think it would 'be of any service unless it [came] down to the question of total and complete abolition of all national armaments'. He even argued that only if Britain disarmed completely would there be no possibility of another war. In an age affected by the loss of life in the First World War, 'the Great War', such views had a resonance, but after Hitler's rise to power in Germany in January 1933, and with Germany's moves towards rearmament, Lansbury's views became unacceptable to most of the British people. Lansbury's pacifist views were rejected by the Labour Party Conference in 1935, when Ernest Bevin of the Transport and General Workers' Union brushed pacifism aside and demanded sanctions against Italian expansionism in Abyssinia. Lansbury's speech had ended with the suggestion that peace must be the ultimate goal: 'This is our faith, this is where we stand, and, if necessary, this is where we will die.' Bevin responded with a personal attack on Lansbury for 'taking [his] conscience round from body to body asking to be told what [he] ought to do with it'. Bevin continued to suggest that Lansbury was hardly the innocent in politics and reminded his audience that '[i]t was not Keir Hardie who formed [the Labour Party], it grew out of the bowels of the Trade Union Congress'. The resolution in favour of sanctions was passed by 2,168,000 votes to 102,000. This led to Lansbury's resignation as Labour Leader on 8 October 1935, despite the Parliamentary Labour Party (PLP) asking him by, 37 votes to 7, to stay on. He retained his seat in the 1935 general election but then refused to stand for the PLP executive in the new Parliament.

From then onwards Lansbury campaigned for his world conference and pacifism. In 1935 he became the President of the Peace Pledge Union and met with all the major world leaders, except for Joseph Stalin. He welcomed, as did many others at the time, Neville Chamberlain's September 1938 Munich Agreement with Hitler which bought peace at the cost of guaranteeing German rights to part of Czechoslovakia.

Lansbury stood out as a man of principle, prepared to sacrifice personal gain in order to advocate the causes of the poor, women's suffrage, and pacifism. However, such a strong faith in principles meant that he was unlikely to act as a Labour Leader for any length of time. He had been thrust into such a role by force of circumstances but, at the age of 73 he was never going to be more than a stopgap before he was forced to retire at the age of 76 to prepare the way for a younger man. Like Ramsay MacDonald, one of his predecessors as Labour Leader, he had put principle before Party – something he had done often throughout his life.

See also: Attlee, Bevin, MacDonald, Mosley

Further reading

Holman, B., 1990, *Good Old George: The Life of George Lansbury*, Oxford: Lion Publishing.

Jefferys, K. (ed.), 1999, *Leading Labour: From Keir Hardie to Tony Blair*, London: I. B. Tauris.

Lansbury, G., 1935, *Looking Backwards – and Forwards*, London and Glasgow: Blackie & Son.

Postgate, R., 1951, *The Life of George Lansbury*, London: Longmans, Green & Co.

Schneer, J., 1990, *George Lansbury*, Manchester: Manchester University Press.

ANDREW BONAR LAW 1858–1923

Andrew Bonar Law was Prime Minister for barely six months, in 1922 and 1923, but, nevertheless, was a tremendously important political figure in the decade leading up to that point. In particular, he became the Conservative Leader in October 1911, revitalizing and reorganizing the failing Conservative Party, and was an important supporter of Lloyd George from 1916 until 1922, when he replaced him as Prime Minister. Bonar Law is also the only person of colonial birth and upbringing to become British Prime Minister, and the first politician from a relatively humble, middle–class, background to rise to the top of the 'greasy pole' of Conservative politics. Indeed, whilst he was Robert Blake's 'Unknown Prime Minister', he was, nevertheless, seminal in the revival of the Conservative Party.

Bonar Law was born at Kingston, New Brunswick, Canada, on 16 September, 1858, the fourth child of the Rev. James Law, a Presbyterian minister, and Elizabeth Kidman. His father was from Portuish in North Antrim, Ireland and returned there in 1877. However, Bonar Law himself was educated at Gilbertfield School, Hamilton, before leaving Canada in 1870 to join his mother's prosperous family business connection in Glasgow and Helenburgh, and he completed his education at Glasgow High School. In 1874 he joined a merchant bank owned by his brothers, and in 1885, at the age of twenty–seven, he bought a partnership into the iron firm of William Jacks. In 1891 he married Annie Pitcairn, who died in 1909.

Bonar Law began his parliamentary career as Unionist MP for Blackfriars Glasgow in 1900. He then lost this seat in the general election of January 1906. In May 1906 he was returned for the 'safe' seat of Dulwich, Camberwell. By this time however he had become the leader of the Unionist section of the Party and he gave up

Dulwich, Camberwell to contest the much more marginal Manchester North West seat in December 1910, in the Unionist free trade heartland. His move misfired but he was returned for Bootle, also in Lancashire, at a parliamentary by-election in March 1911. Finally, he contested and won the Glasgow Central seat in 1918, representing it until his death in 1923.

In politics Bonar Law was identified with the two vital issues of tariff reform and Ulster Unionism. The latter issue arose from his Irish Presbyterian background, whilst the tariff reform issue arose from the fact that, as a Canadian by birth, he was attracted by Joseph Chamberlain's Imperial Preference tariff arrangements. As a businessman he was fully aware also of the imperfect nature of the free trade policy and believed that the revenue from protective measures could be used to finance the social legislation needed to tackle the poor social conditions of the British working class. Driven by this interest, his maiden speech, in February 1901, was in defence of Joseph Chamberlain, Cecil Rhodes and British ambitions in Africa, while on 22 April 1902 he spoke in favour of Sir Michael Hicks-Beach's duty on corn.

Bonar Law was a talented politician and soon came to the forefront of political decision-making. He became Parliamentary Secretary at the Board of Trade, which placed him an ideal position from which to press for imperial preference. He spoke in favour of the Sugar Bounty Convention and supported Joseph Chamberlain's Imperial Preference campaign when it was launched in May 1903. The Liberal landslide of the 1906 general election saw him lose his seat but he was quickly returned for the 'safe' Dulwich seat in May 1906. With the illness and retirement of Joseph Chamberlain, Bonar Law and Austen Chamberlain emerged at the head of the 157 Unionist MPs who dominated the much-diminished Conservative and Unionist Party of that time.

Although Bonar Law was considered an extreme tariff reformer, a 'wholehogger', he was also a pragmatic man and advocated the holding of a referendum on tariff reform. He also acknowledged that there was no possibility of removing the 1911 Parliament Act, passed by the Liberals to restrict the legislative blocking abilities of the House of Lords. Having been returned to Parliament in 1911, after a brief absence, he was elected Leader of the Unionists in November, following the resignation of Arthur Balfour. Yet, since the Unionists were still divided between the protectionists and free traders, the potential for electoral disaster existed. Ever the pragmatist, Bonar Law dropped the commitment to the referendum pledge at a Shadow Cabinet meeting in April 1912 and, though the same meeting indicated the need for a food tax, accepted that this issue would have to be submitted independently to the electorate. Thus, tariff reform became rather less important to the Unionist cause.

Bonar Law did maintain his commitment to tariff reform but he now placed much greater emphasis upon the maintenance of the Union with Ireland to keep his forces together in their desire to defeat the Liberal Party. He pressed the issue of Ulster Unionism from 1911 until the wartime 'all-party' truce began in July 1914. He endorsed the Ulster Unionist demand that Ireland remain part of Britain, both in his speeches and in his support for the military-style drilling which took place at the Balmoral demonstration on 9 April 1912 and for the Blenheim Pledge of 29 July 1912, when he could not conceive of limits to the lengths he would go to protect Ulster. Although he seemed to be contemplating the possibility of some type of direct attack upon parliamentary sovereignty, and the possibility of civil war, he was prepared to compromise, contemplating the prospect of some form of exclusion for Ulster from any Home Rule Bill for Ireland. These issues dominated the events of early 1914, when there were discussions on how the Army Act could be amended to prevent military intervention in Ulster.

It was only the outbreak of the First World War in August 1914 that put an end to the increasingly internecine conflict within British politics, which was still evident in the Buckingham Palace talks of 21 and 23 July 1914 between the Conservative Party and the Liberal government. Nevertheless, within six weeks of the outbreak of the war, on 15 September, the truce was temporarily halted. Asquith had put forward the third Home Rule Bill on the statutes, but suspended its implementation until the end of the war. Bonar Law reacted badly, leading his Party out of the Commons. In the wake of the Easter Rising he was also involved in negotiations organized by Lloyd George to find a settlement. However, since these talks failed he was not placed in the embarrassing position of dividing his Party. He came to accept that Home Rule would occur and, therefore, in 1920, supported the fourth Home Rule Bill – the Government of Ireland Bill. He gave the Anglo-Irish Treaty of December 1921 his support, comfortable in the belief that the Northern Unionists would not be coerced and, indeed, would be guaranteed in what became Northern Ireland

The conduct of the First World War was the other major issue that dominated Bonar Law's political career. He led the patriotic opposition to the Liberal government from August 1914 to May 1915, before he was drawn into a Coalition Government under Asquith, acting as Secretary of State for the Colonies. Bonar Law continued to lead the Conservative and Unionist Party, although he was under serious attack from Edward Carson, and became increasingly disillusioned at Asquith's running of the war. When Asquith resigned, on 5 December 1916, Bonar Law advocated his replacement by David Lloyd George, for whom he became Deputy Prime Minister. Bonar Law also accepted the post of Chancellor of the Exchequer. From then onwards, he acted as Lloyd George's junior, retaining the post of Chancellor until January 1919 when he became Leader of the Commons until March 1921.

As Chancellor of the Exchequer, Bonar Law was a member of the War Cabinet, mainly responsible for organizing the financing of the war effort. He replaced short-term loans with long-term war loans, which raised £2,000 million between January and March 1917. In October 1917 he announced the issue of war bonds for an unlimited amount, which was also successful. He was barely involved in the detailed administration of Britain during the First World War but gave Lloyd George his strong support at times when the latter's authority was challenged.

At the end of the war, Bonar Law and the Conservative and Unionist Party could have won the 1918 general election, given that the Liberal Party was divided and the Labour Party was still emerging. Yet Bonar Law decided to support the continuation of a Coalition Government under the premiership of Lloyd George. Why he did this has been subject to speculation, ranging from the fact that the Coalition had won the First World War, to the possibility that the Coalition would ensure that the Liberals remained divided, and the fact that the 1918 Representation of the People's Act had tripled the electorate. Indeed, Martin Pugh maintains that the alliance of the Conservative Party and Lloyd George 'provided the surest means of effecting the transition from war to peace on the basis of a vast new electorate' (Pugh, 1982, p. 175). In the event, this was confirmed when the Coalition Government won 474 seats, and thus had a majority of 252 seats.

In the new Coalition Government, Bonar Law became Lord Privy Seal but remained Leader of the House. He was one of the signatories of the Treaty of Versailles, on 28 June 1919, although he played little part in the negotiations. Indeed, Bonar Law appears to have been withdrawing from the highest level of British politics. This may have because he had had to endure a number of personal tragedies, including the death of his two sons in the First World War in 1917, and was now suffering from ill health. He decided to retire as Conservative Leader in 1921, although he remained an MP.

In October 1922 the Conservative Party, despite the opposition of Austen Chamberlain, its new Leader, decided to withdraw its support for Lloyd George, over a range of policy issues and scandals. Lloyd George resigned and Bonar Law, at once re-instated as the Leader of the Unionist Party, agreed on 23 October 1922 to allow his name to be put forward for Prime Minister. His premiership lasted little more than six months and his government failed to tackle the four main issues of the day: American loans; German reparations; high unemployment; and a shortage of housing. He resigned on 19 May 1923, suffering from cancer of the throat, and died on 30 October 1923.

Bonar Law's career was always marked by the impression that he lacked ambition. Yet above all, and despite his rhetoric which made him a trenchant Unionist, he was a pragmatic politician. He was a most effective Chancellor of the Exchequer, a powerful Leader of the Unionist Party, and a formidable Leader of the House of Commons. He could also be ruthless, if needed, being prepared to ditch the Coalition Government in December 1915 and again in October 1922. He was certainly one of those politicians who combined the almost contradictory tendencies of ambition and deference. Dubbed the 'Unknown Prime Minister' by Robert Blake, Bonar Law's lasting contribution to politics is that he reorganized the Conservative and Unionist Party on the eve of the First World War when it looked as though they, rather than the Liberals, might disintegrate.

See also: Chamberlain (Joseph), Lloyd George

Further reading

Blake, R., 1955, *The Unknown Prime Minister: The Life and Times of Andrew Bonar Law, 1858–1923*, London: Eyre & Spottiswoode.

Blake, R., 1985, *The Conservative Party from Peel to Thatcher*, London: Fontana.

Pugh, M., 1982, *The Making of Modern British Politics 1867–1939*, Oxford: Basil Blackwell.

Ramsden, J., 1978, *A History of the Conservative Party. Vol 2: The Age of Balfour and Baldwin, 1902–1940*, London: Longman.

DAVID LLOYD GEORGE (FIRST EARL LLOYD-GEORGE OF DWYFOR) 1863–1945

David Lloyd George was one of the most important British politicians of the early twentieth century. Having earned his reputation initially as a Welsh non-conformist radical it was his inspirational role in shaping the Liberal social reforms of 1906 to 1914 and his wartime premiership that earned him lasting admiration. Nevertheless, he earned the odium of those who saw him as responsible for splitting the Liberal Party in 1916 and causing its political decline. He was also a man of many political contradictions: identified with the Liberal Party he advocated centre party politics driven by vital issues; opposed to the Boer War he was a 'war-monger' during the First World War; and opposed to the privileges of the House of Lords between 1909 and 1911 he was ennobled in 1945. Indeed, Lloyd George was a truly dominating, controversial, and inconsistent politician.

David Lloyd George was born in Chorlton-upon-Medlock near Manchester on 17 January 1863, the second child of William George and Elizabeth Lloyd. His father, a school teacher, died in 1864 and he was adopted by his uncle, Richard Lloyd, a master shoemaker and Baptist lay preacher. Raised as a son by 'Uncle Lloyd', he always used the double surname. He was raised as a Baptist in rural north Wales, near Criccieth, but was educated at the Anglican Llanystumdwy National School. He was then apprenticed as a clerk to a law firm in neighbouring Portmadoc and was eventually licensed as a solicitor in 1884, going into the business of his brother William George. In 1888 Lloyd George married the wealthy Margaret Owen of Criccieth, a devout non-conformist who raised her five children in Criccieth whilst her husband philandered, with Frances Stevenson, in London. Nonetheless, their marriage lasted until her death in 1941.

Lloyd George's political career began in 1890 when he was returned as MP for Caernarvon and he continued to represent that seat until 1945. His early political reputation rested upon his attempt to disestablish the Welsh (Anglican) Church, Welsh Home Rule, and the local-option arrangement for the prohibition of drink. However, he eventually abandoned purely Welsh issues and his commitment to non-conformity (he was elected President of the Baptist Union in 1908) did not much survive the First World War. His political profile rose when he was associated with Sir Henry Campbell-Bannerman and that section of the Liberal Party which deplored the Boer War and rejected British involvement in it, since the war was seen to be both imperialistic and expensive. Lloyd George's career progressed further when he led the Liberal campaign against the 1902 Education Act which removed the *ad hoc* school boards and replaced them with local education authorities (LEAs), and further permitted voluntary schools (such as those owned by the Church of England and the Catholic Church) to receive financial aid. Indeed, he led a protest whereby many non-conformists, particularly in Wales, refused to pay the school rates proportion of their local rates.

Lloyd George became President of the Board of Trade when a Liberal government was formed in December 1905, ahead of the Liberal landslide general election of January 1906. For the next two years he and Winston Churchill worked towards social reform. Faced with the need to lighten the crippling burden of poverty being imposed upon the Poor Laws they introduced legislation to reduce that burden, providing old age pensions (1908 Act), employment exchanges for the unemployed from 1909 onwards, and both health and unemployment insurance through the National Insurance Act of 1911. The rising social and political challenge of the newly formed Labour Party and the radical ideas of social harmony, advocated by the 'New Liberals' may also have encouraged moves in this direction. Lloyd George introduced his 'People's Budget' in 1909, which raised taxes upon the rich to pay for the government's financial contribution to these reforms, a move which provoked a strong reaction from the House of Lords which rejected the Budget. Two general elections were fought in 1910 to resolve the issue but it was not until Lloyd George and the Liberal government threatened to create sufficient Liberal peers to force through the legislation that the Lords capitulated and accepted the Parliament Act of 1911 which stripped the House of Lords of the right of its ultimate veto over financial legislation. Lloyd George described the end of the veto as 'the dream of Liberalism for a generation realized at last'. Nevertheless, during the crisis he had been prepared to consider the need for compromise and was actively engaged in considering the need to form a coalition government.

At this time Lloyd George also became concerned about Britain's foreign policy. Although he had gained something of a reputation for pacifism during the Boer War he was now very concerned about German aggression. In 1911 he warned the Germans of the danger of war. He also became concerned at the development of 'National Efficiency' and sought cross-party unity on this issue. However, his political career was almost ended in 1912 when he became involved in the Marconi scandal, in which he was accused of buying Marconi shares on the basis of his inside knowledge of government contracts with the company.

Lloyd George's political reputation was revived during the First World War (1914–18), and he was later referred to as 'The Man Who Won the War'. Indeed, in 1914 he helped ensure that there was unity within the Liberal Party on the war issue and he was instrumental in ensuring that the Coalition Government was formed in May 1915, with H. H. Asquith as its Prime Minister. He himself was appointed Minster of Munitions, and removed trade union restrictions and introduced women as dilutees (in craft trades) and substitutes (in less skilled and unskilled occupations) to increase production and to increase manpower for the army. However, he became particularly hostile towards the policy of slow attrition being fought on the Western Front and with the military fiasco at Gallipoli in 1915. As a result he was increasingly at odds with Asquith and even more belligerent as the possibility of peace negotiations was discussed following the enormous loss of life at the Battle of the Somme in 1916. Lloyd George now became more determined that there should be a military 'knockout blow' against the Germans on the Western Front. He contemplated resignation in December 1916 but, with the support of some Liberals and the Conservative Party, he was appointed Prime Minister shortly after Asquith resigned in December 1916. Whether this was a result of Asquith miscalculating that his resignation would unite the government behind him, whether he had a nervous breakdown, or whether there was a conspiracy to topple Asquith, is still open to question. Whatever the reason for the change, the impact of Lloyd George's assumption of the premiership was twofold: it changed the pattern of the war and it divided the Liberal Party.

Both A. J. P. Taylor and John Grigg have suggested that Lloyd George brought about a revolution in government during the war and his war memoirs, written up in six volumes in the 1930s, tended to stress this view. As Minister of Munitions he greatly extended the role of the state. As Prime Minister he created a small War Committee to more effectively organize the nation's manpower and war effort. He enlisted the help of leading British businessmen in the new government departments he created in 1917. He appealed to the Trades Union Congress, outlining his war aims to them on 5 January 1918. And he organized reconstruction committees to discuss post-war developments. Indeed, when the Armistice came on 11 November 1918 it appeared that Lloyd George had reached the zenith of his political power, an impression that seemed to be endorsed by his political victory at the general election of December 1918 and the creation of a Conservative-dominated post-war Coalition Government of which he was Prime Minister.

Shortly afterwards Lloyd George was involved in the Paris Peace Conference, which produced the Treaty of Versailles settlement and attempted to play down French insistence upon large reparation payments from Germany. He accepted the ideas of the American President Woodrow Wilson, who was at that time promoting the idea of an international peacekeeping organization, later to become the League of Nations. Subsequently, he was involved in a succession of international conferences on European recovery; helped to establish a Jewish homeland in Palestine; and attempted to restore trading relations with Russia after ending the military intervention against the communist regime that had occurred at the end of the First World War. His Coalition Government also introduced legislation on housing and became involved in industrial relations, particularly the miners' strike of 1921.

There is no doubt that Lloyd George was an immensely successful wartime leader and a prominent and respected post-war leader. Nevertheless, he relied upon Conservative support, which began to evaporate after the war. In particular, he signed the Irish treaty of 1921 which gave Dominion status to Catholic-dominated southern Ireland whilst giving Protestants in the northern six counties something equating to Home Rule within Britain. This annoyed many Conservative MPs who were opposed to the Irish settlement and who were alienated further by his controversial involvement in the sale of honours.

Inevitably, Lloyd George felt himself to be a prisoner of the Conservatives. It was they who had ensured that he became Prime Minister in the first place and it was the body of the Liberal Party, led by Asquith, who were his main political opponents. The Maurice debate of May 1918, in which Lloyd George dismissed the accusation that the government was supplying misleading statistics on the level of armed forces in France, demonstrated to him that whilst he had some Liberal support it was the Conservatives that carried him through. The December 1918 'Coupon' election, so named because some 150 Liberal candidates were 'couponed', or committed, to support or at least not to oppose Lloyd George on any major issue in the immediate post-war government, reminded him that it was the largely victorious Conservatives and the wartime situation which permitted him to continue in office. Feeling vulnerable Lloyd George attempted to build up his own National Liberal Party, the money for which would come from the sale of honours and the building up of the Lloyd George Fund. Nevertheless, the Asquithian Liberal Party maintained its hold on the Liberal electorate and its constituency organization whilst Lloyd George's National Liberals had money but little or no organization. Therefore, when the Conservatives came to remove Lloyd George as Prime Minister in October 1922, in a move supported by Stanley Baldwin and other junior ministers who feared that the Chanak incident (in which Lloyd George seemed to support Greece against Turkey and involved British troops in keeping the peace) might lead Britain to war against Turkey, Lloyd George lacked any real party base and was unable to resist.

Many contemporary Liberal politicians attributed the inter-war problems of the Liberal Party to Lloyd George's actions in becoming Prime Minister in 1916, and to the Liberal split which resulted. Many historians have also claimed the same. Although it is not at all clear that the Liberal Party would have survived as a major party in the face of the combined challenge of the Labour and Conservative parties, it is clear that the Liberal Party split at least hastened its decline and that this split continued to undermine the Party during the inter-war years. Attempts to bring the Asquithian and Lloyd George Liberals together in 1923 were half-hearted, even though they worked together, with two headquarters, in the 1923 general election. The 1924 general election, forced upon the first, and minority, Labour government by the withdrawal of Liberal support, was a disaster for the Liberal Party which was reduced to a rump of forty MPs. It forced Lloyd George to attempt to re-organize the Liberal Party but the schisms of the past meant that there was much resistance within the Party to his ideas and little significant improvement in the Party's position.

Lloyd George used his political funds to finance the London newspaper the *Daily Chronicle*, and to finance a number of Liberal books, including the Liberal Yellow Books, on the coal and agricultural industries and on industrial reconstruction, some of them with the aid of the famous economist John Maynard Keynes. Having effectively become Leader of the Liberal Party in October 1926, on Asquith's retirement, Lloyd George pushed forward with his policy document *Britain's Industrial Future* (1928) which became the basis of the 1929 general election document *We Can Conquer Unemployment*. Through these documents Lloyd George committed the Liberal Party to use the 'idle balances' in the banks to pay for a wide programme of structural rebuilding and investment in Britain, to enable Britain to expand out of slump and 'conquer unemployment'. Admirably Keynesian in style, this policy saw the Liberals recover some political ground in an election which saw the return of the second, again minority, Labour government, which was supported by the Liberals for more than two years.

Seriously ill in 1931, with a prostate gland problem, Lloyd George effectively abandoned the Liberal leadership at the time of the August crisis, which saw the end of the Labour government and the formation of the National Government led by Ramsay MacDonald. Sir John Simon and Sir Herbert Samuel, representing the Right and the Left of the Party, respectively, entered the National Government but Lloyd George stayed out. Within a year Samuel, and the free trade section of the Party, had left although Simon remained. Indeed, by the mid 1930s the Liberal Party was divided between the protectionist Simonites, in the National Government, the free traders led by Samuel, and the Lloyd Georgeites, mainly the family and friends of Lloyd George.

By now rather an effete political figure, Lloyd George did attempt to develop a new political party. In the late 1920s he had discussed with Philip Snowden, of the Labour Party, the possibility of creating a new party of the centre. In 1934 and 1935 he revived the idea, once again with Snowden who had left the Labour Party in 1931. They both worked together to develop what became Lloyd George's 'New Deal' based upon Roosevelt's New Deal. However, the policies failed to attract electoral support and in the 1935 general election the Lloyd George Liberals were reduced to a mere four MPs.

Apart from writing his memoirs on the First World War, Lloyd George attempted to act as the independent and experienced international statesman, visiting Hitler in 1936, advocating re-armament, supporting the Republicans during the Spanish Civil War, and opposing Neville Chamberlain's appeasement policies. When the Second World War began he advocated Britain negotiating a peace with Germany because of Britain's ill-preparedness for war, and he later refused a place in the Cabinet of Winston Churchill and the offer of becoming British Ambassador to the United States. Instead he advised Churchill until 1943, when his health began to fail him. That same year he married Frances Stevenson (1888–1972) his long-time secretary and mistress, his wife Margaret having died in 1941. He died of cancer on 26 March 1945, shortly after being raised to the House of Lords as Earl Lloyd George of Dwyfor.

David Lloyd George was both a colourful and an accomplished politician who in a recent poll of political commentators was regarded, along with Winston Churchill and Clement Attlee, as one of the three most successful twentieth-century prime ministers. His work in creating the pre-1914 Liberal welfare state marks him out as a formidable politician, and his premiership during the First World War brought about fundamental changes in the running of governments as well as earning him the accolade 'The Man Who Won The War'. Nevertheless, to Liberals he seemed to be an untrustworthy defender of their principles and was considered by many to be the reason for their political decline. The problem is that whilst he sought to be a politician of issues rather than of party, he was unable to create the broad-based coalitions that he sought. In the end, he relied upon the Conservatives to continue as Prime Minister between 1918 and 1922 and when his value was spent he was discarded. Having reached his political zenith in 1918 he was politically burnt out by 1922, although he remained one of the few politicians with the imagination to tackle the vital inter-war issue of unemployment.

See also: Asquith, Baldwin, Churchill, Eden, Macmillan

Further reading

Grigg, J. (ed.), 1985, *Home Front and Foreign Fields: British Social and Military Experience in the First World War*, London: Methuen.
Morgan, K., 1974, *Lloyd George*, London: Weidenfeld & Nicolson; 1922, Oxford: Clarendon
Packer, I., 1998, *Lloyd George*, Basingstoke: Macmillan.
Pugh, M., 1988, *Lloyd George*, London: Longman.
Taylor, A. J. P., 1965, *English History 1914–45*, Oxford: Clarendon.
Turner, J., 1992, *British Politics and the Great War: Coalition and Conflict 1915–1918*, New Haven and London: Yale University Press.
Wrigley, C., 1992, *Lloyd George*, Oxford: Blackwell.

JAMES RAMSAY MACDONALD 1866–1937

No twentieth-century British political leader has been more reviled than Ramsay MacDonald, Britain's first Labour Prime Minister. He was Prime Minister in 1924 and again between 1929 and 1931. However, his decision to offer the resignation of the second Labour government and to accept the King's commission to form a National Government during the financial crisis of August 1931 provoked much animosity among his former supporters and sustained the myth that he had planned to ditch the second Labour government all along. It has long been an axiom that his actions in 1931 marked him as a traitor, and William Lawther MP remarked that MacDonald was 'bereft of any public decency'. To many Labour activists, the man who created the Labour Party had helped to destroy it as a political force in the 1930s. His reputation was thus one of a traitor until, in more recent years, David Marquand and Duncan Tanner revived his reputation and assessed his very considerable contribution to the growth of the Labour Party.

MacDonald was born at Lossiemouth in Scotland on 12 October 1866, the illegitimate son of Anne Ramsay and, possibly, John MacDonald, a ploughman. He was educated at a local school and expected to become a teacher but, in the 1880s, took up various clerical posts in Bristol and London.

MacDonald acquired wide political experience between 1885 and

1892. He joined the Social Democratic Federation (SDF), a quasi-Marxist organization, whilst he lived in Bristol, was employed by Thomas Lough, a Liberal Radical MP, and circulated in socialist circles. He had ambitions of becoming a Liberal MP but his candidature for Southampton was thwarted in 1894 and he turned, instead, to the Independent Labour Party (ILP), the first major socialist party to be committed to electoral politics, in July 1894 becoming the ILP and Labour Electoral Association candidate in Southampton, on whose behalf he was thoroughly trounced in the 1895 general election.

During the early 1890s MacDonald was introduced to Sidney Webb and joined the Fabian Society, a body of largely middle-class socialists committed to gradual social change through parliamentary and municipal politics. MacDonald acted as a Fabian lecturer in 1892, touring South Wales, the Midlands and the North East. In 1896 and 1897 he was also a member of the Rainbow Circle, which first met in the Rainbow Tavern, Fleet Street, London, and brought together some collectivist Liberals such as Herbert Samuel, who believed that the old Liberal Party was about to disintegrate. The group published papers and, briefly, the *Progressive Review*, in the hope of encouraging the formation of a new centre party in British politics. This desire, as well as MacDonald's interest in foreign policy, were two abiding passions which MacDonald pursued throughout his political career.

Marriage to Margaret Gladstone in November 1896 provided MacDonald with the financial security he needed to develop his political career, since Margaret brought with her a settlement of up to £300 per year. The couple moved to 3 Lincoln Inn Fields, London (a building which still has no plaque to MacDonald and the Labour Party), which was later to be a base for the Labour Representation Committee (LRC), an alliance of socialists and trade unionists later renamed the Labour Party, in its formative years. MacDonald's married life was short-lived for Margaret died on 8 September 1911, although she bore MacDonald six children.

MacDonald's career began to blossom in the 1890s. He joined the Executive Committee of the Fabian Society in 1894 and sat on the National Administrative Committee of the ILP in 1896. He remained a prominent member of the ILP until the First World War, often acting as Chairman, or Secretary. Thereafter, he drifted away from the Party, being particularly at odds with it in 1926 and 1927 over its impractical and controversial 'Socialism in Our Time' campaign, although he did not formally resign until May 1930. His contribution to the ILP would fill most lifetimes but his real claim to fame arose from the fact that he was largely responsible for the early development of the Labour Party.

The LRC was formed in February 1900 and formally changed its name to the Labour Party at the beginning of 1906. MacDonald was Secretary and Chairman until 1914 and was Chairman of the Parliamentary Labour Party (PLP) from 1911 to 1914. From the start, he was committed to winning trade union support for the embryonic organization and was helped in this respect by the attack upon trade unions funds represented by the Taff Vale Judgment of 1901. Yet such support only emerged slowly and, with only four MPs in 1903, MacDonald embarked upon a series of eight secret meetings with Jesse Herbert, confidential secretary to Herbert Gladstone, the Liberal Chief Whip, to arrange the infamous 'Lib–Lab' pact of 1903. This allowed the Labour Party candidates a straight run against the Conservatives in about thirty parliamentary seats in return for a similar arrangement for the Liberals. As a result at the January 1906 general election only five of the twenty-nine successful LRC candidates faced Liberal opposition.

The general election result was a personal triumph for MacDonald who was able to run a Party which now had its own Parliamentary Party, initially led by James Keir Hardie, although led by MacDonald himself from 1911 to 1914. MacDonald also helped to steer the Party in a gradualist, and eventually socialist, direction by creating a Socialist Library to which he contributed his own books, such as *Socialism and Society* (1905) and *Socialism and Government* (1909). The dominating theme of his work was that a form of Social Darwinism ensured that private organizations would get bigger, that the state would have to intervene, and that socialism would emerge from the success, not the failure, of capitalism. Because of the influence of MacDonald and the Webbs during the First World War, these essentially Fabian views became the defining influence in the socialism espoused by the Labour Party after 1918.

From 1906 until 1918, MacDonald was MP for Leicester, sometimes Secretary of the Labour Party and, for nearly four years, Chairman of the PLP. However, he was strongly criticized for helping lead the Labour Party and the PLP into alliance with the Liberal Party. Nonetheless, his reputation for radical socialism was restored, briefly, by his opposition to Britain's involvement in the First World War. This led to a venomous attack on him by the British press, the most notable one being by Horatio Bottomley's attack in *John Bull*, in which the editor published a copy of MacDonald's birth certificate revealing MacDonald's illegitimacy and asserted that MacDonald was both an impostor and a traitor and should be taken to the Tower of London and shot at dawn. Not surprisingly, MacDonald's political stand on the war led to the loss of his Leicester parliamentary seat in the 1918 general election.

In the immediate post-war years, relieved of his parliamentary duties, MacDonald concentrated his efforts on building up the Labour Party. However, he was returned to Parliament as MP for Aberavon in 1922 and, shortly afterwards, became Leader of the PLP, winning narrowly over J. R. Clynes by 61 votes to 57. When Stanley Baldwin failed to win support for his protectionist measures in the 1923 general election, MacDonald was invited to form the first Labour government at the beginning of 1924. It was a minority government and lasted little more than ten months, although it was the first Labour government and thus an important landmark in the rise of the Labour Party. Within this government, MacDonald took the post of Foreign Secretary, becoming the first Prime Minister to assume the role since Robert Cecil, the third Marquess of Salisbury. The government achieved little other than the introduction of the Wheatley Housing Act of 1924, which provided government subsidies on a large scale for the construction of municipal housing.

The defeat of the first Labour government at the general election of 1924 occurred in the climate of the infamous 'Zinoviev Letter', or the 'Red Letter Scare', which suggested that the Soviet Union was intending to use the Labour Party in its revolutionary objectives. Whether this letter was real or a fake, it seems to have made only a small difference to a Party that seemed certain to be, and was, defeated.

During the next five years MacDonald led a Labour Party to which, according to Philip Snowden, he was becoming a stranger. Indeed, there seemed a possibility that he might be replaced by Snowden or some other leading Labour figure. Yet in the May 1929 general election, MacDonald was returned for the parliamentary seat of Seaham and, at the head of the largest party, formed his second, minority, Labour government in June 1929. Unfortunately within six months of its return the Wall Street Crash had occurred and, as a result of the world recession, official figures for unemployment in Britain rose from about one million to three million in less than two years. The Labour government grossly overspent its budget in providing unemployment benefits and precipitated a financial crisis in August 1931. The Cabinet attempted to find the spending cuts demanded by Opposition parties and the Sir George May Committee but split over the decision to cut unemployment benefit by 10 per cent. MacDonald offered the resignation of his government to King George V but returned on 24 August 1931 with a mandate to form a National Government, which was to include both the Conservative and the Liberal parties as well as any 'National Labour' support he could muster.

These actions led L. MacNeill Weir to suggest that MacDonald was never a socialist, that he was an opportunist who had schemed to ditch the Labour government and that he was guilty of betrayal (Weir, 1938). However, David Marquand has suggested that such accusations are, at best, half-truths. Indeed, he has argued that MacDonald was probably as good a socialist as any other leading figure in the Labour Party and that he was a principled opportunist (he gave up the Labour leadership to oppose the First World War), who did not scheme to ditch the Labour government but may have been guilty of betraying his former Labour supporters.

From 1931 to 1935 MacDonald was Prime Minister of a National Government, which a few months after its formation won a landslide victory at the 1931 general election. Throughout that period his political power depended upon the Conservative Party, which encouraged moves towards protectionism. However, MacDonald was allowed to indulge himself in foreign policy and was deeply involved in two conferences in 1932 – the Geneva Disarmament Conference and the Lausanne Conference, which was concerned with German reparations. Thereafter, his career declined and he found himself attacked by both his former colleagues, such as Philip Snowden, and his new political friends. He went into physical and mental decline and was forced to resign as Prime Minister on 7 June 1935. Subsequently, he lost his seat at the 1935 general election, to Emmanuel Shinwell who had put him forward as PLP Leader in 1922. He was found a seat for the Scottish Universities but thereafter played a diminishing role in the activities of the National Government. On 9 November 1937 he died of heart failure while cruising in the Caribbean on the *Reina del Pacífico*. His body was returned to Britain and cremated on 26 November and his ashes interred in the Spynie graveyard, near Lossiemouth, next to those of his wife.

MacDonald was clearly a central figure in the emergence of the Labour Party during the twentieth century. Yet he was also a principled politician, who sacrificed his prominent position in the Labour Party to oppose British involvement in the First World War. Although he re-established his position within the Party during the 1920s it became clear in the financial crisis of 1931 that he would, once again, put principle before Party. Indeed, in the end, playing the role of statesman, he put the needs of the nation first and thus gained the enduring hatred of a Party that he himself had largely shaped.

See also: Baldwin, Churchill, Samuel, Simon

Further reading

Barker, B. (ed.), 1972, *Ramsay MacDonald's Political Writings*, London: Allen Lane.
Laybourn, K., 1988, *The Rise of Labour*, London: Arnold.
Marquand, D., 1977, *Ramsay MacDonald*, London: Cape.
Tanner, D., 1991, 'Ideological Debate: Edwardian Labour Politics: Radicalism, Revisionism and Socialism', in Biagini, E. and Reid, A. (eds), *Currents of Radicalism*, Cambridge: Cambridge University Press.
Weir, L. M., 1938, *The Tragedy of Ramsay MacDonald. A Political Biography*, London: Secker & Warburg, pp. vii–xii.

(MAURICE) HAROLD MACMILLAN (FIRST EARL OF STOCKTON) 1894–1986

Harold Macmillan was a curiously old-fashioned, almost Disraelian, Conservative Prime Minister who combined an interest in Empire with a commitment to the welfare state. Although he is associated with the slogan 'You've never had it so good', his premiership hid the fact that Britain was declining and was not tackling the economic challenges she faced. Indeed, in the 1950s and early 1960 he helped to create an age of illusion.

Macmillan was born on 10 February 1894, the third child of Maurice Macmillan and the American Helen Belles. His paternal grandfather was a Scottish crofter but his father was active in the successful Macmillan book publishing company. The young Harold was educated at Eton and Balliol College, Oxford. When the First World War broke out he volunteered for the army and entered the Grenadier Guards.

Although seriously wounded in the First World War, Macmillan recovered and, in the post-war years, went to Canada as an aide to the Duke of Devonshire, later marrying Dorothy, the Duke's daughter. This was a marriage than never quite worked and, from the late 1920s, Dorothy was involved in a relationship with Bob Boothby, then a Conservative MP. Nevertheless, the marriage to Dorothy provided Macmillan with a way into politics and helped him to win the Stockton-on-Tees parliamentary seat in 1924. He held this seat until 1929, lost it in the Labour election victory, but won it again in 1931, holding it until 1945. Stockton-on-Tees suffered economic depression and high unemployment in the 1930s, and its experiences ensured that Macmillan would press for the 'Middle Way' in British politics through his 'Middle Opinion' group, which argued the need for both state and capitalist intervention to help revive the economy. For a time his name was even associated with that of Oswald Mosley and the formation of the New Party in 1931, although such support waned before Mosley formed the British Union of Fascists in 1932. At this stage, however, Macmillan had not made his mark politically and was also associated with Winston Churchill, then experiencing his period in the political wilderness. Indeed, it was not until the Second World War that Macmillan began to make an impression, and then in part as a result of his friendship with Churchill.

In Churchill's wartime government, and between 1940 and 1941, Macmillan was appointed Parliamentary Secretary at the Ministry of Supply, and then appointed Under-Secretary of State for the Colonies. In December 1942 he was appointed Minister Resident at the Allied Force Headquarters, Algiers. This was a post that saw changes in both location and responsibility as the Allied forces advanced in North Africa. Macmillan dealt with De Gaulle, arranged the Italian surrender and became UK High Commissioner to the Advisory Council for Italy. He was then, variously, Resident Minister of State in Italy and Greece.

At the end of the war, Macmillan was involved in implementing the Yalta Agreement, whereby anti-Soviet Russians were released from prisoner-of-war camps and sent back to Russia. That they were being sent back to their deaths was an observation made only shortly before Macmillan retired as Prime Minister in 1963. Indeed, some writers accused Macmillan of knowingly conspiring to send these Allied prisoners to their death in the so-called Klagenfurt Conspiracy.

In Churchill's caretaker government at the end of the war, Macmillan was appointed to the post of Secretary of State for Air. However, he lost his Stockton seat at the general election of 1945. Shortly afterwards he returned to the House of Commons as MP for the London seat of Bromley, Beckenham and Penge, which he represented from 1945 until his retirement until 1964. This period of his life was closely associated with the idea of political consensus and, in this respect, Macmillan played his part, particularly in relation to his commitment to the welfare state.

When Winston Churchill formed a Conservative government in 1951, Macmillan became Minister of Housing and Local Government and he set a target of 300,000 houses to be built per year. When Sir Anthony Eden replaced Churchill in 1955 Macmillan became

Minister of Defence and was, after Eden and R. A. Butler, seen as the third most important figure within the Conservative Party. Following the 1955 general election he became Foreign Secretary but was quickly appointed as Chancellor of the Exchequer, thus allowing Butler to move to the Home Office; Macmillan held the post until 1957.

Macmillan's political future was determined in 1956. In that year the Egyptian leader, Nasser, nationalized the Suez Canal, which the British and French felt threatened their interests in the Middle East and Far East. Eden set up a Suez Committee, on which Macmillan sat, to organize, with the French, the regaining of the Canal. Following an initial Israeli invasion, the British and the French organized a combined military operation to invade the Canal Zone. This provoked a run on the pound and a financial crisis which forced the British to accept American demands to withdraw in favour of United Nations forces. The collusion between the Israeli, French and British forces was played down and Macmillan maintained that Britain withdrew its forces because the job was done.

There was dissension within Conservative ranks because of the British withdrawal from Suez, and though Macmillan was deeply involved in events it was Eden, the Prime Minister, who bore the brunt of criticism. Eden was ill, was admitted to hospital, and was replaced, in his absence, by R. A. Butler. Meanwhile Macmillan turned his mind to the succession. Indeed, on 22 November 1956 both Butler and Macmillan addressed the 1922 Committee of the Conservative back benchers in the House of Commons. Macmillan enlivened them whilst Butler bored them. Eventually, on 9 January 1957, Eden indicated to Queen Elizabeth II his intention to resign on the grounds of ill health and Macmillan, along with the other Cabinet Ministers, was involved in meetings and soundings which led to Macmillan's appointment as Prime Minister on 10 January 1957. He was one month short of his sixty-fourth birthday, and was replacing a prime minister who was almost three and a half years younger.

Floating on the support and indulgence generally available for new prime ministers, Macmillan soon overcame the embarrassment of the Suez withdrawal. He restored relations with Dwight Eisenhower, the President of the United States, and obtained the, soon to be obsolete, Blue Streak Missiles from the US. In touring the Commonwealth in 1958, where colonialism was giving way to national movements, he detected 'the winds of change'. One of his high points was the Nassau Agreement of December 1962, when John F. Kennedy, the then United States President, agreed that Britain could have Polaris submarines. At the same time, Macmillan presented the image that he could deal with the Russians and he was involved in various conferences to ease tensions, the most important being the Nuclear Test Ban Treaty in July 1963. Successful in most areas, he nevertheless failed in his bid, mounted in August 1961, to get Britain into the Common Market.

Macmillan was also a fervent believer in the need to maintain the British welfare state, even if the economic development of Britain was insufficient to maintain more than the minimal provision. As Chancellor of the Exchequer between 1955 and 1957, he had done little to change this. As Prime Minister, he now opposed the anti-inflationary measures of his first Chancellor, Peter Thorneycroft, who wished to make cuts in the welfare state. This led to the resignation of Thorneycroft, Nigel Birch and Enoch Powell in January 1958, which Macmillan famously described as 'a little local difficulty'. Derrick Heathcoat Amory replaced Thorneycroft and was himself replaced by Selwyn Lloyd. Under Amory the economy expanded too rapidly and Britain was facing inflation by the late 1950s. Nevertheless, Macmillan won the 1959 general election with a much misquoted statement, revived during the election from a speech made in 1957: 'Let's be frank about it; most of our people have never had it so good'.

In the early 1960s Macmillan's government faced mounting economic criticism. He sacked one-third of his Cabinet, including Selwyn Lloyd, in the 'Night of the Long Knives' of March 1962. Jeremy Thorpe, the Liberal MP, quipped that 'Greater love hath no man than he lay down his friends for his life.' Yet what brought the Macmillan's administration down was not this but the Profumo Case. John Profumo, a junior minister at the War Office, was consorting with Christine Keeler, a prostitute, who was further associated with Captain Ivanov of the Russian Embassy. Sex, security risks and political embarrassment, prompted by the fact that Profumo assured both Macmillan and the House of Commons that there had been no 'impropriety', when there had been, led to further scandal and embarrassment.

Facing an operation for cancer of the prostate, Macmillan offered his resignation on 9 October 1963. He was replaced by Lord Home (Sir Alec Douglas Home). He was ennobled as the first Earl of Stockton in 1984, although at the time he was out of sorts with the Thatcher administration: in the previous year he had likened privatization to 'selling off the family silver'. He died on 29 December 1986.

Macmillan was an able Prime Minister and formidable political leader, with a streak of ruthlessness about him. He was also something of a transitional figure, presiding over Britain's declining Empire, committed to defence and also wishing to preserve the welfare state. These approaches were largely conditioned by his experiences in connection with Empire, unemployment and appeasement during the 1930s. Yet he was hardly an innovator and the word 'illusion' comes more to mind about his period in office than 'innovation'. The illusion that all was well with Britain, when this was clearly not the case, was something his successors could not perpetuate.

See also: Churchill, Eden

Further reading

Carlton, D., 1981, *Anthony Eden: A Biography*, London: Allen Lane.
Carlton, D., 1988 *Britain and the Suez Crisis*, Oxford: Blackwell.
Clarke, P., 1991, *A Question of Leadership. Gladstone to Thatcher*, London: Hamish Hamilton.
Evans, H., 1981, *Downing Street Diary: The Macmillan Years 1957–1963*, London: Hodder & Stoughton.
Horne, A., 1988, *Macmillan. Vol 1: 1894–1956*, London: Macmillan.
Howard, A., 1987, *RAB: The Life of R. A. Butler*, London: Cape.
Knight, R., 1986, 'Harold Macmillan and the Cossachs: Was There a Klagenfurt Conspiracy?', *Intelligence and National Security* I: 234–54.
Lamb, R., 1955, *The Macmillan Years 1957–63: The Emerging Truth*, London: John Murray.
Macmillan, H., 1933, *Reconstruction: A Plea for a National Policy*, London: Macmillan.
Macmillan, H., 1966, *Winds of Change, 1914–1939*, London: Macmillan.
Macmillan, H., 1967, *The Beast of War, 1939–1945*, London: Macmillan.
Macmillan, H., 1969, *Tides of Fortune, 1945–1955*, London: Macmillan.
Macmillan, H., 1971, *Riding the Storm, 1956–1959*, London: Macmillan.
Macmillan, H., 1972, *Pointing the Way, 1959–1961*, London: Macmillan.
Macmillan, H., 1973, *At the End of the Day, 1961–1963*, London: Macmillan.
Macmillan, H., 1984, *War Diaries. Politics and War in the Mediterranean. January 1943–May 1945*, London: Macmillan.
Pimlott, B., 'Is The Postwar Consensus A Myth?', *Contemporary Record*, 2 (summer): 12–14.
Sampson, Anthony, 1967, *Macmillan: A Study in Ambiguity*, London: Allen Lane.
Turner, J., 1994, *Macmillan*, London: Longman.

JOHN MAJOR 1943–

John Major is something of a political enigma. He emerged, with limited political experience, to become Conservative Leader and Prime Minister in 1990, successfully fighting off many political challengers to his position throughout the early and mid 1990s (referring to his Conservative opponents as 'bastards'), before being heavily defeated in the 1997 general election. He promptly resigned as Leader and immediately entered political obscurity. Indeed, Kenneth Baker suggests Major published his autobiography in 1999 in order not to be ranked alongside Sir Anthony Eden, Neville Chamberlain and Arthur James Balfour as one of the Conservative Party's least successful premiers of the twentieth century (*Observer*, 7 October 1999). However, Baker, in generous mood, asserts that 'For a Brixton lad to spend longer in Number 10 than either Asquith or Lloyd George is no mean feat.'

John Major was born at Brixton in London on 29 March 1943, the younger son of Thomas Major and Gwendolyn Minny Coates. His father was Abraham Thomas Ball, later to take the stage name Major, a master bricklayer in his early life, a juggler, acrobat and comedian in the theatre throughout his mid-life, and a businessman at the end. His mother, Tom Major's second wife, also worked in the theatre. Despite his background, Major was educated at Rutlish Grammar School, left school at sixteen to work as a clerk and eventually ended up working in the banking sector.

Major's political career began when he helped form the Brixton branch of the Young Conservatives in 1965 and was elected to Lambeth Borough Council in 1968, where he eventually became Chairman of the Housing Committee. It was at about this time, in 1970, that he married Norma Johnson.

Major was unsuccessful in his candidature for Camden, St Pancras North, in 1974, but became MP for Huntingdonshire in 1979, holding the seat until 1983 when he became MP for the newly created Huntingdon constituency, which he has represented ever since. He rose swiftly in the Conservative ranks, and was made Private Secretary to the Minister of State at the Home Office in 1981. Successively, he was Assistant Whip, Whip (1983–5), Under-Secretary at Social Security (1985–6), Minister of State at the Department of Health and Social Security (1986–7), and eventually Chief Secretary to the Treasury (1987–9), a Cabinet post. Having filled the junior and less senior posts of government, Major then rose swiftly to the top in little more than sixteen months, between July 1989 and November 1990. During that period he filled the post of Foreign Secretary (July to October 1989), and Chancellor of the Exchequer (October 1989 to November 1990) before defeating both Douglas Hurd and Michael Heseltine in the 1990 Conservative leadership contest to replace Thatcher, who had resigned after failing to secure the required first ballot majority over Heseltine. Major then held the position of Prime Minister from November 1990 to May 1997.

Although an astute politician, and a good administrator, there was an element of political fortune which saw Major replace Geoffrey Howe, Nigel Lawson and Margaret Thatcher. As Baker reflects, when Major opened his first Cabinet meeting in 1990, with a diffident smile, he asked the rhetorical question: 'Well, who would have thought it?' Indeed, who would have thought it? In the first place Margaret Thatcher would have preferred to replace Nigel Lawson at the Treasury with Nicholas Ridley but chose Major because he was more prepared to conform to the needs of that office. Major was, at the time, her Foreign Secretary. In effect, having appointed Major to two of the most significant offices of state in swift succession, Thatcher had almost certainly picked her successor.

When he became Chancellor, and on his first day of office, in a speech at Nottingham Major coined the famous adage that 'The hard truth is that if the policy isn't hurting it isn't working.' Indeed, such was his concern to control inflation that in the year or so of his tenure interest rates increased by 15 per cent.

Major also had to deal with the European Monetary Union. In the single European Act, signed by Margaret Thatcher in February 1986, Thatcher committed Britain to joining the Union. Yet the French sought the creation of a single currency which Thatcher felt would be an unacceptable surrender of sovereignty and Nigel Lawson supported the emergence of competitive currencies which might veer towards one currency. In a speech on 20 June 1990 John Major offered the 'hard ecu' as his contribution to diverting the French away from the single currency. The ecu was to be a basket of currencies which would be re-valued against the Deutschmark every so often. The idea of the hard ecu was that when such devaluation occurred, the share of the devalued currency within it would be at once reduced and thus the ecu would not become weaker. It was an idea which all European Economic Community governments rejected and which even Thatcher disowned.

Britain eventually made the decision to enter the Exchange Rate Mechanism (ERM) on 8 October 1990, within a 6 per cent band of the central rate and at 2.95 DM to the pound. It was a situation which rebounded on 16 September 1992, later known as 'Black Wednesday', when Major's government was forced to suspend membership of the ERM.

Given the brevity of Major's experience in high office, it is no wonder that many were surprised at the ease with which he moved through the Conservative Party and upwards into government. Until he became Prime Minister it was difficult to appreciate what he stood for, except that he shared with Thatcher a loathing of inflation and a commitment to rolling back the welfare state. In other respects, he was more open to persuasion, more willing to gain consensus, and less driven by a fixed ideology. His pragmatism led him to drop the poll tax Thatcher had introduced as a way of financing local government, and he was less confrontational with Europe than Thatcher had tended to be. Yet he gained a reputation for toughness, through his support for the Gulf War in 1991, when the United States, Britain and other nations drove Saddam Hussein's forces out of Kuwait, and Major's determination was even more evident in the way in which he supported Boris Yeltsin in Russia in 1991. Major's success in the 1992 general election also indicated that he was more than a caretaker Prime Minister, even though his overall majority was narrow and disappeared during the course of that term in government.

Indeed, Major faced numerous problems within the Conservative Party, particularly over Europe. Major's position on Europe was always one that stressed the need to protect British interests. However, within his Party were Euro-sceptics who were opposed any measures that might lead to European integration. Major signed the Maastricht Treaty in December 1991, which edged Britain towards some further measure of integration. However, as already indicated, it was blown off course on 16 September 1992 when the sterling crisis led to Britain's withdrawal from the ERM. Major pressed ahead with the Bill to ratify the Maastricht Treaty, but it failed to reach conclusion until the end of 1994, and then only in the teeth of opposition from the Euro-sceptics, eight of whom the Conservative Whip had forced to resign (although they were restored to the Party within four or five months) and one other who resigned voluntarily from the Party. They objected to the larger financial contribution that Britain would have to make to the European Community as well as the threatened moves towards integration. As a result the narrow Conservative majority in the House of Commons disappeared and, in December 1994, the government was defeated in the vote on the increasing of VAT on domestic fuel. This proved an embarrassment for Major's government, which was already reeling from divisions, allegations of extra-marital affairs, and the abuse of parliamentary privilege. With two Conservative MPs accused of accepting cash for tabling parliamentary questions, Major had been forced to respond by putting Lord Nolan at the head of the Committee for Standards in Public Life, which moved the government to ban paid advocacy by MPs and to require the disclosure of incomes earned from services offered as an MP. The findings of the Nolan report divided Conservative MPs and further scandals increased the perception of the widespread presence of 'sleaze' in British politics. In 1996, the publication of a critical report by Sir Richard Scott into the actions of junior ministers in deciding guidelines for the export of arms-related equipment to Iraq placed even more pressure upon Major's government.

Some of these pressures had forced Major to resign as Party Leader in the summer of 1995, and to provoke a leadership contest in which he was to be one of the candidates. The final straw had been his meeting, in June 1995, with more than fifty Euro-sceptic Conservative MPs – the 'Fresh Start Group' – who seemed to have little respect for his position. In the event, John Redwood was Major's only opponent in the contest and Major won convincingly by 218 votes to 89 votes – the other twenty-two Conservative MPs failed to register a vote. Nevertheless, the Euro-sceptics continued to pressure Major to take a tougher line on European integration and the single European currency, whilst Kenneth Clarke, the Chancellor of the Exchequer and a strong pro-European, threatened to resign if he did so.

Despite the obvious difficulties faced by Major's governments, there were some achievements on other fronts. Major was praised for his handling of the Northern Ireland situation, in particular his brokering of 'The Downing Street Declaration' in December 1993, whereby he and the Irish Prime Minister Albert Reynolds attempted to persuade the 'men of violence' on both sides to enter the democratic process. This led to the cease-fire in 1994 by the Irish Republican Army and loyalist paramilitary groups, and the publication of a consultative document for future government in Northern Ireland in February 1995. So began the movement towards power sharing which developed further under Tony Blair, his successor as Prime Minister in 1997.

Nonetheless, failures seemed to outnumber successes and the Conservative Party was defeated in the general election of 1 May 1997, which brought Tony Blair to power at the head of a Labour Party which had won a landslide victory. The general election campaign had seen the Conservative Party split, with about two-thirds of its more than 320 MPs declaring their firm opposition to the idea of a single currency for Europe. When the Conservative defeat occurred, Major resigned as Prime Minister and then as Conservative Party Leader. Since then he has remained a relatively obscure figure on the Conservative back benches, making the occasional announcement in favour of closer ties between Britain and Europe and favouring the unsuccessful Kenneth Clarke in the Conservative leadership campaign decided by a ballot of members on 13 September 2001.

Major was Prime Minister for seven years in difficult circumstances. He struggled to maintain a parliamentary majority after 1992 and was faced with intense factionalism within the Conservative Party, which forced him to declare a Conservative leadership contest in 1995. Given the situations he faced, it was a remarkable feat to last so long. It is even more remarkable when one reflects, from the vantage point of 2002, how far the Conservative Party has gone along the road of being unelectable ever since Major's departure.

See also: Thatcher

Further reading

Junor, P., 1996, *John Major: From Brixton to Downing Street*, London: Penguin.
Major, J., 1999, *John Major: The Autobiography*, London: HarperCollins.

HERBERT (STANLEY) MORRISON (LORD MORRISON OF LAMBETH) 1888–1965

Alongside Clement Attlee and Ernest Bevin, Herbert Morrison was one of the three most powerful political figures in the two Labour governments of 1945 to 1951. His real importance to the Labour Party was as the organizer of the political victory of 1945 and of the nationalization programme that emerged. He was also Attlee's deputy and is considered by some historians to be the finest administrator that the Labour Party has ever produced. Nevertheless, Attlee remained as Leader of the Labour Party long enough to see off Morrison's political ambition to be Labour Leader.

Morrison was born in London on 3 January 1888, the youngest of seven children of Henry, a police constable, and Priscilla Lyon. He worked as a shop assistant before carving out a career in politics. Initially he joined the quasi-Marxist Social Democratic Federation (SDF) in 1907 but left and joined the Brixton branch of the Independent Labour Party (ILP) in 1910. From 1910 until 1913 he was also Chairman of the Brixton branch of the National Union of Clerks and became involved in local politics. During these years he developed a clear socialist perspective, advocating public works to deal with unemployment and supporting the women's suffrage movement.

During the First World War Morrison adopted an anti-war stance, became closely involved with in the ILP's peace activities and, though blind in his right eye which would have exempted him from military service, attended the Military Service Tribunal and agreed to work on the land. In 1919 he married Margaret Kent, the daughter of a railway clerk, by whom he had a daughter. Thereafter, he rose quickly in Labour circles, becoming a member of Hackney Borough Council and Mayor in 1920 and 1921. He was also a member of London County Council between 1922 and 1945, and was its Leader from 1939 to 1940. Yet it was parliamentary activity that began to occupy his real interests.

Morrison joined the National Executive of the Labour Party in 1920, was MP for South Hackney between 1923 and 1924, from 1929 to 1931 and, again, between 1935 and 1945, before becoming MP for East Lewisham 1945 to 1950 and South Lewisham 1950 to 1959. He was also Minister of Transport in the Labour government of 1929 to 1931 and Minister of Supply for a few months in 1940 before becoming Home Secretary and Minister for Home Security between 1940 and 1945, and a member of the Churchill's War Cabinet in 1942. Yet Morrison's finest hour came when he was made Lord President of the Council, Leader of the House of Commons, and Deputy Prime Minister in Attlee's two Labour governments from 1945 to 1951. In 1951 he was a relatively unsuccessful Foreign Secretary and, following Labour's defeat, continued to act as a Deputy Leader of the Labour Party from 1951 to 1955. He was never able to become Leader of the Labour Party for that role was assumed by Hugh Gaitskell in 1955.

As Lord President of the Council, Morrison had the responsibility of masterminding the whole process of government nationalization and also of overseeing the spending of government departments. This latter role led him into conflict with Aneurin Bevan over the rapidly rising expenditure of the National Health Service (NHS). Morrison had already opposed Bevan's scheme in Cabinet in 1945 and 1946 and was unhappy when the NHS, begun in July 1948, more than doubled its anticipated expenditure in its first year of operation. With the prospect of a further increase, of well over £350 million, and with the potent warning of his civil servants that Britain could be heading for another financial crisis similar to that of 1931 which had ended the existence of the second Labour government, Morrison opposed Bevan's attempt to protect the NHS from cuts.

By any standards, Morrison's political career was impressive, whether in organizing the London Passenger Transport Board in the 1930s, organizing air raid precautions during the Second World War, pushing forward bills nationalizing the coal industry and railways in the Attlee's post-war Labour governments, or in promoting the Festival of Britain in 1951. He was largely responsible for the formulation of

Labour's nationalization programme, and his book *Socialization and Transport* (1933) committed Labour to the idea of a corporate public body as the model for state control. Morrison was, above all, a supreme party organizer, keeping the Labour back benchers happy by creating subject committee groups among them. He certainly gave cohesion to the Labour Party and Attlee's post-war Labour governments.

Nevertheless, there were many personal and political failures in Morrison's life. His first marriage failed, and he appears to have had several flirtations, including one with Ellen Wilkinson. Margaret, his first wife, died of cancer in 1953 and he married Edith Meadowcroft in 1955. Politically, his main setbacks occurred at the hands of Attlee, who defeated him for the Labour Party leadership in 1935, and thwarted his attempts to become Leader in 1939 and 1945. Attlee delayed his own retirement long enough to enable Hugh Gaitskell to become Leader in 1955. Morrison was not liked by some of the leading Party figures. Most famously, when someone suggested that Morrison was 'his own worst enemy', Ernest Bevin is supposed to have retorted 'Not while I'm around'. Morrison was also considered out of his depth as Foreign Secretary.

Morrison stood down as MP in 1959, whereupon he was elevated to the House of Lords as Lord Morrison of Lambeth. He was also made President of the Board of Film Censors in 1960, a post he held until his death on 6 March 1965.

Morrison was a brilliant administrator and one of the key figures behind the Labour Party's policy of nationalization in the early twentieth century. Nevertheless, his intransigence and his propensity to create political enemies meant that he was never able to achieve his greatest goal – to be Prime Minister.

See also: Attlee, Bevan, Bevin

Further reading

Donoghue, B. and Jones, G. W., 1973, *Herbert Morrison: Portrait of a Politician*, London: Weidenfeld & Nicolson.
Morgan, K. O., 1987, *Labour People: Leaders and Lieutenants, Hardie to Kinnock*, Oxford: Oxford University Press.
Morrison, H., 1933, *Socialization and Transport*, London: Constable.
Morrison, H., 1943, *Looking Ahead. War-time Speeches*, London: Hodder & Stoughton.
Morrison, H., 1949, *How London is Governed*, London: People's Universities Press.
Morrison, H., 1960, *Herbert Morrison, An Autobiography of Lord Morrison of Lambeth, PC, CH*, London: Odhams Press.

OSWALD (ERNALD) MOSLEY 1896–1980

Sir Oswald Mosley is best remembered as the founder of the British Union of Fascists, in 1932, and the demonic figure of British fascism. However, his political career was far from fixed in the fascist mould of the 1930s for, pursuing a political career through several political parties, he sought to change the government of Britain radically in such a way that it would tackle the economic problems that blighted Britain's economy during the inter-war years. That he failed to do so owes much to the economic and political problems of that period but also something to the quixotic nature of his character. On his death, in December 1980, A. J. P. Taylor, the famous historian, wrote in an obituary in the *Observer* that 'Mosley sought to play the Great Dictator' but concluded that an East End Londoner, Charlie Chaplin, played the role better. That is true, although it underestimates the remarkable contribution Mosley made to British inter-war politics.

Mosley was born at London on 16 November 1896, the eldest of the three sons of Sir Oswald Mosley and Katherine Maud Mosley (formerly Edwards-Heathcote). From the age of five, however, he was brought up by his mother alone who had separated from his father. In 1909 he entered Winchester, where he became famed for his boxing and fencing skills, leaving in 1912. He then went to Sandhurst in January 1914, but was soon expelled. In October 1914, shortly after the beginning of the First World War, Mosley was commissioned in the Sixteenth Lancers and then joined the Royal Flying Corps as an observer from December 1914 until April 1915. He then injured an ankle in a crash whilst trying to obtain a pilot's licence and then, after recuperation, returned to the Sixteenth Lancers. Because of the continuing problem of his ankle he was invalided out of the armed forces in March 1916, although recently released records suggest that the army felt that the debilitating nature of his condition was probably exaggerated.

Removed from the front, Mosley spent the rest of the war working for the Ministry of Munitions and the Foreign Office. Cultivating his political connections within the Conservative Party he became candidate for the Harrow division of Middlesex, and was returned to the House of Commons in December 1918, with a majority of 10,943 from a total vote of 16,957. His Conservative credentials were strengthened further in 1920 when he married Cynthia Blanche, the second daughter of Lord Curzon of Kedleston, the former Viceroy of India and Foreign Secretary in the Coalition Government led by

David Lloyd George (1918–22). Although totally inappropriate for the office, Curzon was one of the three leading Conservatives, along with Stanley Baldwin and Austen Chamberlain, who might well have succeeded Andrew Bonar Law as Conservative Leader and thus Prime Minister in 1923. Well connected and wealthy, Mosley seemed to have a glowing future within the Conservative Party. However, in the House of Commons he associated with a group of new and young Conservative members, known as 'The Babes', who were increasingly critical of the economic inaction of Lloyd George's Conservative-dominated Coalition Government. Then, in 1920, he opposed the government's policy on Ireland, which was leading to the division between the Northern counties and the rest of Ireland. As a result he decided to stand for Harrow as an Independent Conservative in the general election of 1922.

Mosley was now drifting away from the Conservative Party. In 1923 he won Harrow, as an Independent, on a much-reduced majority, and in March 1924 joined the Independent Labour Party (ILP), which was affiliated to the Labour Party. At this juncture he decided to abandon his Harrow constituency, and in the 1924 general election stood for the ILP/Labour Party cause at Birmingham Ladywood, in opposition to Neville Chamberlain who was the sitting candidate. In the event he was defeated by a mere 77 votes in a Tory heartland. Nevertheless, he continued to cultivate the Birmingham area, being strongly in support of the Birmingham workers during the General Strike of 1926. Eventually, in December 1926, he was returned to the House of Commons after having won a by-election in the Smethwick constituency with a particularly large majority.

During his absence from Parliament, Mosley had been building up his political reputation. He became friendly with both Fenner Brockway, the ILP journalist and leader, and with James Ramsay MacDonald, the Leader of the Labour Party. He attended ILP summer schools at Easton Lodge, the lodge house to the estates of the widowed Countess of Warwick, one-time lover of Edward VII, who had joined the quasi-Marxist Social Democratic Federation in 1904. In the early and mid 1920s, the lodge house entertained Ramsay MacDonald, H. G. Wells, and many ILP and socialist intellectuals in a bout of intellectual debate and physical exercise (the tug-of-war). It was at the Lodge in 1925 that Mosley and John Strachey put forward their programme of state intervention to stimulate the economy out of slump, based upon Keynesian ideas, which later appeared in a book entitled *Revolution by Reason* (1925). In particular, Mosley advocated that banks be forced to loan money to the working classes at a low interest rate in order to stimulate economic demand and industry. It was also at this stage that Mosley began to be talked of as a possible future Labour Leader, especially given that MacDonald, who became a close friend, seemed to be distancing himself from the Labour Party in the mid and late 1920s.

Mosley succeeded to the baronetcy in 1928 and in 1929 was returned again for Smethwick, his wife Cynthia (Cimmie) being returned as Labour MP for Stoke-on-Trent. Mosley was appointed to the post of Chancellor of the Duchy of the Lancaster in the second Labour government that emerged. This was not a Cabinet post at that time but gave him ministerial responsibility without a department. In effect, he became a government troubleshooter and was attached to the Unemployment Committee headed by Jimmy Thomas, the Lord Privy Seal, which was designed to encourage government departments to push forward schemes that would go some way to reduce unemployment levels which had risen since the 1929 Wall Street Crash. Coming into conflict with Thomas, and Philip Snowden who was Chancellor of the Exchequer at that time, Mosley put forward schemes for a significant increase in expenditure. He circulated these throughout government in early 1930, as the 'Mosley Memorandum', and when they were rejected resigned from office on 20 May 1930.

Mosley put his expansionist ideas forward at the Labour Party Conference at Llandudno in October 1930, where they were narrowly defeated. Subsequently he wrote them up at the end of 1930 as the 'Mosley Manifesto'. Indeed, his ideas were supported by a number of prominent politicians, including the Conservative Harold Macmillan and the socialist Aneurin Bevan. Mosley formed his 'New Party' on 28 February 1931 to promote his ideas and initially drew support from Bevan, John Strachey and others. However, much of this support evaporated when it became clear that the New Party was employing 'Biff Boys' to protect its meetings and voting in favour of the Anomalies Bill/Act of July 1931 which was effectively removing the right of married women to claim standard or extended unemployment benefits to which they had hitherto been entitled. The final straw for the New Party was the general election of October 1931, which saw its twenty-four candidates defeated.

In 1932 Mosley visited Italy to study the fascist experiment of Benito Mussolini. Returning to Britain he decided to form his own British fascist movement based upon the economic ideas he had previously advocated and upon the streamlining of British parliamentary democracy. Indeed, he advocated the creation of a Cabinet of five and a parliamentary system based upon the return of MPs, in accordance with the numbers of people employed in different industries or services, which would transcend normal party politics. To many these ideas, which had already appeared in his Manifesto, were tantamount to the advocacy of some type of dictatorship, and one cartoon of the day had Mosley standing next to Mussolini under the title Moslini, with Mussolini asking Mosley of the Cabinet, 'Why bother with the other four?' On 1 October 1932 Mosley formed the British Union of Fascists (BUF) and called for sacrifices from its supporters so that 'a great nation might live'.

For the first two years BUF progressed well. In 1933 and early 1934 Mosley spoke three or four times a week advocating the strengthening of British armed forces, the changing of the constitution, and the need to expand the economy. Small as the BUF was, it is clear that it was attracting interest, especially following Hitler's assumption of power in Germany in January 1933. Inevitably, his activities led him into conflict with Marxist groups, such as the Communist Party of Great Britain (CPGB), which were being instructed by Moscow to form a 'United front against Fascism'. Although the focus of most fascist groups was directed against European fascism, the London branch of the CPGB, in association with Jewish supporters and activists in the East End of London, decided to organize a demonstration against Mosley's triumphalist meeting at Olympia on 7 June 1934. This led to extreme violence which dissuaded many, including the press barons Lord Rothermere and Lord Beaverbrook, and, respectively, their newspapers the *Daily Mail* and the *Daily Express*, from continuing their support of Mosley.

In the wake of Olympia the BUF lost members and came increasingly under the influence of William Joyce and other anti-Semitic and anti-Jewish influences. This led to numerous clashes, the highpoint being the 'Battle of Cable Street' in London in October 1936 when protesters, many of them Communists and Jews, fought to prevent Mosley organizing a fascist march through the East End of London. In May 1937 fascist candidates campaigned, and were defeated, in the East End of London municipal elections on blatantly anti-semetic lines.

Nevertheless, the events at Cable Street had led the Stanley Baldwin National Government to introduce the Public Order Act which forbade the wearing of military or para-military uniforms, thus banning the wearing of the 'blackshirt' by a section of Mosley's supporters. The distinctiveness of the movement disappeared with this decision and the BUF found its ability to organize meetings further limited by the Act, which allowed the police to prevent, delay or alter the dates, times, and routes of marches and meetings. The resulting loss of membership and the financial crisis within the movement led Joyce, and other anti-Semites, to form a splinter group, the National Socialist League, in 1937. The name was chosen to distinguish it from the BUF which had become the British Union of Fascists and National Socialists in 1936.

During this period of political turmoil Cynthia Mosley died of peritonitis in 1933 and, three years later, Mosley married Diana Mitford Guinness, the third daughter of Baron Redesdale and one of the famous Mitford sisters whose political persuasions covered the full range of Right to Left in British politics.

The BUF declined in the late 1930s as Mosley began to lose interest in the fascist movement and his lecturing commitments decreased. This was almost fatal for a movement based upon identification with one individual. Nevertheless, he did increase his activities just before the outbreak of the European War, in September 1939, which led to the Second World War. At this point he declared that 'The War We Want is the War on Want'. Once war broke out, however, he found that some of his supporters joined the armed forces and in May 1940 he and his wife were arrested and detained under Regulation 18B, which allowed for the imprisonment without trial of anyone believed 'likely to endanger the safety of the realm'. The Mosleys were eventually released in November 1943.

After the end of the Second World War, Mosley justified his inter-war activities in his books *My Answer* (1946) and in his autobiography *My Life* (1968). Until 1966 he attempted to revive his fascist movement through a body called the Union Movement. This emphasized European unity based upon racial criteria. Occasionally, there were reminders of the old days as, for instance, with the 'Battle of Ridley Road', Dalston, in 1947–8 when anti-fascists disrupted the meetings of the British League of ex-Servicemen and the Union Movement.

Nevertheless, for most of the post-war years Mosley operated in exile from his home at Orsay, near Paris. He fought the North Kensington parliamentary constituency in the 1959 general election, hoping to derive some support for his ideas in the wake of the Notting Hill race riots in 1958. He also fought the parliamentary contest for Shoreditch in the 1966 general election. On both occasions his support was so small that he lost his deposit. Although Mosley then withdrew from active politics he still believed that he would be called to play a European-wide role when the great social crisis finally occurred. The call never came and he died, an almost forgotten political figure, on 3 December 1980.

In 1968 Mosley wrote his autobiography, *My Life*, to put the record straight. To many critics it was a partial assessment of his career, forgetting and re-interpreting his role in the events of the 1930s. Nevertheless, it reminded his readers of his political width and depth. Robert Skidelsky's book *Oswald Mosley* appeared in 1975 and revived interest on Mosley's career to such an extent that he became an occasional journalist for the *Sunday Telegraph*. The reality, of course, is that despite his ability his political life was a failure. As A. J. P. Taylor suggested in the obituary he wrote, Mosley failed to become the Great Dictator, but this was only partly as a result of his own political instability and more a product of the established, stable and democratic nature of British politics. He was the wrong man at the wrong time.

See also: Baldwin, Bevan, Chamberlain (Neville), MacDonald, Macmillan

Further reading

Lewis, D. S., 1987, *Illusions of Grandeur: Mosley, Fascism and British Society, 1931–1981*, Manchester: Manchester University Press.

Mosley, O., 1968, *My Life*, London: Nelson.

Mosley, N., 1982, *Rules of the Game: Sir Oswald Mosley and Lady Cynthia Mosley, 1896–1933*, London: Secker & Warburg.

Mosley, N., 1983, *Beyond the Pale. Sir Oswald Mosely and Family, 1933–1980*, London: Secker & Warburg.

Skidelsky, R.,1975, *Oswald Mosley*, London and Basingstoke: Macmillan.

Thurlow, R., 1987, *Fascism in Britain: A History, 1918–1985*, Oxford: Blackwell.

Thurlow, R., 2000, *Fascism in Modern Britain*, Stroud: Sutton.

EMMELINE PANKHURST 1858–1928

Emmeline Pankhurst, and two of her daughters Christabel (1880–1958) and Sylvia (1882–1958), were famous for their forceful advocacy of women's suffrage in the early twentieth century. Initially supported by her husband, Richard Marsden Pankhurst, Emmeline was active as a Radical and then as a Labour supporter before pursuing the cause of women's suffrage in a violent manner, dividing an Independent Labour movement which was not always happy with her actions or the explicit middle-class bias of her policies.

Emmeline was raised in Manchester, a member of the radically inclined Gouldon family. At the age of twenty she married the Radical lawyer Richard Marsden Pankhurst (1835–98), and became involved in suffrage and feminist politics. She gave birth to five children – Christabel, Sylvia, Frank, Adela, and Harry – but still had time to become involved in activities connected with gaining the suffrage for women and establishing property rights for married women. She was active for a time with Manchester Poor Law Guardians and, with her husband, was a prominent early member of the Independent Labour Party (ILP); her husband and other rich supporters underwrote the campaign of the ILP in the general election of 1895. Emmeline took up politics more directly on her own account after the death of her husband in 1898 and, finding the ILP reluctant to support her particular policies on votes for women, formed the Women's Social and Political Union (WSPU) in 1903 to organize women on behalf of suffrage.

The WSPU began to campaign for women's suffrage amongst the northern industrial towns and organized mass demonstrations at such places as the House of the Resurrection, at Mirfield near Huddersfield, where there was a quarry which formed a natural amphitheatre that could cater for an audience of several thousand. However, after the 1906 general election the WSPU moved to London where Emmeline organized the famous 'Mud March', in which 3,000 women carried banners, stepped out to the beat of brass bands, and marched from Hyde Park to Exeter Hall demanding votes for women. However, it restricted its demands to gaining votes for women on the same basis as men, that is, on the 'limited franchise' rather than the complete enfranchisement of all people of aged twenty-one and over, which still seemed a distant prospect.

Almost equally obsessional about the issue, James Keir Hardie raised the limited franchise question at the Labour Conference in 1907. The conference, held in Belfast, voted against it by 605,000 votes to 268,000, suggesting that it was a retrograde step. The Conference was not impressed by the fact that the WSPU had advised voters to elect the Unionist candidate rather than the Labour candidate in the Cockermouth parliamentary by-election. A similar fit of petulance, by Hardie occurred at the ILP Conference of Easter 1907, when he annoyed delegates by supporting the limited franchise and demanding a telegram of support be sent to WSPU women who had recently been imprisoned. Ramsay MacDonald, other leading Labour leaders and the Conference all objected to Hardie's action.

Whilst Hardie seemed to be willing to follow Emmeline Pankhurst and the 'limited franchise' without question, others were clearly not willing to do so. In 1907 Teresa Billington-Greig (1877–1964), Charlotte Despard (1844–1939), and others were upset by the antidemocratic ideas of both Emmeline and Christabel, and the way in which they had abandoned both the ILP and the Labour Party. Thus they broke away to form the Women's Freedom League. Even Sylvia Pankhurst, who had interrupted her art studies to support the WSPU, became disillusioned with her mother and sister, although she did not go her own way until 1912.

Until 1909 the WSPU tactics had been relatively peaceful and mainly confined to heckling Cabinet Ministers and to organizing minor disturbances at political meetings. From then onwards, however, their tactics became more militant. They began to throw stones at meetings and in the summer of 1909 militant suffragettes began hunger strikes in prison, demanding that they be treated as political offenders rather than ordinary criminals. The move eventually led the authorities in 1913 to resort to force-feeding.

In 1910, when it appeared that a bill enfranchising women might be carried through Parliament, the WSPU dropped its militancy. Yet when Asquith abandoned the measure, the Conciliation Bill, the WSPU advocated militancy. On 18 November 1910, which became known as 'Black Friday' Emmeline Pankhurst led a suffragette march from Caxton Hall to Parliament Square, where they claimed they were attacked and sexually molested by the police and some civilian bystanders in a six-hour confrontation.

The Conciliation Bill was raised again in 1911, and the WSPU stopped their militant action, but once more returned to their militant activities when the Bill failed once again. This provoked Emmeline Pankhurst, in March 1912, to smash the windows of 10 Downing Street, the official residence of the Prime Minister, a move which led to widespread window smashing throughout London. This resulted in the arrest of 217 suffragettes, including Emmeline and her friends Emmeline (1867–1954) and Frederick (1887–1961) Pethick Lawrence. They were charged with incitement to riot and sentenced to nine months' imprisonment. As a result they began a hunger strike and became so ill that they were released.

At this point the suffrage movement began to divide. Emmeline decided to continue with her militant action and threatened arson. However, the Pethick Lawrences, who had financed the WSPU, disagreed and took their newspaper, *Votes for Women*, away from the WSPU. Christabel went to Paris and edited her own paper *The Suffragette* in its place. Also at this point Sylvia broke away from her mother to work with the East London Federation of Suffragettes, which was largely working class in its support and still affiliated with the ILP. She also began to produce *The Woman's Dreadnought*.

Meanwhile, Emmeline and the WSPU continued with their lawbreaking and, in 1913, set alight Lloyd George's country house. As a result, Emmeline was arrested and eventually sentenced to three years' imprisonment. To forestall any attempt at gaining early release through a hunger strike, the government passed the infamous 'Cat and Mouse' Act which enabled them to release and then re-arrest Emmeline. This occurred so many times that Emmeline served only 30 days of her sentence between April 1913 and April 1914.

The First World War saw Emmeline and Christabel bury themselves in the war effort, in contrast to Sylvia, who pursued her socialist objectives, changed the title of her paper to *The Workers' Dreadnought* and committed herself to supporting the Bolshevik Russian Revolution in 1917. Emmeline and Christabel launched the 'women's right to serve' campaign in opposition to the trade unions who seemed reluctant to allow women to work in engineering and munitions factories. This began in May 1915, with the support of the Minister of Munitions, in munitions factories, and culminated in a 'national procession' in July 1915, funded by the government. Both Emmeline and Christabel began to travel abroad to promote the British cause on the First World War, although this may have been part of a wider feminist campaign of gendered patriotism that did not set aside feminism. Nevertheless, few feminists followed them down that road as they appeared to more or less abandon their feminist activities as the war progressed. In 1917 Emmeline and Christabel transformed the WSPU into the Women's Party, with the slogan 'Victory, National Security and Progress', but neither were involved in the negotiations which led to the 1918 Franchise Act guaranteeing the vote to women aged thirty and over. Indeed, the Women's Party gradually faded away as Christabel failed to gain a seat in Parliament in the 1918 general election and as Emmeline left for Canada. Emmeline spent seven years in Canada lecturing on behalf of the National Council for Combating Venereal Disease. She returned to Britain in 1925 and joined the Conservative Party, and was adopted as candidate for Whitechapel much to the regret of her daughter Sylvia. In fact Emmeline died in 1928 and was never able to contest the seat.

There is no doubt that Emmeline Pankhurst, and her daughters Christabel and Sylvia, raised the issue of women's suffrage to a major political issue in the early twentieth century. She, and they, obviously provided the context out of which the decision to give some women the vote occurred in 1918. Nevertheless, there were other pressures in play and they were not the only forces demanding women's suffrage, and it may well be that other, more moderate forces, played an equally important role. Emmeline's intransigence did, however, undermine support for her cause from time to time and it is clear that her later move to the Conservative Party damaged her reputation for radical action.

See also: Hardie, Lloyd George

Further reading

Alberti, J., 1989, *Beyond Suffrage: Feminists in War and Peace*, Basingstoke: Macmillan.
Pankhurst, E., 1914, *My Own Story*, London: Nash.
Raeburn, A., 1973, *The Militant Suffragettes*, London: Joseph.

HARRY POLLITT 1890–1960

Harry Pollitt was the General Secretary of the Communist Party of Great Britain (CPGB) between 1929 and 1956, except for a break of two years between 1939 and 1941. He was probably the most influential British Marxist of the twentieth century, although Rajani Palme Dutt, the Marxist intellectual, and Tom Mann, the trade union leader, could make some slight claim to that title. Although occasionally inclined to reject the lead of Moscow, as in the case of its advocacy of opposition to the Second World War, Pollitt was normally a faithful representative of the views of the Communist International (or Comintern), and of Joseph Stalin and his successors. Indeed, after Pollitt resigned as General Secretary of the CPGB in 1956 he reiterated that he supported Russian actions in Eastern Europe and was a faithful supporter of the Soviet Union.

Pollitt was born at Droylesdon, near Manchester, on 22 November 1890. He was the son of Samuel Pollitt, a blacksmith and Mary Louise (Charlesworth) Pollitt, a cotton weaver. Harry was the second of six children. He was educated at a local elementary school until he was thirteen, and also at a Moravian Sunday School. He began his working life as a half-timer in a local weaving mill in 1902 and became a full-timer, at thirteen, in 1903 and then moved into engineering and became an apprentice plater for seven years, between 1907 and 1912. After that he worked as a plater in various boiler, constructional and locomotive shops throughout Britain. Indeed, he became a member of the Boilermakers' Society in 1912, serving as Secretary of the London district from 1919, and was Chief Speaker and paid Organizer of the River Thames Shop Stewards' Movement in 1917.

Pollitt's political interests drew him into the socialist-oriented Independent Labour Party (ILP) in 1906 at a time when the ILP and the Labour Party had made significant political gains in the general election. Indeed, he established a reputation as a socialist speaker in his speaking tours of Lancashire and Yorkshire between 1911 and 1914. However, when some members of the ILP joined with the Democratic Party (the old Social Democratic Federation) to form the 'one socialist party', the British Socialist Party (BSP), in 1911, Pollitt joined the new organization. In this organization he opposed the pro-war stance of its leader, Henry Mayers Hyndman. However, in 1916, Hyndman was ejected from the BSP and the anti-war section of the Party began a staunchly anti-war campaign in which Pollitt played a major role.

Shortly after the end of the First World War, Pollitt rose to prominence as national organizer of the 'Hands off Russia' campaign. This event arose because Britain and the other Allied powers had intervened in Russia and were actively supporting the 'White Russians', that is, those opposing the Red Russians or Bolsheviks in the Russian civil war. The 'Hands off Russia' campaign began on 10 May 1919 when some stevedores and dockers refused to supply coal to the SS *Jolly George*, which was loaded with munitions for Poland to help the White Russians. Over the following months a Central Council of Action was formed, by the Trades Union Congress (TUC) and the Labour Party, and about 350 local councils of actions came into existence. Demonstrations were held throughout August and on 17 August 1919 the 'Hands off Russia' campaign issued a leaflet demanding *Peace with Soviet Russia*. In the event, the Allied invasion of Russia came to an end and the campaign ended.

Pollitt was a founder member of the Communist Party of Great Britain (CPGB) when it was formed in London in July/August 1920 and reformed in Leeds in 1921. At first he was merely a young and active agitator and the CPGB was led by an old guard, led by Albert Inkpin, who was General Secretary between 1920 and 1929. Pollitt earned his reputation, which grew rapidly, as an industrial and trade-union activist. He was an organizer, agitator and editor for the British Bureau of the Red International of Labour Unions and became a formative figure in the creation of the National Minority Movement (NMM) in Britain, a CPGB organization which had as its purpose the capture of trade-union support. However, although it claimed about one million trade union members in 1926 it had declined, on its own admission, to fewer than 3,000 members when it became defunct in

1933. For their part the trade unions, especially after the 1926 General Strike, were positively hostile to the NMM.

By 1922, Pollitt was a rising young star in the CPGB and was drawn into writing a report on the party structure with Rajani Palme Dutt. The 'Dutt–Pollitt' Report suggested that all the branches of the CPGB should be organized along the lines of workers' soviets, with everyone having a specific duty, rather than along the lines of other British political parties which were essentially talking shops. Although this Report had some impact at first it is doubtful whether these pro-active branch activities survived much beyond the late 1920s and the Report was less effective than has often been suggested.

In 1925 Pollitt was imprisoned, with eleven other members of the CPGB, for seditious libel, incitement to mutiny and seduction of members of the armed forces. Some were imprisoned for six months but Pollitt was one of those imprisoned for twelve months. This meant that he, and some other leading members of the CPGB, were out of circulation at the time of the General Strike of May 1926, in which the CPGB supported the industrial action taken by the TUC but criticized its calling off of the dispute on 12 May as the 'greatest crime ever committed' in the history of the working class.

Once released from prison, Pollitt re-established his position within the CPGB and was appointed General Secretary in 1929 at a time when the old leadership was being swept away. By then, however, the CPGB had given up its attempt to work with the trade unions and the Labour Party and was moving into its 'Class Against Class' phase (1928–32/3). As a result, the membership of the CPGB often fell to less than 3,000 and its influence, both within the trade unions and the Labour Party, declined almost to the point of extinction. Indeed, the declining significance of the CPGB was amply demonstrated when Pollitt stood against James Ramsay MacDonald, the Labour Leader, in the Seaham constituency at the 1929 general election and was soundly trounced.

A Workers' Charter movement was begun in order to create a direct link between the CPGB and the workers and to make the Class Against Class policy a success. The purpose was to offer policies, such as shorter hours and more pay to the workers, in the hope of attracting support from the trade unions to the CPGB. In fact the movement failed, and in a panic to achieve success the CPGB offered some new initiative, based partly upon the Workers' Charter, practically every week. In addition, there was a campaign to support independence for India, advocated by leading CPGB figures such as Rajani Palme Dutt and S. Saklatvala.

Realizing that the CPGB was becoming politically obscure, and accepting that its ability to affect the outcome of industrial disputes was greatly diminished by its lack of influence within the trade unions, Pollitt led a British delegation to the Comintern at the end of 1931/ early 1932. It secured the 'January Resolutions' for the CPGB, which, exclusively, allowed the CPGB to ignore part of the Class Against Class policy and to attempt to work, once again, with and within the British reformist trade unions. From 1932 onwards, then, the CPGB became more outward looking. Yet it was the rise to power of Hitler in Germany in January 1933 that led to the abandonment of the whole policy and to the Comintern advocating a 'United Front' policy against fascism with other socialist parties and, from 1935, a 'Popular Front' policy with all parties opposed to fascism. Neither policy gained much support within Britain, despite Pollitt's determined attempts to make them work. Indeed, the famous Olympia conflict of 7 June 1934 between the CPGB and the British Union of Fascists was largely a product of the London district of the CPGB forcing the issue. Part of the reason for the failure is that Pollitt, and many other leading figures in the Party, took European fascism more seriously than they did British fascism. The other reason was that the Labour Party would not, on any account, work with the CPGB. Pollitt's defeats in the parliamentary contests at Clay Cross (1933) and Rhondda East (1935) simply reflected the huge obstacles he had to overcome.

This general antipathy towards the CPGB and its policies was demonstrated most effectively in the case of the Spanish Civil War, which began on 19 July 1936 with the fascist invasion of Spain and local fascist risings, and ended with the defeat of the Spanish Republican government on 1 April 1939. In line with Comintern policy on Spain, Pollitt called for British volunteers to join a British Battalion of the International Brigade in Spain (*Daily Worker*, 5 December 1936), an initiative which eventually attracted about 2,300 volunteers. Pollitt also went to Spain on five separate occasions to talk to the volunteers. He also sought to work with the ILP and the Socialist League in forming a Socialist Unity campaign to press for the end of the British government's policy of non-intervention in Spain. None of this worked and the fragmentation of socialist support, with deep hostility emerging from the Labour Party, worsened the situation.

Unfortunately for Pollitt's campaign, the Moscow Show Trials occurred in 1937 and 1938, and saw Stalin arrange for the trial and execution of his political opponents. Secret messages were sent from Moscow to Pollitt to get him to convince a disbelieving British public that those executed were in fact traitors to the Soviet Union. In the end, however, there was little Pollitt could do to persuade a sceptical British public of such an unlikely explanation.

At the outset of the Second World War, in September 1939, Pollitt directed the CPGB to support Britain's war effort against Nazi Germany, publishing his political line in the pamphlet *How to Win the War* (CPGB, 1939). However, within a month the CPGB was instructed to change this line by Stalin and the Comintern as a result of Stalin's concern to protect the German–Soviet non-aggression pact signed on the eve of war. Pollitt was unhappy with this arrangement and resigned as General Secretary of the CPGB, although he later fought a parliamentary by-election at West Ham/Silvertown in 1940. At the meeting at which this new policy emerged, Pollitt stated: 'I am a loyal supporter of the CI.... I am opposed to this thesis. I believe that in the long run it will do the Party very great harm' (CPGB, Central Committee minutes, 2 October 1939). He was re-instated as General Secretary in 1941, following the German invasion of the Soviet Union, known as Operation Barbarossa, and he turned the CPGB into the most patriotic of all British political parties in its pursuit of the war effort.

In 1945, at the end the Second World War, Pollitt pursued the policy of working with the Labour Party which had effectively been adopted in 1933 and extended in 1935, even though the Labour Party did not reciprocate. Therefore, instead of putting forward fifty or more candidates at the 1945 general election the CPGB put forward only twenty-one – of whom two were returned. Pollitt himself was narrowly defeated in East Rhondda.

The change of direction for CPGB parliamentary policy continued when, in 1951, after many years of evolution, the CPGB published *The British Road to Socialism*. This groundbreaking document appeared to offer an option of a democracy that had emerged from the 'People's War' (the Second World War) that allowed Pollitt to offer an agenda for Communist politics in Britain which had a decidedly parliamentary slant. It suggested that it was now possible for the working class to win control over the capitalist state in Britain by constitutional means, In other words, the idea of the parliamentary cul-de-sac was abandoned and the parliamentary road to socialism took the place of the proletarian dictatorship as advocated by Marx, Engels and Lenin.

Despite Pollitt's occasional differences with the Moscow line he always regarded himself as a faithful follower of the Comintern and Joseph Stalin. Indeed, when Stalin died in 1953 Pollitt was a member of the Guard of Honour at his funeral. He resigned from the post of General Secretary of the CPGB in May 1956, three months after

Krushchev made his secret attack upon Stalin at the Twentieth Congress of the Communist Party of the Soviet Union. When that speech, at which he was not present, was formally released in June 1956, Pollitt reflected that he could not denigrate a man whom he had admired above all others.

Pollitt died on 27 June 1960, on the liner *Orion* on his way back from Australia. By that time the CPGB had split over the Soviet invasion of Hungary in November 1956 and the dispute over free speech within the Party. These were problems which he recognized from his own, quite successful, period as General Secretary of the CPGB, during which time he always accepted the Moscow line, even if he was sometimes hesitant in so doing. Not surprisingly, then, to many Britons Pollitt was 'Moscow's man in Britain', an impression he did little to remove.

See also: Bevin

Further reading

Laybourn, K. and Murphy, D., 1999, *Under the Red Flag*, Stroud: Sutton.
Mahon, J., 1976, *Harry Pollitt. A Biography*, London: Lawrence & Wishart.
Morgan. K., 1989, *Against Fascism and War*, Manchester: Manchester University Press.
Morgan, K., 1993, *Harry Pollitt*, Manchester: Manchester University Press.
Pollitt, H., 1940, *Serving My Time*, London: Lawrence & Wishart.
Pollitt, H., 1947, *Looking Ahead*, London: The Communist Party.
Thompson, W., 1992, *The Good Old Cause: British Communism 1920–1991*, London: Pluto Press.

(JOHN) ENOCH POWELL 1912–98

John Enoch Powell is best remembered for both his 'Rivers of Blood' speech against immigration and for the fact that he adopted monetarist and anti-welfare state positions in the late 1950s, well before the revival of those views by Margaret Thatcher in the 1970s and 1980s. However, Powell was not a successful minister and his controversial career, based upon an uncompromising advocacy of his principles, meant that he never reached the political heights for which he seemed destined. Indeed, Powell sat in the Cabinet for a mere fifteen months in a parliamentary career of thirty-seven years.

Powell was born at Birmingham on 16 June 1912 to Ellen Mary (née Breese) and Albert Enoch Powell, who were both teachers. He was born in Flaxley Lane, Stechford, Birmingham. A particularly bright boy, Enoch was educated at King Edward School, Birmingham, where he earned a reputation for being an independent thinker. In 1929 he passed his Higher School Certificate with distinctions in Latin, Greek and Ancient History and then went on to Trinity College, Cambridge, where he was recognized as a formidable scholar and a recluse: 'This was not because I disliked my fellows, that's not the point at all', he explained, 'It was that I didn't know there was anything else to do'. (Heffer, 1998, pp. 14–15). Nevertheless, he did take out life membership of the Cambridge Union, in order to eat dinner there on a Saturday night, but he never attended its debates and played no part in politics. Instead he was greatly influenced by the lectures of A. E. Houseman, the Kennedy Professor of Latin, who had been responsible for *A Shropshire Lad*, a collection of lyrics published to great acclaim in 1896. Powell's academic rise was swift and in October 1934 he became a Fellow of Trinity, at the very young age of twenty-two. In 1937, aged only twenty-five, he became Professor of Greek at Sydney University in Australia, giving his inaugural address in May 1938.

Powell resigned his academic post in 1939 and joined the British army on 20 October 1939 to fight in the Second World War . He regarded this as one of the finest things he ever did for it gave him the opportunity to wipe away the shame of appeasement which he felt stained British politics. He was a supreme patriot with a strong sense of duty and, in the army, rose from private to brigadier, and spent some of his war in India and Malaya.

After the Second World War Powell started a career in politics, the third career of his short life. He instructed his father to use his (Oswald's) proxy parliamentary vote against the candidate who supported Churchill and whom he felt was erratic, and declared that the return of Attlee in 1945 was the right decision. However, he soon veered towards the Conservative Party: 'I was born a Tory … a Tory is a person who regards authority as immanent in institutions' (Heffer, 1998, p. 99). Powell was appointed to the Secretariat of the Conservative Party, at £900 per year, with the responsibility of briefing the Conservative Shadow Ministers. His immediate colleagues in that body were Reginald Maudling and Ian Macleod, both of whom became distinguished and leading politicians and ministers within the Party and its governments. The Secretariat he joined united with the Conservative Party's Research Department in 1948.

As early as 1948 Powell was criticizing the British welfare state, which had come into existence in July 1948 with the formation of the National Health Service and the introduction of the National

Insurance Act. Indeed, by 1947 he was already comparing 'Labour Britain' with the 'appeasement Britain' of 1938 and throughout 1948 was levelling enormous criticism at Nye Bevan, accusing him of misrepresenting the facts on both housing and health.

Powell, despite his rising political profile, struggled to get into Parliament. He failed to win the Normanton parliamentary by-election in the winter of 1947, but was eventually returned as MP for Wolverhampton South West in the general election of 1950, holding that seat until he resigned from the Conservative Party in 1974.

As already suggested, Powell's political career was hardly impressive. He was Parliamentary Secretary at the Ministry of Housing between December 1955 and January 1957, Financial Secretary to the Treasury from January 1957 until January 1958, and spent three years as Minister of Health from July 1960 until October 1963. As Minister of Health he was promoted to the Cabinet in July 1962. By the autumn of 1963 his ministerial career was over. Yet he became a towering political force within the Conservative Party, largely because of his controversial political opinions. He was, as already suggested, one of the first politicians to challenge the post-war consensus, defending the free market, warning about the dangers of race relations legislation and opposing Britain's attempt to become a member of the European Economic Community (EEC) in 1961 and Britain's eventual entry in 1973.

Powell's political career was severely undermined by his outspoken approach to politics and his reluctance to compromise his principles. For instance, in January 1958 he resigned from the Treasury team when Harold Macmillan and the Cabinet refused to accept the attempt by Peter Thorneycroft, the Chancellor of the Exchequer, to reduce public expenditure and increase interest rates to 7 per cent. In October 1963, Powell was invited to join Lord Home's Cabinet but refused because he supported the rival claims of R. A. Butler for the Conservative Leadership and, thus, for the premiership. In 1965 Powell stood against Edward Heath for the leadership of the Conservative Party but won only a miserly fifteen votes. Most important of all, his infamous 'Rivers of Blood' speech of 20 April 1968, warning of the dangers of continued immigration of the New Commonwealth citizens into Britain, ended his direct political influence on the decision-making bodies and groups within the Conservative Party.

In many ways, the 'Rivers of Blood' speech was the defining moment of Powell's political career, bringing about his political nemesis. In the speech, which took place in the upper rooms of the Midland Hotel in Birmingham (Heffer, 1998, pp. 449–59), Powell began by suggesting that the function of statesmanship is to 'provide against preventable evils'. Then, addressing the immigration question in Britain, he stated: 'If I had the money to go I wouldn't stay in this country. I have three children.... I shan't be satisfied till I have seen them all settled overseas. In this country in 15 or 20 years time the black man will have the whip hand over the white man.' Suggesting that the number of (recent) immigrants would be three and a half million within fifteen or twenty years, Powell stressed the need for 're-emigration' of these immigrant groups and warned of the fear that was beginning to stalk the British streets. He added that 'Like the Roman, I seem to see the River Tiber foaming with blood' (Heffer, 1988, p. 454). Powell thus predicted that continued immigration would lead to 'a total transformation to which there is no parallel in a thousand years of British history' (*The Times*, 23 April 1968).

This speech was an attempt to move the Conservative Party to the Right and to make a populist appeal to the middle ground of middle- and working-class opinion. However, Powell's tactics misfired and Edward Heath sacked him as Shadow Secretary of State for Defence the very next day. For the following two decades Powell was treated as a political leper both in Conservative and British politics, and was denied access to the main channels of Conservative Party influence.

Nevertheless, in the wake of Powell's speech there were a number of strikes against what he had described as the 'privileging' of the immigrant under the Race Relations Act. There were also unofficial strikes in support of Powell's right to free speech and some support for his racist remarks.

Powell continued to be a popular platform speaker but the gulf between him and Edward Heath, and thus the Conservative Party, widened when he opposed Heath's attempted entry into the EEC in the early 1970s, much as he had opposed Macmillan's attempt to do the same in 1961. Powell further opposed the policies which led Heath's government of 1970–4 into incomes policies and intervention in industry, which ran counter to the commitment to the free market which he espoused and which dominated the Conservative manifesto of June 1970.

During this period, Powell was increasingly identified with a movement which became known as 'Powellism'. The movement focused upon the tensions between state sovereignty and national identity, the individual and the state, and the whole purpose of politics in the 1970s progressed. However, despite being a right-wing Conservative he found little satisfaction in the emergence of Margaret Thatcher as Conservative Party Leader in 1975 and Prime Minister in

1979. He disliked Thatcher's support for Higher Education in terms of financial value to the nation, professing an interest in education for its own sake. He was also opposed to capital punishment

By the late 1970s Powell had left the Conservative Party. He was opposed to many of the policies of the Heath government and was bitterly opposed to Heath's decision to call a general election in February 1974, in response to the miners' strike which sought to dismantle the prices and incomes policy operated by the Conservative government. From a free-market position Powell felt that the general election had been called to defend the statutory incomes policy which would have to be abandoned in order to get the striking miners back to work. He also distanced himself further from the Conservative Party by asking his supporters to vote Labour in the future. As a result, he effectively left the Party in February/March 1974. He was briefly out of the House of Commons from March until October 1974 when, after another general election, he was elected as an Ulster Unionist for Down South, a seat he held until his defeat in the 1987 general election. As an Ulster Unionist he supported the direct rule of Northern Ireland from Westminster and was opposed to the Protestant Unionists power sharing with the Republican Roman Catholics.

For the rest of his political career, Powell preached many of the free-market ideas later taken up by Margaret Thatcher, but he was never identified with her in any personal sense. He continued to advocate the continuance of the union of Northern Ireland and Britain and the increased control of New Commonwealth immigration into Britain. However, after his parliamentary defeat in 1987 he withdrew from active politics. He died on 8 February 1998.

In assessing Powell's political career, it is clear that he was an influential political figure. Many of the policies introduced by Thatcher in the 1970s and 1980s were foreshadowed by Powell's political activities in the 1950s and 1960s.

Yet, whilst Powell possessed a first-rate mind it is clear that he was a man who held his principles dearly and not prepared to compromise. This meant that he refused political office on a number of occasions in his life and resigned on two occasions. Powell once said of all political careers that 'at the end of a lifetime in politics ... when a man looks back, he discovers that the things he most opposed have come to pass and that nearly all the objects he set out with are not merely not accomplished, but seem to belong to a different world from the one he lives in' (Heffer, 1998, p. 961) He added, in reflective mood, that 'All political lives ... end in failure, because that is the nature of politics and of human affairs.' These reflections are not altogether true, for whilst in some respects Powell's political life was a failure, many of the issues he espoused still command attention, whether for good or ill.

See also: Eden, Heath, Macmillan

Further reading

Heffer, S., 1998, *Like the Roman: The Life and Times of Enoch Powell*, London: Weidenfeld & Nicolson.

Lindop, F., 2001, 'Racism and the Working Class in Support of Enoch Powell in 1968', *Labour History Review*, 66, 1 (spring).

Powell, 1965, *A Nation Not Afraid*, ed. J. Wood, London: Hodder &; Stoughton.

Powell, 1969, *Freedom and Reality*, ed. J. Wood, London: Batsford.

Powell, E., 1971, *The Common Market: The Case Against*, Kingswood: Elliot.

SIR HERBERT (LOUIS) SAMUEL (FIRST VISCOUNT SAMUEL) 1870–1963

Herbert Samuel, who became the first Viscount Samuel in 1937, was a leading figure in the Liberal Party during the early twentieth century, becoming Leader between 1931 and 1935. He was a Minister in the Liberal government and wartime administrations of 1905 to 1916 and also High Commissioner of Palestine between 1920 and 1925. He was, indeed, deeply involved in the Jewish community and a Zionist, much respected by the Jewish settlers. Politically, Samuel is associated with the Asquithian free-trade wing of the Liberal Party and often found himself in opposition to David Lloyd George, even though he favoured government-inspired social reform of New Liberalism in his younger years.

Samuel was born at Liverpool on 6 November 1870, the son of Edwin Samuel, a very wealthy Jewish banker, and Clara Yates, his wife. Samuel's parents moved to London in 1871, where Edwin activated his partnership in Samuel & Montagu, one of the great London banks. However, Edwin died in 1877, leaving an estate of about £200,000, as well as his holdings in Samuel & Montagu and his leasehold properties. Herbert, although orphaned, was therefore raised in considerable wealth, with his three brothers and a sister, by his mother.

Samuel was educated at University College School, London, and at Balliol College, Oxford, where he gained a first-class degree in modern history. Whilst at Oxford he came under the influence of Graham Wallas, an empiricist and prominent member of the Fabian Society, which was committed to the gradual extension of state control and the improvement of social conditions. It was probably at this stage that Samuel developed his commitment to 'meliorist' ideas, which he defined as ones which considered that the present was better than the past and that the future may be better still. In any case, he was also greatly influenced by Sidney Webb, a leading figure in the Fabian Society who was committed to social reform. It was through this type of connection that he became deeply involved in the activities of a group of Radicals, including Ramsay MacDonald, Charles P. Trevelyan and both Beatrice and Sidney Webb, who met in the Rainbow Tavern in London and formed the 'Rainbow Circle'. The *Progressive Review* was produced between 1896 and 1897 as a journal to represent the views of the Circle. However, Samuel, Trevelyan, and other Liberal Radicals wished radicalism to remain within the Liberal Party whilst MacDonald and the Webbs began to favour Hardie's ideas that the Labour movement should focus upon a separate political party which was independent of the Liberal Party.

With the acrimonious break-up of the Rainbow Circle and the end of the *Progressive Review*, Samuel began to develop his own progressive ideas in pamphlets and, finally, in his book *Liberalism* (1902), in which he outlined many of the social reforms eventually introduced by the Liberal government from the end of 1905 to 1914. Indeed, throughout the late 1890s and early twentieth century Samuel undertook a punishing programme of lectures – 502 between 1893 and 1902 – to shape, influence and revive the Liberal Party organizations and attitudes. (It must be remembered here that the Liberal Party was out of office between 1895 and 1905.)

Samuel entered Parliament in 1902, as Liberal MP for Cleveland, a seat he held until 1918. At first he made his name because of his humanitarian concerns. Indeed, in 1903, he denounced the 'barbarism' of King Leopold of the Belgians in the Congo and, in 1904–5, working alongside Roger Casement, bitterly opposed the Conservative scheme for the importation of Chinese labour to work in the gold mines of South Africa. It was this latter controversy that, with others, brought down the Conservative government of Arthur Balfour in December 1905.

Between 1905 and 1909, Samuel became Under-Secretary at the Home Office, at first in the Campbell-Bannerman government and then in the Asquith government. He helped to draft and present social reform legislation and was associated particularly with the Probation Act of 1907, which created a national system of probation officers, and with the Children's Act of 1908, which codified much of the existing legislation governing the treatment and protection of children. In 1909, he was appointed Chancellor of the Duchy of Lancaster, effectively a minister without a portfolio or ministry who was given a specific task by the Prime Minister. This raised him to the Cabinet and thus earned him the distinction of becoming the first Jew who had not converted to another religion to occupy a seat in the Cabinet. He was subsequently Postmaster-General from 1910 to 1914 and, again between May 1915 and January 1916, and was largely responsible for the nationalization of the telephone service. He was also President of the Local Government Board from February 1914 to May 1915, where his attempted reforms were abandoned as a result of the First World War. He was also, briefly, Home Secretary between January and December 1916 and found himself in conflict with many former Radical friends who felt that civil liberties were being removed in pursuit of victory in the First World War. The internment of Irish dissidents also presented problems for his reputation, and he was deeply involved in the case of Sir Roger Casement who was found guilty of high treason and executed on 3 August 1916, having been arrested in April 1916 as he landed from a German submarine. However, Samuel's ministerial and Cabinet posts came to an end in December 1916 when, instead of accepting office under David Lloyd George, he decided to support Asquith, the deposed Prime Minister, on the opposition front bench. It was a logical decision for someone so concerned with the extension of state control.

His interest at this time had, in any case, moved towards Zionism. His interest in the area seems to have emerged before the First World War and, in 1915, he put to the Cabinet the need for a British-sponsored homeland in Palestine, a plan outlined in the memorandum *The Future of Palestine*, which demanded 'the restoration of Jews to the land to which they are attached by ties as ancient as history itself'. He hoped that Palestine could provide a home for at least three or four million of Europe's Jews. Undoubtedly, he played some part in influencing the Balfour Declaration of November 1917, a single-sentence statement stating that

> His Majesty's Government view with favour the establishment in Palestine of a national home for the Jewish people, and will use their best endeavours to facilitate the achievement of this object, it being clearly understood that nothing shall be done which may prejudice the civil and religious rights of existing non-Jewish communities in Palestine, or the rights and political status enjoyed by Jews in any other country.

Samuel thus became the obvious choice for the first High Commissioner in Palestine under the League of Nations mandate, a post which he held from 1920 to 1925. In many ways, he laid the basis for the modern Israeli state during this formative period, although the Arab anti-Zionist riots of 1920 and 1921 forced him to restrict Jewish immigration according to the 'economic absorptive capacity' of Palestine. Nevertheless, he was seen by many as a 'Nehemiah leading his people home from exile' (Wasserstein, 1992, p. 249). Hymns of redemption were composed in his honour and carpets were woven bearing his image.

When Samuel ended his period as High Commissioner he expected to retire into writing and developing his philosophical ideas, proposing to live in a house on Mount Carmel in Palestine. However, he was quickly drawn back into public life as head of the Royal Commission on the Coal Industry, which was set up in August 1925 in order to examine the future of the British coal industry in the light of the threatened industrial action of July 1925. The Commission reported in March 1926 and suggested that the industry should be rationalized, that government coal subsidies could not be continued, and that the wages of the coal miners, already much reduced in the previous five years, would have to be temporarily reduced further. It was a report which was rejected by both the coal miners and the coal owners and it failed to prevent the conflict which led to the General Strike of the Trades Union Congress (TUC) between 3 and 12 May 1926. Nevertheless, whilst on holiday around Locarno, in Italy and Switzerland, Samuel was called back by the TUC to help negotiate a settlement to the strike. His negotiations with the TUC, which led to the production of the 'Samuel Memorandum', which largely reiterated the main points of the Report of the Royal Commission on the Coal Industry, was sufficient to encourage the TUC, in the face of opposition from the coal miners, to call off the General Strike at 12.10 pm on the 12 May 1926. The Baldwin Conservative government, however, felt no need to be bound by the Memorandum, and the TUC had effectively surrendered without guarantee.

In the late 1920s Samuel was drawn back into the Liberal Party, from whose internal discussions and quarrels he had been distanced by his role in Palestine. Indeed, during the 1920s he had kept up his close contacts with Labour figures, such as Beatrice and Sidney Webb, and had become rather distant from the Liberal leaders. He now became the Liberal Party's organizational chief in 1927, securing £300,000 from the Lloyd George Fund to fight the general election of May 1929 and £35,000 per year for administration. Eventually, the Liberal Party improved its position enormously from its disastrous showing at the 1924 general election, winning fifty-nine seats instead of the forty of 1924, and Samuel himself was returned to Parliament as MP for Darwen. Along with Lloyd George, he operated a Lib–Lab arrangement which kept Ramsay MacDonald's second Labour government in office. When the Labour government fell, in August 1931, Samuel was instrumental in helping to form MacDonald's National Government, in which he became Home Secretary and, incidentally, Liberal Leader. Despite Liberal losses in the October 1931 general election, and many differences within the new National Government, Samuel remained Home Secretary until the end of September 1932, when he resigned because of the continued protectionist policies that were being adopted. Samuel remained Liberal Leader until the 1935 general election when he himself was defeated and the Liberal Party reduced to nineteen seats. Thereafter, he never held office again and, raised to the Lords in 1937, instead spoke in the House of Lords, broadcast on the BBC and wrote philosophical works.

Samuel will be remembered as one of the key figures in the Liberal Party as it declined during the inter-war years and as a Zionist who helped to lay the foundations of the state of Israel. It will probably be forgotten that, although he was often closely associated with the free-trade section of the Liberal Party, he was one of the formative figures in the creation of the New Liberalism, with its emphasis upon social reform, which David Lloyd George helped develop in the early twentieth century.

See also: Lloyd George, Simon

Further reading

Wasserstein, B., 1992, *Herbert Samuel: A Political Life*, Oxford: Clarendon.

SIR JOHN (ALLLESBROOK) SIMON (VISCOUNT SIMON OF STACKPOLE ELIDOR) 1873–1954

Sir John Simon was one of the leading political figures of the Liberal Party during the early twentieth century, although he ended his career within the Conservative Party. Indeed, as his political career developed he drifted from the Left of the Liberal Party to the Right, eventually joining the National Government in 1931, leading the Liberal Nationals section into the National Government and, ultimately, into the Conservative Party. Rooted in his Liberal past, however, he fulfilled the role of Foreign Secretary in the 1930s in an entirely non-aggressive manner, which marked him out as one of the originators of the appeasement policy towards fascism. Indeed, his tenure as Foreign Secretary was described as 'disastrous' and 'surely the worst in modern times' (*The Times*, 12 January 1954).

John Simon was born of Welsh parents at Manchester on 28 February 1873. He was educated at Fettes College and then, from 1892, at Wadham College, Oxford, where he studied Classics. He became President of the Oxford Union, obtained a first-class degree in 1896 and was elected a Fellow of Souls College, Oxford. Two years later he was called to the Bar, and became a King's Counsel. Indeed, he was a very successful barrister and, in 1909, became the standing counsel to the University of Oxford.

By that time, however, Simon was already carving out a political career. In 1906 he became Liberal MP for the Walthamstow Division of Essex and rose quickly in Liberal circles, his legal training helping in his appointment as Solicitor-General in 1910. It was a post he held until 1913, when he became Attorney-General (with a seat in the Cabinet). He was also appointed as a Privy Councillor in 1912.

Like many pacific Liberals, Simon was unhappy about Britain's involvement in the First World War. His political output was one geared towards securing peace through international negotiations and, with other leading Liberal figures, he seriously considered resigning from the wartime Liberal government. Nevertheless, he remained in government, refusing the post of Lord Chancellor in the wartime Coalition Government, formed in May 1915, but accepting the post of Home Secretary. It was a short-lived appointment, lasting a mere seven months after which he resigned when Asquith's government introduced military conscription in January 1916. This period of office had, in fact, been painful to him since he had to sanction the police seizure of pamphlet stock of the Union of Democratic Control, a body which had been formed at the beginning of the Great War to protect civil liberties and which contained some of Simon's old friends. From 1917 onwards, and despite his hesitancy, he nevertheless spent the rest of the war with the Royal Flying Corps in France.

Simon remained a supporter of Asquith and opposed Lloyd George's 'Coupon' Coalition Government arrangement in 1918. As a result he lost his seat in the 1918 general election. He contested the Spen Valley parliamentary by-election in November 1919 and

December 1920 but, faced with a Coalition Liberal opponent who divided the potential Liberal vote, he was defeated by the Labour candidate, Tom Myers. In 1922, however, the situation had changed and he was returned for Spen Valley, a seat he held from 1922 until 1940, first as a Liberal until 1931 and as a National Liberal thereafter.

Until 1931, Simon remained a Liberal. He was staunchly opposed to Lloyd George because of the way in which he had divided the Liberal Party in December 1916, but he recognized that ideas and inspiration had returned to the Party when he rejoined in 1923. However, the Liberal Party remained divided – despite its moves towards unity in the 1920s. The Asquithian free-trading section was led by Sir Herbert Samuel in the late 1920s; David Lloyd George led his own section of the Party and published many policy initiatives, encouraging state intervention in certain circumstances; while Simon led an increasingly right-wing and nationalistic section of the Party. The differences between the three sections were evident on many occasions. For instance, during the General Strike of May 1926, Lloyd George condemned the actions of the Baldwin government, Sir Herbert Samuel attempted to bring about a settlement between the coal miners and the coal owners, and Simon condemned the miners' strike and the General Strike in the House of Commons on 6 May. Indeed he suggested that the latter was unlawful and that 'every trade union leader who has advised and promoted that course of action is liable to damages to the uttermost farthing of his personal possessions'. Such a comment should not be surprising, for by the mid 1920s Simon had come to see socialism as the ultimate political evil.

In 1927 Simon became Chairman of the Indian Statutory Commission which, within the context of widespread unrest and nationalism, undertook to examine the way in which constitutional progress could be achieved in India. In June 1930 the Simon Report suggested that there should be an enlarged electorate in India and the need for responsible government in the provinces and a conference between the ruling princes of the native states of India, the government of India and the British government on the future form of a central government. The report carried little weight in the context of civil unrest and disobedience in India but did lead to a Round Table Conference in London in November 1930. The Indian National Congress Party abandoned this conference but the princes of the Indian states did agree to the formation of an all-Indian federation in the near future.

By 1931 Simon was a disgruntled member of the Liberal Party which was propping up Ramsay MacDonald's second Labour government. In March of that year, he opposed Lloyd George's decision to continue to support the Labour government. However, when the government collapsed in the financial crisis of August 1931 and the National Government was formed, under Ramsay MacDonald, he gave his full support to the new administration. Yet the formation of the National Government brought about the final fragmentation of the Liberal Party. David Lloyd George, the Liberal Leader, stayed outside the National Government and led a faction of Liberal MPs who were increasingly dominated by his own family and close friends. Sir Herbert Samuel entered the National Government but withdrew with the Liberal free traders when, in 1932, it became blatantly obvious that the Conservative-dominated National Government was becoming staunchly protectionist. Simon himself joined the National Government and, with about twenty-five supporters, formed the Liberal Nationals – a group which formally proclaimed its separate existence on 5 October 1931. The loyalty of the Liberal National group to the National Government was cemented by Simon's appointment as Foreign Secretary, a post he held until 1935, and by the fact that he made the political somersault of abandoning his support for free trade and accepting the need for protectionism.

As Foreign Secretary, Simon supported the principles of disarmament and non-interventionism. This suited the political mood and style of MacDonald, the Prime Minister, but meant that he did not confront the fascist dictators and Simon is, rightly, regarded as one of the initiators of the policy of appeasement.

Indeed, Simon was ineffective in dealing with the Japanese invasion of Manchuria in September 1931, and the creation of the state of Manchukuo in March 1932. The League of Nations did nothing to counter this and Simon was more concerned with placating the Japanese government than the Chinese government. He participated in the Geneva Disarmament Conference in 1932, but found that the rivalry between France and Germany prevented any meaningful action being taken and, in 1933, was involved in a Four-Power Pact (Britain, France, Italy and Germany), which effectively circumvented the League of Nations and agreed to revise the peace treaties (particularly the Treaty of Versailles) in favour of Germany. Responding to those concessions which would pave the way for German re-armament, Hitler announced, on 17 May 1933, that a European war would be 'madness', thus encouraging Simon to look further towards appeasement as the means of avoiding another European conflict.

When the Disarmament Conference resumed on 14 October 1933, Simon offered an arrangement for five years' international supervision of arms, without disarmament or re-armament, after which there would be disarmament, thus bringing all nations to an equal footing with Germany. In fact, Hitler decided not to attend the conference, announced that he intended to withdraw Germany from the League of Nations, and waited for a possible French invasion of the Ruhr and a Polish invasion of East Prussia. Nothing happened and the Conference was proclaimed at an end in May 1934.

It was in the wake of such events that Simon had second thoughts about disarmament. In 1935 he met Pierre Laval, the French Foreign Minister, and helped produce a joint statement suggesting the need for a freely negotiated agreement between Germany and the other powers and an armaments agreement to replace the Treaty of Versailles. Yet this did not seem to attract much positive response from Hitler and, on 4 March 1934, Simon issued a nine-page White Paper, *Statement Relating to Defence*, which reiterated that Britain was committed to collective security through the League of Nations and would continue to make efforts to bring about a reduction in armaments. But, in the absence of any foreseeable agreement, it declared that Britain had to strengthen her armed forces. Simon's involvement in foreign policy then came abruptly to an end. Lloyd George, in a letter to Smuts, Deputy Prime Minister of South Africa, on 31 July 1935, wrote: 'Simon has disappeared from the Foreign Office an acknowledged failure' (Dutton, 1992, p. 221).

When Stanley Baldwin replaced MacDonald as Prime Minister in 1935, Simon was appointed Home Secretary and Deputy Leader of the House of Commons, during which time he was involved in the abdication crisis of Edward VIII and the coronation of King George VI. When Neville Chamberlain replaced Baldwin as Prime Minister in 1937, Simon became the Chancellor of the Exchequer and was one of Chamberlain's inner cabinet. As Chancellor of the Exchequer he financed a substantial increase in the size of the Royal Air Force, although he tried to observe the Treasury policy of balancing the Budget. Yet, like Neville Chamberlain, the then Prime Minister, he still entertained the idea that peace in Europe could be maintained by agreements with Hitler and he endorsed the famous Munich Agreement of September 1938 by which Chamberlain surrendered Czechoslovakia to German expansionism in order to preserve peace in Europe.

It was only when Adolf Hitler invaded Poland in September 1939 that Simon changed his mind. Up to that point he had been willing to reach some form of compromise with Hitler and Mussolini, but the invasion led him, and other Cabinet Ministers, to insist that Neville Chamberlain should declare war on Germany. However, he played only a small part in the Second World War. In May 1940 he became Lord Chancellor in Winston Churchill's wartime Coalition Government, and was awarded the title of Viscount Simon of Stackpole Elidor. He retired from politics in 1945 and died of a stroke on 11 January 1954.

Simon was an excellent lawyer, but as a politician he lacked the ability to make decisions when in office and was too strongly associated with the process of appeasement in the 1930s that led to Hitler's political expansionism. Whilst he held three of the four major offices of government, and may have come near to securing the post of Prime Minister in 1937, it is clear that he never secured a reputation as a statesman of stature.

See also: Baldwin, Chamberlain (Neville), Churchill, MacDonald

Further reading

Dutton, D., 1992, *Simon: A Political Biography of Sir John Simon*, London: Arum.

Heuston, R. E. V., 1987, *Lives of the Lord Chancellors, 1940–1970*, Oxford: Clarendon.

MARGARET (HILDA) THATCHER (BARONESS THATCHER OF KESTEVEN) 1925–

Margaret Hilda Thatcher is Britain's only female Prime Minister. A powerful and determined politician, she gave her name to an ideology, Thatcherism, which stood for a limited but firm government, the rolling back of the welfare state, the end of consensus politics, and a staunchly anti-European and independent attitude on many vital issues. She was the longest-serving Prime Minister of the twentieth century and the only one to have ever been removed from office as a result of a ballot of Party MPs. She was the first Prime Minister since Lord Liverpool (the longest continuously serving Prime Minister of the nineteenth and twentieth centuries) to have won three successive general elections. Yet, above all, her period as Prime Minister (1979–90) transformed the nature and pattern of British politics. Indeed, she was one of the most combative of Prime Ministers in the twentieth century, challenging the post-war political consensus that had operated since 1945 in her attempt to restore what she described as 'Victorian Values'.

Margaret Hilda Roberts was born on 13 October 1925, the younger daughter of Alfred Roberts and Beatrice Stephenson, into a family of lower-middle-class grocers. She was raised as a Methodist. Her father was an ex-Liberal who became an Independent councillor and Mayor of Grantham, in Lincolnshire, and greatly influenced Margaret with his emphasis upon thriftiness and a belief in the free-market economy. She was educated at Kesteven and Grantham Grammar School, where she was known as 'Snotty Roberts', and from there went on to Somerville College, Oxford, where she ended with a second-class honours degree in Chemistry. She worked for a period in commercial and industrial chemistry (1947–51) and then married a fellow Methodist, Denis Thatcher, in 1951, by whom she had twins in 1953. During these years Thatcher read for the Bar and passed her exams to become a lawyer in 1953, practising for a few years in the field of tax law.

Thatcher's active interest in politics began at Oxford and she quickly became involved in parliamentary politics, losing in the Dartford parliamentary constituency at the general elections of 1950 and 1951. She eventually secured the Conservative candidature of Finchley in 1958 and represented that seat from 1959 to 1992, when she was raised to the House of Lords. Initially, she was promoted to a minor post in October 1961 and was, successively, Conservative Party spokesperson on Pensions, Housing, Energy, Transport, Education and the Environment between 1961 and 1970, entering the Shadow Cabinet in 1967. She then became Secretary of State at the Department of Education and Science in the government of Edward Heath, between June 1970 and February 1974. She campaigned for the extension of nursery education but also felt that the Ministry of Education was 'self-righteously socialist' and was spending too much money on education. Not surprisingly, she earned a reputation for being a 'cutting minister' when she transferred a small amount of money from the provision of school milk to science. The furore that resulted led to the catchy phrase 'Thatcher, Thatcher, milk snatcher'. At that point she appeared to be an unpopular political figure, and with the defeat of the Conservatives in the general elections in 1974 it seemed her political star was on the wane. Yet she stood against Edward Heath for the leadership of the Conservative Party in 1975 and won by 130 votes to 119, in what was effectively a back-bench revolt against Heath. She then won the second ballot against William Whitelaw, who subsequently became Deputy Leader of the Con-servative Party and Deputy Prime Minister and the subject of Thatcher's comment that 'Every prime minister needs a Willy'.

As Opposition Leader (1975–9) Thatcher moved gradually to replace the old Heathite 'One-Nation' Tories with figures of the New

Right, such as Sir Keith Joseph and Rhodes Boyson, who favoured the free market of writers such as Milton Friedman and von Hayek. She herself had been influenced by such ideas by her father and had identified with them when she became Vice-Chairman of the Centre for Policy Studies in June 1974. Her moment to introduce such ideas came when she won the 1979 general election, defeating a deeply unpopular Labour government led by James Callaghan, which had just faced a 'Winter of Discontent' of industrial disputes. Thatcher's first ministry (1979 to 1983) lacked sureness of touch but displayed determination, particularly in seeing off the old Heathite Tories such as Francis Pym. Faced with inflation well in excess of 20 per cent per annum she moved to redistribute income in favour of the rich (in Geoffrey Howe's tax cutting Budget of 1979) and then to control the supply of money, supporting the 1981 Budget which actually did the unheard-of action of raising taxes during a recession. The result was that unemployment, which was just over one million in May 1979, rose rapidly to more than three million by 1983, despite numerous changes that removed many people from the unemployment register. The government became deeply unpopular and was soon falling behind the Labour and Liberal Parties in the opinion polls, and struggling to keep ahead of the Social Democratic Party (SDP), formed in 1981. However, the outbreak of the Falklands War resulted in victory for Thatcher's government in the 1983 general election. In it, Thatcher sent a British military expedition to repossess the Falklands Islands from the Argentineans in the spring and summer of 1982, which culminated in Britain's recapture of the Falkland Islands on 14 June of that year. As a result of Britain's military success Thatcher's popularity rose to 80 per cent in the opinion polls. There were, however, other factors which helped Thatcher to secure her second general election success in 1983. The most obvious was that inflation fell from 21.8 per cent in April 1980 to 3.7 per cent in June 1983, revealing the success of her anti-inflationary policies.

Thatcher's second ministry (1983–7) was far more successful than the first. Insofar as it had direction it became increasingly committed to the privatization of public services and the reduction of public expenditure, particularly on the welfare state. In this process Thatcher pressed forward with a whole range of legislation designed to reduce the power of the trade unions and uphold her commitment to government control and intervention. Her government introduced eight acts (most notably the Employment Acts of 1980, 1982, 1988, 1989 and 1990, and the Trade Union Act of 1984) between 1979 and 1990 which were designed to weaken trade union power, deregulate the economy and remove the checks on British employment which it was felt had been responsible for the relative economic decline of Britain since the Second World War. The 1980 Employment Act introduced a limited definition of legal picketing; the 1982 Act permitted only closed trade union shops where 85 per cent of the workforce favoured them; the 1984 Trade Union Act forced unions to hold secret ballots, preferably postal, before legal industrial action could take place. These and other measures posed a direct challenge to established trade union rights. Indeed, the issue seemed to come to a defining moment with the coal miners' strike of 10 March 1984 to 5 March 1985. Fighting against the closure of pits the miners were defeated in part by the intransigence of Arthur Scargill, their leader, who succeeded in dividing the mining unions, but also because of the Conservative government's use of the law to restrict and punish the National Union of Mineworkers. Thatcher was determined that the miners would not bring down her government as they had done with Heath in February 1974. After the strike British trade unionism recognized the need to rethink its policies along a less confrontational route which could take advantage of the new legislation.

Thatcher was lucky to defeat the miners, the lack of union unity helping her cause. Her luck held out when on 12 October 1984 she narrowly missed death when an IRA bomb exploded at the Grand Hotel, Brighton, during the Conservative Party Conference, killing five people and injuring thirty-two. She was also fortunate in other developments. She helped to broker the Anglo-Irish Agreement of 1985 which allowed the Irish Republic a role in the politics of Northern Ireland, and she was active at the time when Mikhail Gorbachev, the Russian President, was making moves towards ending the Cold War towards the end of 1984 and in the early months of 1985. However, Thatcher's apparent invincibility and good fortune was tested to its limits by the Westland Affair in 1985 and 1986. After a prolonged debate over the future of the Westland Helicopter company, which Thatcher felt could only be saved by merging with the American firm of Sikorsky, Michael Heseltine, the Minister of Defence, resigned on 9 January 1986. Whilst this was damaging, the subsequent debate was more so, with Heseltine accusing Thatcher of adopting a presidential style of government and of deliberately leaking information. This led to a government defence which saw the resignation of the Home Secretary, Leon Brittan, for misleading the House of Commons. The Westland affair could have damaged Thatcher's political future but, in the end, changed little, and the improving economy, cuts in income tax, and continued problems within the Labour Party ensured that Thatcher won the general election of 11 May 1987, with a majority of 102.

Thatcher began her third term (1987–90) in an almost unassailable position, with the economy doing well, the higher levels of income tax down to 40 per cent by 1988, increased public spending and a public spending surplus. Yet in November 1990 she was replaced by John Major as Conservative Leader and Prime Minister. Her resignation as Prime Minister was prompted by a number of events.

The economic situation of the country began to worsen from 1981 onwards and her Party and some of her supporters began to doubt her policies on Europe. On 20 September 1988 she made a speech in Bruges in which she declared her opposition to any diminution of the sovereignty of the United Kingdom, building upon her reputation for toughness which had won Britain reductions in her financial contributions to Europe between 1984 and 1986. This put her in conflict with the sympathies of a section of her Party led by Kenneth Clarke and also with many of the sections of industry which supported a greater role in Europe. Also, Geoffrey Howe, her Chancellor of the Exchequer who resigned due to differences with her over Europe, delivered a dramatic resignation speech in the House of Commons on 13 November 1990, in which he stated: 'We have paid heavily in the past for late starts and squandered opportunities in Europe. We dare not let it happen again. If we detach ourselves completely, as a party or a nation, from the middle ground of Europe, the effects of this will be incalculable and very hard ever to correct.' It was clear that the government was divided at its highest level and that Thatcher's style of leadership was being questioned. Indeed, Howe asked how Cabinet unity could be maintained 'when every step forward risked being subverted by some casual comment or impulsive answer'.

The attack by Howe weakened Thatcher's position even further, but particularly in light of Thatcher's failures in connection with the poll tax in 1989 and 1990. Personally committed to abolishing the property-based rates, Thatcher advocated a system (the community charge, popularly known as the poll tax) whereby every adult paid the same local rates for the same local services. The scheme was first introduced into Scotland in 1989, where it was considered unjust since it required 'a widow in her flat to pay the same as a lord in his castle'. Yet the Conservative Party Conference insisted upon its introduction in England and Wales (1990) within one year rather than over a four-year period. However, opposition to it was intense, both in terms of demonstrations (the most important being in London on 31 March 1990) and non-payment. Indeed, when John Major replaced Thatcher he quickly abandoned the poll tax and returned to the old property-based system of raising money for local authorities,

Thatcher's resignation was a dramatic end to her political career. Under Conservative Party rules the leadership could be contested every year. In 1989 Sir Anthony Meyer, a back-bench candidate, lost to her by 314 votes to 33. In November 1990, after being attacked by Geoffrey Howe, who had just resigned as Foreign Secretary, Thatcher's leadership was attacked by Michael Heseltine. She obtained 204 votes to Heseltine's 152 but fell four votes short of the majority required for outright victory in the first round. Pressured to resign by various Ministers, including Kenneth Clarke, she made way for a new Leader to be elected rather than face further political humiliation, but was dismayed by what she believed was the betrayal of her former followers. Her resignation resulted in a brief rise in support for the Conservative Party in the opinion polls. In 1992 she accepted a life peerage in the House of Lords as Baroness Thatcher of Kesteven and has remained a presence in Conservative politics ever since, opposing Britain's closer involvement with the European Economic Community and endorsing William Hague's leadership of the Conservative Party in 1997.

Thatcher's period as Prime Minister saw the undermining of a general consensus that had existed in parliamentary politics since 1945. In particular, it removed the close links between trade unions and government, challenged the welfare state and promoted the privatization of government-owned public services and industry. Above all, her period in office promoted a free-market attitude in British society and established in the minds of the British public that lower rates of taxation would allow individuals, and not the government and public service institutions, to determine supply and demand conditions of the market. Thatcher's survival at the top of British politics owed much to fortunate events, such as the Falklands War and the miners' strike, both of which demonstrated her toughness and won her patriotic support. Yet there is still no doubting her impact upon both British politics and the politics of John Major, her Conservative successor. Indeed, Tony Blair, Labour's Prime Minister since 1997, undoubtedly dropped the public ownership part of Labour's traditional Clause Four in 1994/5, recognizing that Thatcherism had made such a policy untenable.

See also: Blair, Heath

Further reading

Evans, B., 1999, *Thatcherism and British Politics 1975–1999*, Stroud: Sutton.

Thatcher, M., 1993, *The Downing Street Years*, London: HarperCollins.

Young, H., 1990, *One of Us: A Biography of Margaret Thatcher*, London: Pan in association with Macmillan.

ELLEN (CICELY) WILKINSON 1891–1947

Ellen Wilkinson, 'Our Ellen', was one of Britain's most important female politicians, becoming Minister of Education in Clement Attlee's post-war Labour government. She was a trade union organizer, in part responsible for the Jarrow March, a journalist, a brilliant orator, and a prominent member of the Labour Party's National Executive. Indeed, she was an important national figure in the Labour Party even if, as Beatrice Webb suggested, she was not an original thinker (Vernon, 1982, p. 1).

Wilkinson was born at Ardwick near Manchester on 8 October 1891 into a respectable upper-working-class family. She was raised as a Methodist, valued education, and worked her way through school until, winning a scholarship, she entered the University of Manchester in 1910, where she obtained in history an upper second-class degree, not the First she expected, and an MA. At university she joined the Fabian Society, although she had already joined the Independent Labour Party (ILP) in 1907, and was active in the University Socialist Federation, which brought her into contact with the leading socialists of the day, including J. T. Walton Newbold, the first Communist MP in the 1920s who was organizing the Manchester Fabian Society at that time, to whom she was briefly engaged, and Herbert Morrison.

During these years, and subsequently, she gained a reputation for being a fiery personality. The fact that she was red-haired and small led to the epithets 'elfin fury', the 'Fiery Atom' and, later, 'Red Ellen' and 'Red Nellie Wilkinson'. For a time she worked for the National Union of Women's Suffrage Societies; she was active in the Women's International League and, in 1915, became the national women's organizer of the Amalgamated Union of Cooperative Employees. She was a powerful and tireless speaker and a ubiquitous crusader for women's rights. During and after the war she became a member of several trade boards. These had been set up in several industries after the 1909 Trade Boards Act, to help maintain industrial peace, and consisted of equal numbers of representatives from employers and employees.

Although initially active in the Communist Party of Great Britain (CPGB), attending its first Conference in July/August 1920 as a representative for the National Guild's League, and in the formation of the Red International of the Labour Unions, Wilkinson won her political spurs for the Labour Party when she was returned as a City Councillor for Gorton South Ward, Manchester, in November 1923. She lost her first parliamentary contest at Ashton-under-Lyne in 1923 but was eventually returned for Middlesbrough East in 1924 and became one of only four women in the House of Commons, and later one of only fourteen women in the House of Commons in 1929. She held that seat until the crushing Labour defeat in the 1931 general election but was returned for Jarrow in 1935, holding the seat until her death.

Ellen was deeply involved in the General Strike of 1926, called by the Trades Union Congress (TUC) in support of the coal miners who faced wage reductions and longer hours of work. From the start, Ellen was involved in a tour of Britain, with her friend Frank Horrabin, to organize meetings and to assess morale. Ellen organized the speakers and conveyed them north of the Humber. They were particularly concerned at the poor communications between the strikers. A few months after this Ellen, along with Frank Horrabin and Raymond Postgate, produced for 'Plebs' a small book entitled *A Workers' History of the General Strike*.

From 1924 until 1939 Wilkinson was closely associated with the British Left, active in the Socialist League and involved in pacifist and anti-fascist movements; and from 1939 onwards she was a contributor to the socialist weekly, *Tribune*. She had been attracted by Oswald Mosley's flamboyant disregard for economic orthodoxy in the 1920s but as she moved towards fascism she began to consider him a pariah. Ellen also aspired to be a journalist and a novelist. Michael Foot, who was closely associated with *Tribune* at this time, considered Ellen to be 'a brilliant journalist' (Vernon, 1982, p. 132). Her first novel, a political one entitled *Clash*, received mildly encouraging notices. Her second novel, the detective story *The Division Bell Mystery*, was equally well received.

Yet Ellen Wilkinson's great claim to fame was the fact that she helped to organize the Jarrow March to pressure the National Government to provide jobs for Jarrow, a town suffering from unemployment. The March began on 5 October 1926 when a contingent of 200 men from Jarrow marched to London to present two petitions to Parliament, demanding the creation of a new steel works for Jarrow. Ellen walked some of the way with the marchers, spoke to them on many evenings, presented their case to the Labour Party Conference at Edinburgh, and led the marching men on the last part of the march to Parliament when the petitions were presented to the Bar of the House. The petition from Jarrow had 11,000 signatures and that from the other Tyneside towns 68,500. The first was handed in by Ellen and the second by Sir Nicholas Gratton-Doyle, the Conservative MP who was the longest-serving MP in the Newcastle area. Wilkinson later wrote of her experiences and the unemployment and poverty problems of Jarrow in *The Town that was Murdered* (1939).

From 1930 onwards, however, Ellen moved more to the centre of Labour politics. In Winston Churchill's wartime Coalition Government she was appointed Parliamentary Secretary to the Ministry of Pensions in May 1940, Parliamentary Secretary to the Home Office in October 1940, and was made a Privy Councillor at the beginning of 1945. In August 1945 she became Minister of Education in Attlee's post-war Labour government. It was in this capacity that she pressed ahead with campaigns for free school milk and secondary education for all. The free milk would be one-third of a pint and provided regardless of class. Indeed, Wilkinson reflected that 'Free milk will be provided in Hoxton and Shoreditch, in Eton and Harrow' (Vernon, 1982, p. 214). Unfortunately, her work in education was cut short by her untimely death, of heart failure, following bronchitis, on 6 February 1947.

Ellen Wilkinson was an influential figure in the Labour Party and earned a reputation as a radical socialist. She was a lively, impetuous and energetic politician who was concerned to challenge poverty and improve the lives of the working classes. Commenting upon this ambition and her drive for change, Jack Lawson, MP, stated: 'Quite simply it arose from the urge of compassion for mankind and a vision of the world as it might be' (Vernon, 1982, p. 238).

See also: Attlee, MacDonald

Further reading

Morgan, K. O., 1987, *Labour People: Leaders and Lieutenants, Hardie to Kinnock*, Oxford: Oxford University Press.

Rubinstein, D., '1979, Ellen Wilkinson Reconsidered', *History Workshop Journal*, 7: 161–9.

Vernon, B. D., 1982, *Ellen Wilkinson, 1891–1947*, London: Croom Helm.

Wilkinson, E., 1939, *The Town that was Murdered*, London: Gollancz.

(JAMES) HAROLD WILSON (LORD WILSON OF RIEVAULX) 1916–95

Harold Wilson was Labour Prime Minister from 1964 to 1970 and again between 1974 and 1976, the first Labour Party Leader to win four general elections. He was thus the Labour Party's longest-serving Prime Minister before retiring in 1976, and subsequently becoming Baron Wilson of Rievaulx in 1983. However, Wilson's premierships occurred at a time when Britain was facing serious economic difficulties and was dominated by major social and industrial problems. As a result, historians, biographers and writers have depicted Wilson in two contrasting lights. On the one hand he is projected as the master of expediency, and indeed intrigue, who was not to be trusted and, on the other, as the man who brought stability to British society in a period when Britain faced serious difficulties with foreign trade and international finance. In 1964, however, his return as Labour Prime Minister brought to an end thirteen years of Conservative government and removed the fear that Labour would never again win office.

Harold Wilson was born on 11 March 1916, into a lower-middle-class family, the son of John Herbert and Ethel Wilson. Harold's father was an industrial chemist at Hollidays in Huddersfield. Harold was educated at Royds Hall Secondary School, Huddersfield, where he was an outstanding pupil, and he was also greatly influenced by the non-conformist radicalism of his grandfather. He went to Jesus College, Oxford, where he obtained a first-class honours degree. It was here that Wilson's political education began. At first he was a member of the Liberal Club but, by the end of the 1930s, he had switched to Labour, although he never became a member of the prestigious Labour Club at Oxford, which had produced Labour political luminaries such as Anthony Crosland and Denis Healey. Given the small and fragmented position of the Liberal Party in the 1930s, it seems that Wilson saw no political future in the Liberal Party and was greatly influenced by G. D. H. Cole, one of the foremost of Oxford's socialist intellectuals and labour historians. In 1939 Wilson married Gladys Mary Baldwin, the daughter of the Rev. D. Baldwin. At this time he was a junior academic at Oxford, although he later became research assistant to William Beveridge. During the Second World War, Wilson became a civil servant, filling several posts until he became the Director of Economics and Statistics at the Ministry of Fuel and Power between 1943 and 1944.

Wilson began his political career at the 1945 general election, when he was returned as MP for Ormskirk. He represented that constituency until 1950 when he switched to Huyton, which he represented until his retirement from the House of Commons in 1983. Once in the House of Commons, Wilson rose quickly in the governmental ranks. He was Parliamentary Secretary to the Minister of Works between 1945 and 1947, in the first Attlee Labour government.

He then became Secretary for Overseas Trade in 1947 before being appointed President of the Board of Trade, a post he held from 1947 to 1951 and which gave him a seat in the Cabinet. This political success was a remarkable achievement for someone who had neither a grounding within the Labour Party nor a background within the politically powerful trade union movement.

What was even more surprising was Wilson's attachment to Aneurin Bevan, one of the leading political figures in the Labour Party and the founder of the National Health Service (NHS). In April 1951 he joined Bevan, then Minister of Labour, and John Freeman in resigning from the Labour government over the threat to impose NHS charges and in order to 'fight for the soul of the Labour Party'. With Bevan and Freeman, Wilson joined 'Keep Left', a left-wing grouping within the Labour Party committed to long-term planning for socialism and to creating a 'Third Force' of European nations to act as a buffer between the United States and the Soviet Union in an attempt to prevent war. Keep Left formed the basis for the Bevanites that divided the Labour Party in the early and mid 1950s. Nevertheless, in 1954, Wilson replaced Bevan in the Labour Shadow Cabinet with responsibilities for foreign policy and defence. To many political observers, this action suggested that Wilson was a pragmatist who cared little for principles and abandoned them at the slightest opportunity. Nevertheless, one must recognize that Wilson lacked the social and intellectual connections which Hugh Gaitskell, Anthony Crosland and the 'Gaitskellites' had acquired in the Labour Club at Oxford. Drawn from a different cultural background, Wilson always had a strained relationship with Gaitskell, who became Labour Leader in 1955 and operated with his friends in the 'Hampstead Set'. Indeed, following Gaitskell's unsuccessful attempt to get the Party to change Clause Four in 1959 and, in 1960, his opposition to unilateral nuclear disarmament, Wilson was provoked into a leadership challenge, partly to offset potential rival challenges to Gaitskell's leadership. He was well beaten by 166 votes to 81, but he had laid his mark as a potential new leader rather than as a stalking horse.

Gaitskell's death in 1963 led to a leadership contest which saw Wilson elected Labour Party Leader, defeating George Brown and James Callaghan in the process. Wilson clearly benefited from the fact that he was not closely attached to the trade unions nor to the middle-class Gaitskellites and could attract support from all sections of the Party. He won a narrow victory in the October 1964 general election, at which he offered the vision of a new egalitarian Britain, based upon a scientific and technological revolution, as well as offering a wider range of social welfare measures.

Wilson's Labour government inherited a balance-of-trade deficit of around £600 million and found it impossible to achieve its objectives. Nevertheless, Labour was able to obtain a majority of almost 100 seats in the general election of March 1966. The omens looked good for the new government, buoyed up by a sense of patriotism as England won the World Cup at football. However, the economic situation soon deteriorated rapidly. There was a seamen's strike which proved protracted, whilst the pound sterling remained under pressure and forced a rather belated devaluation in November 1967 which constrained the economic growth policies of Wilson's government. Trade union resistance to the attempt to impose wage controls and unofficial strike activity, evidenced by Barbara Castle's White Paper *In Place of Strife* (1969), also created intense conflict within the Labour movement. Nevertheless, the Wilson government did introduce a range of progressive legislation connected with homosexual, and both sex and racial, equality.

Wilson's government also faced a torrid time in dealing with foreign affairs. The European Economic Community (EEC) refused the renewed effort of Britain to join it in 1967, Wilson's effort to act as a mediator in the Vietnam War proved abortive, and the white government of Rhodesia unilaterally declared independence from the British Commonwealth. Wilson's support for President Johnson's policy on Vietnam, along with Britain's close relationship with America, disillusioned many of his supporters and provided the mainstay of student unrest and political action in 1967 and 1968.

Wilson called a general election for June 1970 at a time when the economy seemed to be recovering. He appealed to the electorate to give him a mandate to implement the necessary social measures which had been won by 'two years of hard slog'. However, the Conservatives, under Edward Heath, were returned to power. Wilson was now Leader of a Labour Party in opposition, and a Party which had begun to divide between its Left and Right. It was divided on many issues, most obviously on joining the EEC, which the Left opposed and the Right, led by Roy Jenkins, supported. However, Labour generally drifted to the Left and this was reflected in the radical commitments envisaged within the 'Labour Programme 1973', which included major extensions to public ownership. Wilson was not particularly happy with this but fought, and won, the general election of February 1974 on the issues of inflation, rising unemployment and Heath's three-day week policy in the face of the miners' strike. However, it was a minority government and did not secure a majority until the general election of October 1974, when it won a majority of three seats.

Wilson was now a much less active leader than he had been in the 1960s. Nevertheless, he was involved in many important developments. He resolved the Left and Right split over joining the Common Market (EEC) by calling a referendum of the British electorate which, by two to one, voted in favour of joining. He scrapped the incomes policy of the Heath government and negotiated a 'social contract' with the trade unions, attempting to regulate wage bargaining in return for an extension of welfare benefits to be paid out of increased taxation on the rich and by large-scale borrowing. However, the world economic crisis of 1975 created economic problems for Britain and forced Denis Healey, the Chancellor of the Exchequer, to increase taxation in his April 1975 Budget in order to borrow money from the International Monetary Fund. As a result, the government failed to honour its part of the 'social contract'. Wilson further annoyed the Labour Left by removing Tony Benn from the vital post of Industry Secretary.

The Wilson government began to falter and was defeated in the House of Commons on two occasions in March 1976. It was at this point that Wilson announced his resignation at the age of sixty. There are many possible reasons for this. He had long suggested that he might retire at that age, although few took him seriously. There is also the possibility that he became frustrated at a possible long-term campaign against him by members of the security services who believed him to be a Soviet stooge. Perhaps he was just tired of the strain of the economic problems that every one of his governments' had faced. Whatever the reason, he retired to the back benches until 1983. He was then raised to the House of Lords as Lord Wilson of Rievaulx. Wilson was not a particularly prominent member of the Lords and suffered serious ill health in his later life. He died on 24 May 1995.

Wilson is a perplexing political character. On the one hand he had immense political skills and is often regarded as a master of political tactics. On the other hand, one has to recognize that Wilson's four Labour governments, brimming with talented people, never became the reforming and socialist agencies they intended to be largely because of the acute economic situation each one faced. There were some important reforms, particularly in the late 1960s, and Wilson managed to keep the Left and the Right of a deeply divided Party together during a period of significant tension. Perhaps he was, of all Labour's Prime Ministers, the best given to crisis management and compromise, belonging as he did to neither section of the Party. It may be that his great contribution was to keep the Labour Party together, although he was unable to reshape it in the way some of his successors have been able to do. The financial difficulties his governments faced also heralded the end of Keynesianism, whereby a large amount of money was spent to tackle unemployment, and initiated moves towards the Thatcherite policy of monetarism, which emphasized the control of inflation and reductions in public spending.

See also: Attlee, Bevin, Bevan, Callaghan, Crosland, Gaitskell, Heath

Further reading

Foot, M., 1968, *The Politics of Harold Wilson*, Harmondsworth: Penguin.

Morgan, A., 1992, *Harold Wilson*, London: Pluto Press.

Pimlott, B., 1992, *Harold Wilson*, London: HarperCollins.

Wilson, H., 1971, *The Labour Government 1964–1970*, London: Weidenfeld & Nicolson.

Wilson, H., 1979, *Final Term: The Labour Government 1974–1976: A Personal Record*, London: Weidenfeld & Nicolson.

INDEX